Gender and
in the
of Muslin

CW00523803

Gender and Patriarchy in the Films of Muslim Nations

A Filmographic Study of 21st Century Features from Eight Countries

PATRICIA R. OWEN

McFarland & Company, Inc., Publishers
Jefferson, North Carolina

Library of Congress Cataloguing-in-Publication Data

Names: Owen, Patricia R., 1946– author.
Title: Gender and patriarchy in the films of Muslim nations : a filmographic study of 21st century features from eight countries / Patricia R. Owen.
Description: Jefferson, North Carolina : McFarland & Company, Inc., Publishers, 2018. | Includes bibliographical references and index.
Identifiers: LCCN 2017043943 | ISBN 9781476667874 (softcover : acid free paper) ∞
Subjects: LCSH: Women in motion pictures. | Sex role in motion pictures. | Social problems in motion pictures. | Motion pictures—Islamic countries—History—21sst century. | Motion pictures—Islamic countries—Catalogs.
Classification: LCC PN1995.9.W6 O87 2018 | DDC 791.43/655—dc23
LC record available at https://lccn.loc.gov/2017043943

British Library cataloguing data are available

ISBN (print) 978-1-4766-6787-4
ISBN (ebook) 978-1-4766-2860-8

Front cover: Muslim woman praying in the mosque
© 2018 1001nights/iStock

Printed in the United States of America

McFarland & Company, Inc., Publishers
Box 611, Jefferson, North Carolina 28640
www.mcfarlandpub.com

Acknowledgments

I wish to thank Taylor Wright for serving as an independent reviewer of films. Her insightful comments were invaluable in compiling the film analyses. We had fun discussing these very interesting films, and we learned an enormous amount of information about a fascinating part of the world. I also want to thank St. Mary's University for awarding a grant that helped to purchase films and other materials and allowed me to complete the research in a timely manner.

Table of Contents

Preface

The research for this filmography began a few years ago when I instructed my students to locate contemporary feature films from non–Western cultures that portrayed issues related to gender. I am a professor of psychology, and this assignment was to be a requirement for a psychology course on gender relationships. The project was of special interest to me because I wanted to depart from the usual Eurocentric course materials in order to broaden awareness and knowledge of gender-related customs and traditions of diverse cultures. As my class soon realized, finding full-length feature films originating in non–Western countries was a daunting task.

Although several academic texts existed that provided scholarly discourses on world cinemas, many of these texts were too limited for our purposes, as they often featured analyses of only a handful of exemplary films, or else their compilations of foreign films, though comprehensive, were not referenced by gender themes. Internet searches yielded dozens of websites listing foreign films associated with diverse regions of the world, but most of these sites proved to be of little use because of insufficient (and sometimes incorrect) information about film plot and availability of films for English-speaking viewers. Ultimately, as neither my students nor I had the time or resources in one brief semester to locate and view foreign films that could be potentially useful for this assignment, the project was abandoned. Hence the beginnings of research for this filmography that focuses on gender issues depicted in films from Muslim-majority countries.

I chose to focus on this region of the world for a reason. There are 49 countries in the world in which Muslims (followers of Islam) constitute a majority of the population. Islam is the second largest religion in the world, with an estimated 1.6 billion followers. However, despite the significant world presence of Muslims, many people in the United States and elsewhere are uninformed about Islam and about Muslim worldviews. What knowledge they do have is often incorrect, fueled by lack of formal education about

1

Islam, distorted media depictions, and current political jingoism. Issues related to gender and gender relationships are especially subject to misconceptions regarding the role of Islam and Muslim practices. As an example, gendered practices such as honor killings are often attributed to Islamic advocacy, though in reality this practice stems from a patriarchal tradition that pre-dated the arrival of Islam on the world scene. Given the challenges in understanding Muslim-dominant cultures and countries, films portraying Muslim culture that originate in Muslim countries are uniquely positioned to provide insight into the lives and worldviews of others. What better way to learn about the ordinary, and sometimes extraordinary, life challenges that people encounter in diverse parts of the world than through the media of film?

This filmography is dedicated to educators, students of film, and indeed any cinephile who finds life to be enriched by foreign films and the window they provide into cultural experiences.

Introduction

This filmography provides an analysis of contemporary feature films with English subtitles that originate in Muslim-majority countries and that feature narrative themes related to gender issues or gender relationships. Gender was selected as an area of focus since it is considered one of the most salient organizing principles of any given society. An understanding of gender provides a powerful tool in comprehending how nations define themselves and others.[1]

The selection of films from Muslim-majority countries was informed by two reasons. First, films from Muslim-majority countries are little known in the West, and this cinematic deficit could serve as one contributor to Western unfamiliarity with the cultural dynamics of Muslim nations.[2] Second, existing internationally focused filmographies present challenges in their usefulness for locating contemporary films that include gender themes and are available to viewers in the United States. Thus, the films covered in this filmography are all accessible to U.S. viewers. All films are indigenous to Muslim-majority countries, and all feature gender-related issues that take place in contemporary times.

CRITERIA FOR FILM SELECTION

As stated above, films selected for this filmography were available for viewing in the United States through rental, purchase, or viewing online (e.g., YouTube). Films were subtitled in English and (if in DVD format) formatted for Region 1. The selection of films was guided by two criteria. First, selected films were contemporary feature films (as opposed to documentaries) that originated in a Muslim-majority country. A film was defined as contemporary if it was produced or released for distribution around the year 2000 or later and if it featured a narrative that took place in modern times.[3] Selected films also contained themes related to gender issues or gender relationships. Many of the gender issues were impacted by patriarchal traditions and religious laws, which were also analyzed. Films were viewed in their entirety by two raters, the author and a university student trained in film analysis. Each of us independently took extensive notes on every film and analyzed each in terms of depictions of gender issues and the presence of patriarchal traditions and religious laws. More than 150 films were viewed; of these, 56 met the selection criteria. (One caveat: Our analysis and interpretation of the gender themes and related issues found in these films comes from a Western perspective. Neither of us is Muslim, and we do not claim any expertise on the faith of Islam.)

Countries Represented

Films originating from countries in the Middle East, the Maghreb (a region of northwest Africa), South Asia, and the Indian subcontinent were selected for analysis. The decision to select films from some Muslim-majority countries and not others was a practical one, as many of the countries that are not represented in the filmography do not have films that meet the selection criteria.

Gender Issues and Gender Relationships

Gender issues and relationships found within the narratives of films were examined with reference to depictions of gender roles and gender-associated attributes. Specifically, the content of films was analyzed for depictions of (a) traditional and nontraditional gender roles and (b) traditional gender stereotypes and nontraditional gender attributes that were associated with female and male film characters.

Female characters in each film were evaluated for the presence of traditional stereotypic feminine traits of passivity/non-agency, dependence, submissiveness/subjugation, incompetence, chasteness, and self-sacrifice. Nontraditional gender attributes were noted if a female character showed independence, self-agency, sexual agency, competence, and dominance. Traditional female roles were noted if the female character's primary and sole obligation was to family and marriage and these responsibilities involved caregiving, nurturance, and domestic tasks. A nontraditional gender role was noted if a female character engaged in work activities that occurred outside of (or in addition to) familial or marital obligations.

Male characters were evaluated for the presence of traditional stereotypic masculine traits of dominance, competence, independence, self-agency, sexual agency, and aggression. Nontraditional gender attributes were noted if a male character demonstrated traits of passivity/non-agency, dependence, incompetence, nurturance, and self-sacrifice. If a male character provided financial support for his family through work outside the home, this was noted as a traditional male role. If a male character was engaged in domestic tasks that involved caregiving, this was noted as a nontraditional male role.

Patriarchal Traditions and Religious Laws

Many gender issues depicted in films occurred in the context of patriarchal-based traditions and/or religious laws. These traditions and laws were analyzed with reference to their impact on gender issues. Patriarchy is defined as a gender-based social system controlled by males and founded on male dominance, power, and authority and female subordination and dependency.[4] Within patriarchal systems, male privilege is affirmed in both public and private (family) spheres by cultural/tribal, religious, and/or national subscription to and acceptance of beliefs about traditional gender roles and attributes. Though patriarchal structures exist in much of the world, scholars refer to Muslim countries of the Middle East, North Africa, and South Asia as the "belt of classic patriarchy."[5] Classic patriarchy, in this conceptualization, refers to "male domination, son preference, restrictive codes of behavior for women … veiling and sex segregation [which] are legitimated on the basis of the *Quran* or *hadith*."[6] What differentiates the "classic" patriarchy of many Muslim-majority countries from other countries with patriarchal systems is the legitimization by law of gender roles and gender relationships. These laws, typically found in a country's personal and criminal codes, are based on combinations of Islamic legal systems (such as Sharia), pre–Islamic tribal customs, and, in some cases, Western law.[7]

A Note About Sharia

Islam is a law-based religion, and Islamic law is concerned with all areas of human life, including the personal (e.g., marriage, divorce, and inheritance) and the public (e.g., criminal behavior, commerce, and politics). Sharia law is Islam's legal system, which provides a code that, some scholars believe, all Muslims should abide by in their daily lives.[8] Sources of Sharia include the Quran (Islam's central text), the Sunna (the words and actions of God's chosen messenger, the Prophet Muhammad), and hadith (the specific narratives of the Prophet's tradition).[9] Only a handful of Muslim-majority countries use Sharia as an authority in their national laws. Within the countries that do follow Sharia, there are different schools of thought or law (e.g., Hanafi, Maliki, Ja'fari) that are used to interpret the Quran and hadith. Hence the legal codes of Muslim-majority countries may differ depending on whether Sharia is followed and, if so, what school has been adopted for judicial interpretations. Of the countries represented in this filmography, Afghanistan, Egypt, Iran, Iraq, and Pakistan include Sharia in their national laws. Algeria and Bangladesh adhere to a more mixed system, in which Sharia is applied to family or personal law and secular laws apply to other areas, and in Turkey, Sharia plays no formal role in governance. Scholars have long debated the immutability of Sharia law, and opinion is divided. For many, Sharia is divine and unassailable, whereas others believe that (as is true for other religions) interpretations of Sharia are human-made and thus subject to contextual readings.[10]

Cautionary Notes

Issues of gender inequality and female oppression were found in the films of Muslim-majority countries, many of which were judged to stem from patriarchal traditions and/or religious laws. Lest readers (or viewers) consider these issues as idiosyncratic to Muslim countries, three cautionary points must be made. First, though patriarchal systems are very much in evidence in films that originate in Muslim-majority countries, it should not be assumed that patriarchy is unique to Muslim-majority countries. As social science scholars attest, almost all countries of the world have in place some form of a culture-specific patriarchal arrangement whereby males are privileged and females disadvantaged.[11]

Second, it must be noted that Muslims, though united in their shared faith and belief in the message of the Quran, are not a monolithic group. As Irshaad Hussain remarks in his blog *Islam from Inside*:

> The focus and emphasis, the extent to which some verses of the Qur'an and hadith overshadow others, the depth (or lack of it) of interpretation varies from group to group.... So we have varieties of traditional Muslims, progressive Muslims, conservative Muslims, liberal Muslims, socialist Muslims, reformist Muslims, secular or cultural Muslims, various sectarian groupings of Muslims.[12]

Just as Muslim people are not homogeneous, Muslim-majority countries are not monolithic, as each country has its own distinctive sociocultural, economic, and political identity and its own distinctive interpretation of Islam with reference to cultural heritage and political agendas.[13] Regarding gender issues, for example, Islamic Sharia law is considered by many scholars to promote gender inequality in laws that regulate marriage, divorce, child custody and guardianship, and inheritance. Mariam Al-Attar states in her essay on Muslim women and violence that "there are many verses in the Qur'an that can be cited in support of women's inferiority, and such verses are used as a basis for family laws [Sharia] that discriminate against women. Progressive Muslim scholars have struggled to interpret verses that were usually understood to endorse women's inferiority."[14] But, as noted above, only a few Muslim countries adhere to Sharia law. Other countries adopt blends of Sharia and secular law, and still others use completely secular civil law.

Despite the existence of national legal systems, either Sharia based or secular, there are certain patriarchal traditions and tribal laws that contradict and assume priority over national law. These traditions, often seen in rural regions, are generally a priori assumed by those unfamiliar with Islamic legal principles as originating from Islam. It is worth noting that while some patriarchal traditions do indeed stem from (or are reinforced by) Islamic teachings, many other traditions do not and, in fact, may be incompatible with Islamic tenets. For numerous traditional practices, debate continues as to their origins and rationale for their continuation in the social structure of a given country or group. For example, a group may justify the practice of honor killings as Islamic, though it is almost universally agreed that this practice (observed in Muslim-majority countries as well as non–Muslim-majority countries) does not stem from Islam, but rather from a centuries-old patriarchal tradition dictating that those who threaten familial honor merit punishment to restore the family reputation.[15] Needless to say, the extent to which the tradition of a given culture or country and the teachings of Islam contribute to a gendered tradition is often difficult to disentangle and frequently subject to debate.

A further caution about viewing films originating in Muslim-majority or other countries is the presumption that gender themes and practices found in these films reflect the reality of that country or culture. Films, of course, represent the filmmaker's interpretation of reality, and that interpretation may not represent real issues of importance in the country of origin. However, while it is difficult to make definitive claims about how fictionalized film corresponds to real life, it should be noted that many filmmakers report drawing on their real-life experiences in their countries of origin.

A last consideration concerns the representativeness of films that receive distribution rights to international markets. Films distributed to Western markets have received distribution resources based in part on acknowledgment by film critics or financiers of their potential to appeal to an international audience and potential for success in international markets. Whether this economic reality influences cinematic content is difficult to ascertain.

ORGANIZATION OF THE FILMOGRAPHY

This filmography features films alphabetically organized from Afghanistan, Algeria, Bangladesh, Egypt, Iran, Iraq, Pakistan, and Turkey. A profile is provided for each country, which includes information as to demography, religion, legal codes, sociopolitical issues relevant to gender, and status of CEDAW ratification. (CEDAW, the Convention on the Elimination of All Forms of Discrimination Against Women, is an international treaty adopted by the United Nations General Assembly in 1981 that has been ratified by 189 countries.)[16] In these country profiles, every effort was made to provide the most current and accurate information available.

Within each chapter, films are alphabetically arranged by the English distribution title, followed by the original title in parentheses. For each film, production details are provided, including date of theatrical or video release, director, list of key characters (with the actors' names in parentheses), film length, setting, and plot synopsis. Film summaries provide information on the patriarchal traditions and religious laws that are featured in the film that may have impacted gender issues. Also provided are analyses of traditional gender stereotypes and nontraditional gender attributes associated with both female and male characters.

It must be noted that while these gender characterizations may appear reductive, gender-associated traits are not mutually exclusive. Women (whether of a Muslim-majority nation or any other nation) do not constitute a monolithic group, and neither do men. Many of the gender practices illustrated in these films are controversial as to origin and contemporary cultural and religious legitimization. Religious and historical scholars have noted the difficulty inherent in attempting to disentangle religious prescriptions from patriarchal tradition, and scholars often provide conflicting opinions about gendered topics. Thus many of the film summaries include a commentary that provides additional thought-provoking and/or controversial information about a gender issue or relevant topic that appeared in the story-line.

Last, an ending summary is provided that integrates the findings of the films across countries with reference to key gender topics. A question of interest explored in the summary involves whether there are commonalities in gender relationships and gendered practices in the films of Muslim-majority countries.

1

CEDAW

CEDAW refers to the Convention on the Elimination of All Forms of Discrimination Against Women, a treaty sponsored in 1979 by the United Nations General Assembly.[1] To date, 187 countries have ratified CEDAW, agreeing to be bound by most of its provisions. Of these, 29 countries have not fully endorsed Article 16, which calls for the elimination of discrimination in all matters relating to marriage and family relations, including the right to enter into marriage; the right to freely choose a spouse; equal rights in marriage and its dissolution; equal parental rights and rights over children; equal personal rights as spouses; and equal rights in ownership, acquisition, management, and disposition of property. Reservations about Article 16 are based on its potential to contravene Sharia law. The following pages provide the language of CEDAW, including an introduction to the content and purpose of the document as well as Article 1 (Discrimination), Article 2 (Policy Measures), Article 5 (Sex Role Stereotyping and Prejudice), and Article 16 (Marriage and Family Life).

CEDAW: INTRODUCTION[2]

On 18 December 1979, the Convention on the Elimination of All Forms of Discrimination against Women was adopted by the United Nations General Assembly. It entered into force as an international treaty on 3 September 1981 after the twentieth country had ratified it. By the tenth anniversary of the Convention in 1989, almost one hundred nations have agreed to be bound by its provisions.

The Convention was the culmination of more than thirty years of work by the United Nations Commission on the Status of Women, a body established in 1946 to monitor the situation of women and to promote women's rights. The Commission's work has been instrumental in bringing to light all the areas in which women are denied equality with men. These efforts for the advancement of women have resulted in several declarations and conventions, of which the Convention on the Elimination of All Forms of Discrimination against Women is the central and most comprehensive document.

Among the international human rights treaties, the Convention takes an important place in bringing the female half of humanity into the focus of human rights concerns. The spirit of the Convention is rooted in the goals of the United Nations: to reaffirm faith in fundamental human rights, in the dignity and worth of the human person, in the equal rights of men and women. The present document spells out the meaning of equality and how it can be achieved. In so doing, the Convention establishes not only an international bill of rights for women, but also an agenda for action by countries to guarantee the enjoyment of those rights.

In its preamble, the Convention explicitly acknowledges that "extensive discrimination against women continues to exist," and emphasizes that such discrimination "violates the principles of equality of rights and respect for human dignity." As defined in article 1, discrimination is understood as "any distinction, exclusion or restriction made on the basis of sex ... in the political, economic, social, cultural, civil or any other field." The Convention gives positive affirmation to the principle of equality by requiring States parties to take "all appropriate measures, including legislation, to ensure the full development and advancement of women, for the purpose of guaranteeing them the exercise and enjoyment of human rights and fundamental freedoms on a basis of equality with men" (article 3).

The agenda for equality is specified in fourteen subsequent articles. In its approach, the Convention covers three dimensions of the situation of women. Civil rights and the legal status of women are dealt with in great detail. In addition, and unlike other human rights treaties, the Convention is also concerned with the dimension of human reproduction as well as with the impact of cultural factors on gender relations....

Aside from civil rights issues, the Convention also devotes major attention to a most vital concern of women, namely their reproductive rights. The preamble sets the tone by stating that "the role of women in procreation should not be a basis for discrimination." The link between discrimination and women's reproductive role is a matter of recurrent concern in the Convention. For example, it advocates, in article 5, "a proper understanding of maternity as a social function," demanding fully shared responsibility for child-rearing by both sexes. Accordingly, provisions for maternity protection and child-care are proclaimed as essential rights and are incorporated into all areas of the Convention, whether dealing with employment, family law, health care or education. Society's obligation extends to offering social services, especially child-care facilities, that allow individuals to combine family responsibilities with work and participation in public life. Special measures for maternity protection are recommended and "shall not be considered discriminatory" (article 4). The Convention also affirms women's right to reproductive choice. Notably, it is the only human rights treaty to mention family planning. States parties are obliged to include advice on family planning in the education process (article 10.h) and to develop family codes that guarantee women's rights "to decide freely and responsibly on the number and spacing of their children and to have access to the information, education and means to enable them to exercise these rights" (article 16.e).

The third general thrust of the Convention aims at enlarging our understanding of the concept of human rights, as it gives formal recognition to the influence of culture and tradition on restricting women's enjoyment of their fundamental rights. These forces take shape in stereotypes, customs and norms which give rise to the multitude of legal, political and economic constraints on the advancement of women. Noting this interrelationship, the preamble of the Convention stresses "that a change in the traditional role of men as well as the role of women in society and in the family is needed to achieve full equality of men and women." States parties are therefore obliged to work towards the modification of social and cultural patterns of individual conduct in order to eliminate "prejudices and customary and all other practices which are based on the idea of the inferiority or the superiority of either of the sexes or on stereotyped roles for men and women" (article 5). And Article 10.c. mandates the revision of textbooks, school programmes and teaching methods with a view to eliminating stereotyped concepts in the field of education. Finally, cultural patterns which define the public realm as a man's world and the domestic sphere as women's domain are strongly targeted in all of the Convention's provisions that affirm the equal responsibilities of both sexes in family life and their equal rights with regard to education and employment. Altogether, the Convention provides a comprehensive framework for challenging the various forces that have created and sustained discrimination based upon sex...

Article I

For the purposes of the present Convention, the term "discrimination against women" shall mean any distinction, exclusion or restriction made on the basis of sex which has the effect or purpose of impairing or nullifying the recognition, enjoyment or exercise by women, irrespective of their marital status, on a basis of equality of men and women, of human rights and fundamental freedoms in the political, economic, social, cultural, civil or any other field.

Article 2

States Parties condemn discrimination against women in all its forms, agree to pursue by all appropriate means and without delay a policy of eliminating discrimination against women and, to this end, undertake:

(a) To embody the principle of the equality of men and women in their national constitutions or other appropriate legislation if not yet incorporated therein and to ensure, through law and other appropriate means, the practical realization of this principle;
(b) To adopt appropriate legislative and other measures, including sanctions where appropriate, prohibiting all discrimination against women;
(c) To establish legal protection of the rights of women on an equal basis with men and to ensure through competent national tribunals and other public institutions the effective protection of women against any act of discrimination;
(d) To refrain from engaging in any act or practice of discrimination against women and to ensure that public authorities and institutions shall act in conformity with this obligation;
(e) To take all appropriate measures to eliminate discrimination against women by any person, organization or enterprise;
(f) To take all appropriate measures, including legislation, to modify or abolish existing laws, regulations, customs and practices which constitute discrimination against women;
(g) To repeal all national penal provisions which constitute discrimination against women.

Article 5

States Parties shall take all appropriate measures:

(a) To modify the social and cultural patterns of conduct of men and women, with a view to achieving the elimination of prejudices and customary and all other practices which are based on the idea of the inferiority or the superiority of either of the sexes or on stereotyped roles for men and women;
(b) To ensure that family education includes a proper understanding of maternity as a social function and the recognition of the common responsibility of men and women in the upbringing and development of their children, it being understood that the interest of the children is the primordial consideration in all cases.

Article 16

1. States Parties shall take all appropriate measures to eliminate discrimination against women in all matters relating to marriage and family relations and in particular shall ensure, on a basis of equality of men and women:
   (a) The same right to enter into marriage;
   (b) The same right freely to choose a spouse and to enter into marriage only with their free and full consent;
   (c) The same rights and responsibilities during marriage and at its dissolution;
   (d) The same rights and responsibilities as parents, irrespective of their marital status, in matters relating to their children; in all cases the interests of the children shall be paramount;
   (e) The same rights to decide freely and responsibly on the number and spacing of their children and to have access to the information, education and means to enable them to exercise these rights;
   (f) The same rights and responsibilities with regard to guardianship, wardship, trusteeship and adoption of children, or similar institutions where these concepts exist in national legislation; in all cases the interests of the children shall be paramount;
   (g) The same personal rights as husband and wife, including the right to choose a family name, a profession and an occupation;
   (h) The same rights for both spouses in respect of the ownership, acquisition, management, administration, enjoyment and disposition of property, whether free of charge or for a valuable consideration.
2. The betrothal and the marriage of a child shall have no legal effect, and all necessary action, including legislation, shall be taken to specify a minimum age for marriage and to make the registration of marriages in an official registry compulsory.

2

Afghanistan

COUNTRY PROFILE

BACKGROUND[1]

The Islamic Republic of Afghanistan is located in Southwestern Asia. The title of "Islamic Republic" (one of five in the world) was adopted in 1956, indicating the country's governance by Islamic Sharia laws (Hanafi school of thought). Afghanistan's form of government is a presidential Islamic republic, and its population is almost entirely Muslim. Afghanistan is home to many different ethnic groups, including the larger groups of Pashtun, Tajik, Hazara, and Uzbek. Only 26 percent of the population reside in urban areas. Afghanistan has experienced many wars and periods of civil unrest throughout its history. More recently, civil wars in the 1990s allowed the Taliban to take control of the country in 1996. The Taliban's strict interpretation of Sharia law led to many draconian regulations that affected the Afghan population, especially females. In 2001, the United States–led invasion forced the Taliban to relinquish control.

SOCIOPOLITICAL AND RELIGIOUS ISSUES RELATED TO GENDER

Efforts have been made to ensure that the information presented here reflects current law and policies. However, many Muslim-majority countries are currently contending with challenges to their civil and criminal laws that stem from competing constituencies of those favoring greater freedoms for women and those espousing conservative Islamic principles. As such, governmental policies are continually evolving, and laws relevant to gender issues may be added, deleted, or amended in subsequent years.

Law

The Afghan constitution[2] was adopted in 2004 and guaranteed equal rights to women, with the caveat that all laws must be compatible with Islamic Sharia civil and criminal law. The constitution contains prohibitions against many Afghanistan patriarchal traditions. CEDAW was adopted by presidential decree in 2009. In general, there is compliance with CEDAW articles as long as they do not conflict with Sharia law and principles. The law provided and strengthened protections for women and addressed issues of rape, child marriage, forced marriage, domestic violence, and denial of education to girls. The Civil Code of 1977 is the source of family law and states that first statutory law prevails, followed by religious law, and then customary laws.

Some key points of the civil code with reference to gender are as follows:

- The minimum marriage age is 16 for girls and 18 for boys, though marriage of 15-year-old girls is allowed provided that the father or a legal guardian approves
- Marriage without the consent of the parties (i.e., forced marriage) is not valid
- Polygyny (a man's right to be married to as many as four women at the same time) is allowed provided the husband can financially support all wives and treat all wives equally
- Men have the right to divorce unilaterally (talaq, or verbal repudiation) without any justification; women can obtain a divorce only under certain conditions, though she can divorce through khul' with husband's consent and with return of bride price
- Fathers are guardians of their children
- In divorce, women have custody of children up to the age of 9 for girls and 7 for boys; if she remarries, she loses custody of the children (if a divorced man remarries, he does not lose custody)
- Women have the right to inherit both as daughters and as widows; a daughter inherits half of a son's share
- Rape is a criminal offense and is punishable by a minimum of five years in prison and a maximum sentence of death in cases where the victim dies from the rape
- Abortion is forbidden except to save the life of the mother

Laws Regulating Homosexuality

The 2016 report on sexual orientation laws compiled by the International Lesbian, Gay, Bisexual, Trans and Intersex Association (ILGA) identified the following items in Afghanistan penal law:

Adultery, Pederasty, and Violations of Honor
Article 427:
(1) A person who commits adultery or pederasty shall be sentenced to long imprisonment.

According to ILGA, "The Afghan Penal Code does not contain any explicit provisions on the criminality of consensual same-sex sexual acts. Article 130 of the Constitution allows recourse to be made to Sharia law, which prohibits same-sex sexual activity in general. Afghanistan's Sharia law criminalizes same-sex sexual acts with a maximum death penalty. However, no known cases of death sentences have been handed out for such behavior since the end of Taliban rule."[3]

Additional Issues

As noted by the Afghanistan Legal Education Project,[4] the laws that govern the lives of Afghan citizens are constituted in three realms: secular, religious, and customary. Secular laws are supposed to take precedence over religious and customary laws. In reality, however, Islamic (Sharia) and customary laws govern the lives of the people, especially those living outside major urban areas. As an example, forced marriages are prohibited by the constitution, but the practice exists in many Afghan provinces that are governed by tribal law. It is estimated that between 60 and 80 percent of all marriages in Afghanistan are forced, most of these involving young girls.[5] Many of these marriages occur as part of a practice called *baad*, in which unmarried girls are given in marriage to tribes to settle disputes. Since these marriages are non-consensual, they are in violation of Afghan laws and Sharia law.

In response to this and other problems encountered by females, Afghanistan endorsed the End Violence Against Women (EVAW) law in 2009. EVAW[6] criminalizes 22 acts as violence against females, including "rape, forced prostitution, publicizing the identity of a victim in a damaging way, forcing a woman to commit self-immolation, causing injury or disability, beating, selling and buying women for the purpose of or under pretext of marriage, baad (retribution of a woman to settle a dispute), forced marriage, prohibiting the choice of a husband, marriage before the legal age, abuse, humiliation or intimidation, harassment or persecution, forced isolation, forced drug addiction, denial of inheritance rights, denying the right to education, work and access to health services, forced labour and marrying more than one wife without observing Article 86 of the Civil Code." Under the law, those who violate EVAW provisions are subject to punishment. Underage marriage, for example, is prohibited and punishable by two to five years of imprisonment. Forced marriage is punishable by one to two years of imprisonment. In 2013, the Afghanistan parliament refused to endorse the EVAW law, but it continues to be in effect as signed by presidential decree.

FILMS

3 Dots (Seh Noktah/Ellipsis)

Year: 2003; *Director:* Roya Sadat; *Cast:* Gul Afrooz—woman in her late 20s; *Setting:* small rural village in Afghanistan; impoverished community

SYNOPSIS

Gul Afrooz is a young widow with three children, living in an impoverished, desolate Afghan village. Her story is one of suffering and misery. She was forced to marry an elderly warlord, but now she is widowed and spends endless days struggling to find food for her starving children. She is being pressured to marry another man who already has a wife, but she refuses to consent, as she will lose her children as tradition dictates.

Gul Afrooz's infant son is dying of pneumonia, and, in desperation, she barters with the village warlords for antibiotics in exchange for smuggling drugs across the border into neighboring Iran. Once across the border, she is caught and sentenced to life in prison for carrying illegal drugs. A final scene shows her crouched in squalid prison cell, alone and in despair as jailors take her infant away. This film is relentlessly depressing.

PATRIARCHAL TRADITIONS AND RELIGIOUS LAWS

Remarriage of Widows

Many marriage customs in Muslim-majority countries have connections to patriarchal and religious traditions (as is true for most other countries in the world). Polygyny, remarriage of widows to the deceased's relatives, and arranged marriages are practices dramatized in *3 Dots*.

As permitted by Sharia law (Afghanistan family laws adhere to Sharia), males are allowed to wed more than one wife, provided the man has the resources to support all of his wives. In *3 Dots*, a married man who resides in the village is honor-bound to marry his brother's widow. Under national law, a wife inherits, but under customary law, she is often denied any inheritance, which may have been the case in this film. Widows then are commonly forced to marry another male relative to keep the inheritance in the family. And if she does not remarry into the same family, she risks losing her children to her deceased husband's relatives.

The man in the movie desires to marry Gul Afrooz, who is also a widow. Gul does not want to remarry, as she could lose her children to her in-laws. However, there is considerable pressure from village elders and the man's mother to accept his offer of marriage. It seems that in a patriarchal society an unmarried woman is perceived as a threat, as the absence of a male provider implies that she is competent without his protection. Further, an unmarried woman is subject to sexual attention from men, which threatens her honor.

Arranged Marriages

Arranged marriages are a way of life and often under control of fathers, who frequently marry young girls to much older men. Two scenes in 3 *Dots* show the fears and despondency that young girls experience about their arranged marriages. In one, a mullah spots one of the girls fetching water. Their eyes meet, but she seems discomfited by his presence. As she discovers later, her father has arranged for her to marry the much older man, and on her wedding day, she bursts into tears. Another scene features a group of young girls fetching water, and they sing about their anxiety and dread:

> Girls pick flowers but don't smell them
> Stay in Father's homes! Don't get husbands!
> Father give us wheat bread
> But husbands sting us like scorpions
> Oh, Father, I am a good girl!
> Don't marry me off to an old man …
> You married me off far away
> I was not content, but you did it by force.
> I didn't agree, but it was my fate.
> You used me as firewood in this furnace.

TRADITIONAL GENDER STEREOTYPES

The men in 3 *Dots* are portrayed as sinister, soulless, greed-driven characters who lack empathy and compassion. Male dominance is illustrated by the gendered division of labor that is obvious in this village. Women work; men don't. A woman such as Gul endlessly toils to ensure the survival of her family. She makes bread to sell, she fetches water from a distant well, she prepares her children's meals, she tends to her sick infant, she assists in the construction of a stone wall, and she gleans brush for the fire. No male was portrayed as working in this film.

NONTRADITIONAL GENDER ATTRIBUTES

Females have limited agency in this film. Gul Afrooz makes heroic attempts to save her family. She refuses to remarry, despite the attempts of the women of the village and the elders to shame her. In addition, she initially refuses to carry drugs for the warlords and resists all sorts of persuasions. But in the end, what else could she do? Her baby is dying and her children have to eat.

CULTURAL RELATIVISM

Different "reads" of the narrative in *3 Dots* are instructive, as they illustrate how diverse interpretations construct the effects of patriarchy on women. Mark Graham[7] argues that the narrative of *3 Dots* provides instruction regarding how traditions must be understood from the perspective of Afghan culture as opposed to a Western orientalist perspective. He claims that Western media have prejudiced consumers to automatically accept the notion that women in Afghanistan are without agency and powerless to control their fates, which are under the control of men. Graham contends that the women of *3 Dots* do indeed have agency and power within the patriarchal system, and that those viewing this film with a Western lens would fail to note this agency. His evidence? A group of girls singing about their fears of forced marriage to old men and familial abandonment demonstrates that females fully accept and participate in this patriarchal tradition. For Graham, the act of articulating a tradition equates to acceptance. And agency? Graham claims that Gul Afrooz has agency, as she labors outdoors unaccompanied by men and free of hijab. Here he confuses agency with engagement in demanding physical labor.

What Graham may not understand is that in rural agrarian societies such as this one, women have no choice. In order for them and their families to survive, they must accept without question the arduous labor that men choose not to do. Gul, along with the other women, carries water from streams, bakes bread, cooks, clears the land of brush, tends to animals, and takes care of the children. It is ironic that, as strong and capable as Gul is, she is undervalued within this rigid patriarchal society. As such, her voice and her agency are muted in the presence of men, who have ultimate control over her destiny.

Act of Dishonour

Year: 2010; *Director:* Nelofer Pazira; *Cast:* Mejgan (Nelofer Pazira)—woman in her 30s; Mena (Marina Golbahari)—15-year-old girl; *Length:* 90 minutes; *Setting:* rural village in Afghanistan; working-class community

SYNOPSIS

Mejgan, a Canadian filmmaker, has returned to her native home in rural Afghanistan to produce a film about life in post–Taliban Afghanistan. She and her film crew discover Mena, a pretty 15-year-old girl who lives in a small stone home, caring for her widowed father and two younger brothers. Mena is happily planning her wedding to Rahmat, a young bus driver who travels the region. According to village tradition and Islamic moral codes, unmarried women are not allowed to interact with unrelated men. As Mena is of marriageable age, her conduct is under surveillance by the villagers, and any hints of impropriety will be reported and subject to censure. Mena and her fiancé are obviously aware of this norm; yet the two engage in innocent and furtive flirtations when Rahmat passes her home and leaves trinkets and other gifts in a hole in the wall of her home.

Mejgan is convinced that Mena would be ideal for a role in her film, but she must be convinced to participate. The problem is that women must follow strict rules about appearing in public, and Mena is aware of the potential danger to her reputation if she were to appear in public knowing that strangers will be in attendance. Eventually, with the permission of her father and the promise of a prized burqa for her wedding night, Mena shows up for filming, fully veiled with her face hidden. The village elders have all along looked upon the foreigners with suspicion, and now their suspicions are confirmed. Mena has committed the grave sin of appearing in public in the presence of males who are not her family members. Now her father's social standing in the village and her family's honor are compromised.

The penalty for dishonoring family is death, and Rahmat, as her intended, is charged with her execution. Mena accompanies Rahmat, armed with a rifle, to the countryside. She knows what has been ordered but protests that she is innocent. Rahmat is torn between his duty to the honor of his village and his affection for Mena. He orders her to stand several yards away and turn her back to him. He raises his rifle but then turns and walks away.

Patriarchal Traditions and Religious Laws

Honor and Honor Killings

The honor of females is of central importance to communities that are highly patriarchal, with honor equated with modest behavior and appearance and sexual purity. A female's honor is ensured by strict regulations that maintain gender segregation in public areas. In *Act of Dishonour*, the village elders are aghast that Mena participated in the film and gossip about her: "Men in the community are saying that if Mena was their daughter they would bury her alive. That being around a foreign man is a form of adultery. They said that the father should punish her, stone her." The women of the village also participate in castigating Mena.

Although condemned by Islam and categorized as a punishable offense under many Muslim-majority countries' penal codes, honor killings are an accepted practice in many rural communities that are rigidly patriarchal and governed by tribal law. Honor killings are committed against females for sexual improprieties that could include socializing with men, eloping, and adultery. In *Act of Dishonour*, Mena is judged by the elders to have committed the serious infraction of being seen (though fully veiled) in the presence of unrelated men. Her punishment is death.

TRADITIONAL GENDER STEREOTYPES

The patriarchal custom of restricting females to the private sphere and apart from public view is evident in *Act of Dishonour*. The rules that regulate the conduct of males and females clearly demarcate the responsibilities and roles of each gender. Women remain in their homes as caretakers of family, and men work outside the home to support their families. These roles are established early. Villagers gossip about Mena: "She is 15 and still not married. God does not approve of it. It is an act of dishonor on her father's part."

The importance placed on gender segregation implies that a female's activities must be restricted. After all, if unrelated males and females were allowed to interact, then the female's chastity and the family's honor could be compromised. Propriety must be observed in the public sphere. In *Act of Dishonour*, woman are not permitted in the mosque, are not allowed to watch cartoons in the makeshift movie room (though pre-pubescent girls can do so with a male's permission), and cannot leave their homes unescorted. A man who is not related to a woman is not allowed to ask her name.

NONTRADITIONAL GENDER ATTRIBUTES

Mena's father is loving and protective of his daughter; yet he orders her death. He, too, is a victim of patriarchal traditions in which defense of honor becomes more important than defense of a daughter's life. Under patriarchal systems, males are constrained by social norms dictating that the achievement of masculinity comes at the expense of freedom to make choices that could ultimately serve a better moral good. As a young boy, Rahmat was honor-bound to kill the man who had murdered his father—he was a child and had no choice. Now he is a man, and he has become aware that matters of honor are more nuanced than what he believed as a child. It cannot be easy for him to relinquish his patriarchal-dictated obligation to kill Mena. Stepping outside the traditions of masculinity requires courage. Yet Rahmat finds courage and chooses not to honor tradition. The film ends on a glimmer of hope that, given courage and awareness of alternative choices, tradition could change.

The Burqa and Miscommunication

Cross-cultural miscommunication can lead to deadly consequences. Mena is a young girl in love with the romanticized notion of marriage and, like many young girls, fantasizes about her wedding. In her culture, the burqa, to be worn on the bride's wedding night, symbolizes the mystery of femininity and sensuality of unveiling. The Western film producer is unaware of the symbolism and refuses to honor his promise and provide her with the burqa she so desires. His position is that he does not want to reinforce a system that tyrannizes and oppresses women and confines them to invisible lives. He sees his refusal as liberating Mena from symbolic enslavement. Does his refusal represent a Western orientalist arrogance? Perhaps. But could his refusal represent his belief in universal humanitarian principles that support equality and justice for both women and men? Perhaps.

FEMALE CLOTHING STANDARDS

There is considerable confusion in the West about female clothing standards in Muslim-majority countries. Terms such as *burqa*, *hijab*, and *chador* are commonly and mistakenly used interchangeably. The following list is a glossary of female clothing styles characteristic of the countries found in this filmography[8]:

- *Hijab*: Can be a generic term for modest Islamic clothing and typically involves a veil or head covering
- *Burqa*: Loose outer garment covering a woman's entire body, including her head; her eyes and mouth are concealed by a mesh panel or woven grille (also called *chadri*)
- *Abaya*: Full-length, robe-like outer garment (usually made of black synthetic fiber) that covers the whole body except the head, feet, and hands; usually worn with a head scarf or niqab
- *Niqab*: A veil that covers the face and entire head but with a place cut out for the eyes; may be worn with an abaya
- *Half niqab*: A veil that is tied on at the bridge of the nose and falls to cover the lower face
- *Chador*: Cape-like garment that covers the head, hair, and body but not the face; does not have slits for arms and hands and is held shut with the hands or teeth or wrapped under the arms; seen most commonly in Iran

A frequently asked question is whether Muslim women are obligated to wear some form of hijab based on Quranic prescriptions. Religious scholars debate this issue, and readings of certain Quranic verses are subject to different interpretations. As Ann Black and her coauthors note, a commonly cited verse is Súra Núr 24:31, which refers to female modesty:

> And say to the believing women that they should lower their gaze and guard their modesty; that they should not display their beauty and ornaments except what (must ordinarily) appear thereof; that they should draw their veils over their bosoms and not display their beauty except to their husbands, their fathers, their husband's fathers, their sons ... or small children who have no sense of the shame of sex; and that they should not strike their feet in order to draw attention to their hidden ornaments.[9]

Black et al. explain traditionalist and modernist interpretations of this verse. The traditionalist position interprets the phrase "should not display their beauty and ornaments" as a command for women to cover their entire body, including hands, face, and especially eyes. Hence, in this view, the burqa or niqab is ideal attire. The modernist position interprets the verse as a command for women to appear modest and only cover their bosoms. Furthermore, the command to "lower their gaze" implies that the face need not be covered. According to modernist beliefs, there is no Islamic prescription that mandates hijab for women.[10]

At Five in the Afternoon (Panj é asr)

Year: 2003; *Director:* Samira Makhmalbaf; *Cast:* Noqreh (Agheleh Rezaie)— woman in her 20s; Leylomah (Marzieh Amiri)—woman in her 20s; *Length:* 105 minutes; *Setting:* large city (Kabul) in Afghanistan; impoverished community

SYNOPSIS

The Taliban regime has been ousted from Afghanistan, and Noqreh (an unmarried woman in her 20s), her father, and her sister-in-law, Leylomah, are living in Kabul, the capital city. The family lives among refugees, and all suffer from the scarcity of food, water, and shelter. Noqreh's father provides a taxi service with his horse-drawn cart. He is a conservative Muslim and bitter about the loss of morals and the laxness of adherence to Sharia among his fellow Afghans. At one point, he refuses transportation to girls for not wearing their head scarfs properly. At another point, he orders a man to turn off his music and its demonic influence. Leylomah, whose husband went missing in the war, frets about her malnourished baby, for whom she is unable to find adequate food and water.

Noqreh attends a girls' school where she and the other girls learn about the Quran and other spiritual materials. When the girls are asked about future careers, Noqreh raises her hand and states that she wants to be president.

She is serious and begins her campaign with the help of a young poet who is known for reciting the works of Federico García Lorca, a famous Spanish poet. Phrases from Lorca's "Lament for Ignacio Sanchez Mejias," with its references to "five in the afternoon," are cited throughout the film.

While Noqreh is campaigning, refugees continue flooding into Kabul, and Noqreh's family is forced to relocate to a deserted, bombed-out palace on the outskirts of Kabul. Here, water is even scarcer, and what little they find is used by the father to wash his feet in religious observance. Eventually, Noqreh must abandon her campaign and migrate with her family across the desert, as her father is in search of a locale that is faithful to the principles of Sharia.

The film ends on a bleak and devastating note. The desert is vast and unforgiving, and the family is sweltering and parched from thirst. The family's horse has died of starvation, and the father, now forced to pull his cart, watches impassively as Leylomah's baby dies of dehydration. At the end, he buries his dead grandchild as Noqreh and Leylomah look on.

TRADITIONAL GENDER STEREOTYPES

Post–Taliban Afghanistan is experiencing social changes, and the tensions between the Islamic traditionalist values and more modern values are evident. The father in *At Five in the Afternoon* represents tradition. He longs for the days when, under strictly enforced Sharia law, his authority and dominance were unquestioned. He reminisces about times when females knew their place in the patriarchal hierarchy and assumed roles that confined them to their homes. In his taxi service, the father will only let women ride in his cart if they are properly veiled. It is sinful for a woman not to cover her face, and he forcefully ejects two women from his cart who removed their veils.

In post–Taliban Afghanistan, females are now allowed to attend schools, but schools must be segregated by gender. Rules demand a modest appearance, and veiling is observed in schools and public areas. The girls are instructed in religious texts with verses from the Quran that reinforce their subordination to male dominance: "Men are women's guardians, for God created some superior to others. Advise women whose opposition and obstinacy you fear. Avoid them in bed and punish them. And don't oppress them if they obey you."

NONTRADITIONAL GENDER ATTRIBUTES

Noqreh wants to become president of Afghanistan. It is unknown where or how she developed the self-confidence to aspire to this position, as most girls raised in the rigid patriarchy of Taliban-run Afghanistan would have likely internalized beliefs about feminine incompetence and lack of agency. But not Noqreh. She is aware of the restrictions placed upon her as a woman in a rigidly patriarchal society, but she doesn't appear to care. In her campaigning, she often is unveiled. She insists that her campaign photo be of her unveiled face, although the photographer states the photo would look much better if her face were veiled. The requisite low-heeled black shoes worn by women in public are exchanged for fancily decorated white high heels. Noqreh also leads refugees to shelter, and she fraternizes with a strange man, a French soldier, whom she interrogates about his knowledge of female world leaders.

"Lament for Ignacio Sanchez Mejias"

The title of this film, *At Five in the Afternoon*, comes from a poem written by Federico García Lorca, a Spanish poet known for his works featuring themes of tragedy and anguish and primitivism. These "At Five in the Afternoon" verses are excerpts from "Lament for Ignacio Sanchez Mejias":

> At five in the afternoon.
> It was exactly five in the afternoon.
> A boy brought the white sheet
> at five in the afternoon.
> A frail of lime ready prepared
> at five in the afternoon.
> The rest was death, and death alone....
>
> The bull does not know you, nor the fig tree,
> nor the horses, nor the ants in your own house.
> The child and the afternoon do not know you
> because you have died forever.
>
> The shoulder of the stone does not know you
> nor the black silk, where you are shuttered.
> Your silent memory does not know you
> because you have died forever.
>
> The autumn will come with small white snails,
> misty grapes and clustered hills,
> but no one will look into your eyes
> because you have died forever.
>
> Because you have died for ever,
> like all the dead of the earth,
> like all the dead who are forgotten
> in a heap of lifeless dogs.
>
> Nobody knows you. No. But I sing of you.
> For posterity I sing of your profile and grace.
> Of the signal maturity of your understanding.

Of your appetite for death and the taste of its mouth.
Of the sadness of your once valiant gaiety.

It will be a long time, if ever, before there is born
an Andalusian so true, so rich in adventure.
I sing of his elegance with words that groan,
and I remember a sad breeze through the olive trees.[11]

Buddha: Collapsed Out of Shame (Buda az sharm foru rikht)

Year: 2007; *Director:* Hana Makhmalbaf (Iranian); *Cast:* Baytak (Nikbakht Noruz)—5-year-old girl; Abbas (Abbas Alijome)—5-year-old boy; *Length:* 81 minutes; *Setting:* small rural village in Afghanistan; impoverished community

SYNOPSIS

The opening scenes of *Buddha: Collapsed Out of Shame* show actual footage of the dynamiting of the Afghanistan Buddhas of Bamiyan by the Taliban in 2001. These Buddhas, considered one of the marvels of the world, were colossal statues carved into cliffs in the 4th century. It has been reported that the reason for the Buddhas' destruction was to rid the country of statues that the Taliban considered non–Islamic.

This film takes place in post–Taliban contemporary Afghanistan, and Baytak, a five-year-old girl, and her mother live in one of the caves where a Buddha once stood. In a neighboring cave, Abbas, a young boy, is getting ready to go to school, and Baytak is insistent that she go as well. But there is a problem: she needs school supplies—namely, a notebook and a writing instrument—and her mother is too poor to afford them. Baytak is determined, however. She sells eggs from the family's chicken in exchange for a notebook, and she pilfers her mother's lipstick for a pen.

Baytak is set for school and follows Abbas, but along the way she encounters a gang of boys who are playacting as Taliban fighters in combat with Americans. The boys accost Baytak and accuse her of engaging in Taliban-prohibited activities. Females, for example, are not allowed to go to school, and Baytak, with notebook in hand, is on her way there. Females are also not allowed to use makeup, and Baytak is in possession of lipstick. For her sins, the boys decide that she must be punished, and the punishment is death by stoning. Baytak is forced into a pit and the boys surround her with stones in hand, waiting for a signal to kill her. The signal never comes, and the boys devise other punishments for her. Baytak knows not to take these boys seriously, and she is finally allowed to leave, only to find that Abbas's school only admits boys. Baytak is then given directions to the all-girls school.

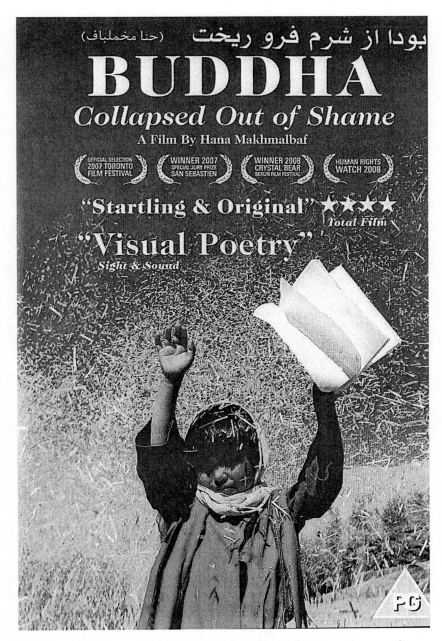

In the ruins of post–Taliban Afghanistan, Baytak (Nikbakht Noruz), a 5-year-old girl, obtains a coveted notebook that will allow her to go to school (*Buddha: Collapsed Out of Shame* DVD cover—released in 2007).

On the way home from school, she again encounters the boys who bullied her. This time she is an enemy soldier, and they pretend to shoot her. As part of the game, she must fake her death in order to go home. Though she refuses, the boys persist. She knows she's outnumbered and eventually plays the game and falls to ground, feigning death.

PATRIARCHAL TRADITIONS AND RELIGIOUS LAWS

Gender Segregation

Gender segregation is a patriarchal-based practice that applies to all areas of the public sphere, including transportation systems, workspace, schools, and, in some regions, parks and sports stadiums. In Afghanistan, girls and boys are segregated in schools after the third grade. State policy calls for gender equality in public schools; however, with scarce financial resources, funding for girls' education is unequal to that for boys. As reported by Saagar Enjeti on April 2, 2015, in the online source *The Diplomat*, Afghanistan suffers from a shortage in supplies and teachers, which disproportionately affects females. Enjeti also cites statistics from the World Bank that indicate the literacy rate for females under the age of 15 is only 32 percent, the lowest in the region.

In *Buddha*, Baytak is desperate to attend school with Abbas. However, when she encounters the teacher, he explains that the school is for boys only and that she must go to the other side of the river to attend the all-girls school. The male-only school is headed by a male teacher, and the female-only school is headed by a female teacher. Both schools appear to have the same number of students and equivalent resources.

TRADITIONAL GENDER STEREOTYPES

In rural Afghanistan, females (old and young) are portrayed as caregivers. The women cook, wash dishes, and collect and filter water for the household. Mothers provide lessons for their young daughters in childcare, teaching them how to feed and care for babies. No males in *Buddha* were seen in the home or laboring in the fields. Rather, males engaged in a variety of occupations in the public sphere. In the local market, they were vendors and tradesmen working as metalsmiths, butchers, and jewelers. Males were also traffic police and teachers. Other than a female teacher in the local girls' school, no females were seen working outside the home.

The violence of boys is a predominant theme in *Buddha*. The gang of boys' interactions with the young girl on her way to and from school represent a microcosm of the larger Afghan society that is emerging from the brutality of Taliban rule. (Certain scenes are reminiscent of the feral children in *Lord of the Flies*.) In one scene, some rag-tag boys are play-acting as Taliban fighters. They encounter Baytak on her way to school and ask her about her notebook. When told it is for school, the boys state that girls do not go to school and tear out the pages. The boys then discover the lipstick she has taken from her mother that will be used for a pen. Baytak is told that she is a sinner, and they shout, "Lipstick is for heathen women. We'll stone her!" In a harrowing scene, the boys dig a pit and force her into it, covering her head with a paper bag. Each boy, with a large stone in hand, surrounds the pit, awaiting the signal to stone her. The signal is not given and the boys release her.

NONTRADITIONAL GENDER ATTRIBUTES

Buddha: Collapsed Out of Shame is a story about Baytak, who is remarkable in her agency and her determination. She has decided that she will go to school, and, despite all the obstacles, that's what she does. She realizes that she needs to have paper and pen, and she decides to sell the family eggs in the market. She runs to the market, populated by crowds of men, and asks numerous men to buy her eggs. Most refuse, but she is undeterred by rejection. She eventually gets enough money for just a notebook, but the problem of the pen is solved by pilfering her mother's lipstick. The male teacher later tells her to go to the other side of river, where the all-girls school is, but she doesn't want to and she lets him know. At first she refuses to playact with the boys who bully her. All she has to do is to engage with them in their war game. They want her to play dead from their pretend assault, but she refuses up until the very end, when, realizing that it's time to go home, she acquiesces and falls to the ground in a pretend death.

Kabuli Kid

Year: 2008; *Director:* Barmak Akram; *Cast:* Khaled (Haji Gul Aser)—man in his late 30s; *Length:* 97 minutes; *Setting:* large urban city (Kabul) in Afghanistan; working-class community

SYNOPSIS

Khaled is a taxi driver in post–Taliban Kabul. A burqa-clad woman and her baby are passengers in his taxi. She urges him to stop, runs out, and disappears into the crowd. Moments later, Khaled finds that she has abandoned the baby on the back seat of his taxi. His search for her is in vain, and he realizes that since there is no one to care for the boy, he has little choice other than to bring the baby to his home. His wife and four daughters are ordered to take care of the baby while he sets out to find help. Although he is desperate for a son, he cannot in good conscience keep the child.

Basically, Khaled is a decent man who strives to do the right thing. He urgently pleads with various organizations, including the police and an orphanage, to take the child in, but to no avail. Eventually, a humanitarian NGO and a local radio station agree to help locate the infant's mother by offering a $100 reward if she reclaims her son. Soon, several burqa-clad women are lined up outside the station, with each woman claiming to be the mother. The real mother is eventually found, and she reveals the troubling events that prompted her to abandon her child.

TRADITIONAL GENDER STEREOTYPES

In *Kabuli Kid*, a clear gendered division of labor is observed in the streets of Kabul. Males are dominant in the public sphere and work in a variety of jobs. Men are taxi drivers, guards, pharmacy clerks, orphanage managers, police, radio announcers, and street vendors. Females are invisible in the public arena, as they are confined to the home in their roles as caretakers of the family.

Khaled is the breadwinner for his family. He is something of a contradiction. He criticizes women who wear burqas ("Why do you women still wear burqas?"), yet he requires his own wife to wear the veil when leaving their home. He also keeps the females of his family in servitude to him. A daughter assists him as he washes his face, and another daughter cleans the floor. His wife serves him water and prepares the family meal while feeding, clothing, and soothing the abandoned baby. Khaled assumes that his wife will be infant's caregiver. There is no discussion; she is given the baby and told to care for him. There is no discussion about adoption plans for the baby. Her opinion, if she has one, is not sought. Females in this household are not allowed to feed the birds; as Khaled tells his daughter, "It's a man's thing." Another "man thing" apparently is watching television, as only males are seen in front of the family's set.

The Patience Stone (Syngué Sabour, pierre de patience)

Year: 2012; *Director:* Atiq Rahimi; *Cast:* The woman (Golshifteh Farahani)— woman in her late 20s; *Length:* 102 minutes

An unnamed narrator (Golshifteh Farahani) is pictured at a moment when she discovers her own agency and realizes that she is no longer in thrall to her abusive husband (*Patience Stone* DVD cover—released in 2012).

SYNOPSIS

In a bombed-out house in what is presumed to be Afghanistan, an unnamed woman tends to her comatose husband, who is ostensibly brain dead from a wound sustained in a war. She is alone, with no money for food for her two young children or medicine for her husband. While caring for her husband, armed militants invade her home. The leader's intent is to rape her, but she lies and tells him that she is a prostitute. He leaves her alone in disgust, as there is no masculine bravado in "raping a whore."

Out of desperation for money and advice, she seeks help from her aunt, who does earn a living through prostitution. The woman confides to her aunt that in her solitude she has been examining her life and the secrets she has held deep inside. All her life, she has been silenced, first as an obedient Muslim daughter and then as an obedient Muslim wife. But now she is compelled to reveal, to confess. Her aunt relates the parable of the patience stone, a stone that, once discovered, must be told everything—all secrets. "Eventually the stone will shatter, and you will be delivered."

The woman discovers that her patience stone is her mute husband, and, throughout the days, as she feeds and bathes him, she reveals her intimate feelings about both her father and the stranger who is her husband. She recalls an event from early in their marriage, when he had just returned from war. During their initial sexual encounters, she found him uncaring and brutal. He prohibited her from kissing him because, she claims, he was scared and did not know how to kiss a girl. The stone must be told everything, and she becomes more empowered in her revelations. Sexual secrets are divulged. She reveals her recent affair with a young militant who, believing her to be a prostitute, requested that she instruct him in the pleasures of sex. Finally, the most powerful secrets are told, and indeed, as her aunt foretold, the patience stone shatters and she is delivered. Her final story is one of sexual emancipation and a search for identity through revenge.

PATRIARCHAL TRADITIONS AND RELIGIOUS LAWS

Arranged Marriages

Arranged marriage is a centuries-old tradition in many parts of the world (see commentary below). In Muslim-majority countries, this tradition dates to pre–Islamic times. Although there can be variation dependent on regional custom, in a typical arranged marriage, the intended spouses and their families or spokespersons meet to ensure that the marriage is consensual and to establish any stipulations required for the marital contract. This procedure was not observed in *Patience Stone*. In this film, the female protagonist's father forces one of his adolescent daughters to wed a man much older than herself as payment for a gambling debt. There was no consent provided and no mutually agreed-upon marital contract.

A proxy marriage was another marital practice observed in the film. In a proxy marriage, the prospective spouse is absent and is represented by a proxy during the marriage ceremony. In some proxy marriages, a bride might not even be aware of the marriage until after the fact. In *Patience Stone*, the woman's husband was absent due to military duty, and her marriage was conducted in the presence of his proxy—a photograph of her new spouse.

Divorce

The woman in *Patience Stone* was miserable throughout her marriage to a distant and often brutal man. Why didn't she divorce him? Divorce for women in many Muslim-majority countries is difficult due to legal proscriptions and patriarchal norms that stigmatize divorced women. In Afghanistan, divorce laws are based on Islamic Sharia, and men and women are not granted the same rights. Men have the right to divorce without any justification and can divorce their wives unilaterally. Women, by contrast, have the right to divorce only if certain conditions apply. In divorce, women are penalized by losing custody of their children when they reach a certain age. A divorced woman will also lose custody of her children if she remarries (see the discussion of *3 Dots* earlier in this chapter).

Not only does the law disadvantage women in divorce situations, but patriarchal norms differentially and detrimentally impact women more than men. In patriarchal societies, women, by virtue of their gender, are in subordinate positions both socially and economically, and marriage offers some protection against their vulnerability. A woman who is divorced is viewed as even more subordinate and vulnerable than one who is unmarried. A divorced woman is also viewed as shameful, as she has violated her social role of wife. Furthermore, she may now be subject to sexual predation by men, which will exacerbate her shame.

Traditional Gender Stereotypes

The protagonist of *Patience Stone* embodies the patriarchal-dictated ideals of daughter, wife, and mother. Her obedience and submissiveness to her father, and later to her husband, demonstrates the subjugation of females to the authority of males. The woman has no identity apart from wife and mother, and this identity is assured as long as she obeys and pleases others.

As is true for many women across the world enduring patriarchal restrictions, entrenched values are not only not questioned but also internalized as acceptable. Women are socialized to believe in their inferior value. In this film, the woman accepted early in her marriage that husbands care more about things (e.g., the husband's affection for his quails) than their own wives and children. She also accepted the belief that a man's sexual needs take priority over her own. In her own words, she was just "a piece of meat."

NONTRADITIONAL GENDER ATTRIBUTES

The unnamed woman is a transformational character in *Patience Stone*. Her individuality, which had long been denied by her loveless and authoritarian father and then her husband, is restored as she reveals her secrets to her comatose husband. As she tells these secrets one by one, the complexity of her inner life is revealed. Memories come flooding back, and with each remembered event, her anger intensifies and another self-truth is revealed. She recalls an especially brutal sexual encounter with her husband, who forced sex on her while she was sleeping. Discovering that she was menstruating (thus defiling him), he beat her. As she relates this event to her comatose husband, she is aware that she is in her menstrual period; she puts her fingers between her legs and wipes her blood on his face. "You were born of this blood," she states. "It is cleaner than the blood of your own body!" With the soldier, she negotiates her sexual agency. She is empowered as she instructs him on what pleasures her. She will no longer be victimized by men.

ARRANGED AND FORCED MARRIAGES

Marriage in Islam is a civil contract, not a religious one. Marriage customs in Muslim-majority countries vary considerably, though most customs involve a marital contract that may list a number of stipulations. Under the precepts of Islam, marriages must be consensual and the bride and groom must agree to the provisions of the marital contract. If one or the other disputes the contract, the agreement is dissolved. Often, family members act as intermediaries in establishing the specific stipulations of the contract. As marriage involves the union of two families, the choice of a marital partner is of utmost importance. In arranged marriages, parents (or tribal elders) select the marital partners, and each must give their consent for the marriage to take place. Many marriages in Muslim-majority countries are arranged, and it is important to distinguish between arranged marriage and forced marriage. Typically, in arranged marriage, the couple is introduced to each other in a family setting and decisions about the acceptability of the marriage are made. In a forced marriage, consent is not freely given. The more egregious examples of forced marriage involve abductions, exchange of child brides to settle tribal disputes, and physical violence. In these cases, coercion obviates any consensual process.

Although on surface, arranged marriages are consensual, consent that is assumed to be "freely" given may be difficult at times to ascertain due to certain social and psychological forces. The traditions of culture and the persuasiveness of one's family may be difficult to combat, especially when those entering marital contracts are young and uninformed. To clarify the distinction between arranged marriages and forced marriages, Abdullahi A. An-Na'im maintains that it may be useful to conceptualize arranged and forced marriages as "falling on a continuum between consent and coercion. This characterization acknowledges the cultural and contextual nature of consent and considers its difference from coercion as a matter of degree and perception, with persuasion playing a key role in the gray area of the continuum."[12]

Stray Dogs (Sag-haye velgard)

Year: 2004; *Director:* Marzieh Makhmalbaf (as Marziyeh Meshkini); *Cast:* girl (Gol-Ghotai); boy (Zahed); *Length:* 93 minutes; *Setting:* large urban city (Kabul) in Afghanistan; impoverished community

SYNOPSIS

A young girl of around 5 years old, her older brother, and a scruffy small dog (which the two rescued from the torments of street kids) spend their days rummaging through mounds of rubbish, looking for rags to sell, food to eat, and scraps of wood for warmth at night. This is post–Taliban Afghanistan, and these children, along with thousands of others, are trying to survive in a war-ravaged Kabul. The children's mother is in prison, but the guards allow the children (and the dog) in at night, so they sleep in her cell and share what meager food resources are available. The mother's crime is alleged adultery, for she remarried when she believed her husband had died in the war. But the mother has since learned that her husband is still alive and has returned as a prisoner. Her children are allowed to visit him, and she coaches them to plead her case, but to no avail.

Upon returning to their mother, the children discover that the prison has new administrators, who prohibit the children from staying with their mother at night. Now, with nowhere to stay, they devise a scheme so they can join her. The boy will steal a bicycle and be arrested, and both he and his

An unnamed girl's (Gol-Ghotai) mother has been imprisoned for adultery. She walks the streets of Kabul, Afghanistan, with her rescued dog, in search of food and shelter (*Stray Dogs* DVD cover—released in 2004).

sister will be sent to her prison. The boy does steal and is arrested, but he is transported to a different prison. In an ending that is bleak, despairing and without hope, the girl and the stray dog are crouched alone outside the fortress walls of her mother's prison and the boy screams from behind bars in a solitary cell in a prison for men, crying for his mother and sister.

PATRIARCHAL TRADITIONS AND RELIGIOUS LAWS

Sex Outside of Marriage: Zina

In Afghanistan, cases of premarital sex and extramarital sex are considered zina offenses, which are serious moral transgressions punishable by imprisonment (Afghan penal code) or death by stoning (Islamic Sharia law). In this film, the mother of the two young children is imprisoned for the crime of adultery. Believing that her missing husband died in the war, she was forced to remarry to feed her children. But the husband has returned as a prisoner of the regime. As the law allows, he has his wife arrested and imprisoned for adultery; according to the law, only he can pardon her and secure her release from prison. As the children can visit their father in jail, their mother coaches them on what to say so their father will forgive her and she'll be freed. She instructs them to not talk about how he beat her but to tell him, "You vanished for five years. We thought you had been killed. Mother couldn't feed us, so she married again so we could eat." The father is unforgiving and replies, "I went to fight the holy war. Your mother married again ... didn't she love me?" Upon hearing that her second husband is dead, he states, "That's good, and if Mother dies, they can make love in hell."

TRADITIONAL GENDER STEREOTYPES

Whether masculine aggression is innately driven or learned through social conditions is irrelevant in patriarchal societies, as males have the prerogative (if not the compulsion) to express aggression when provoked. There are several scenes in *Stray Dogs* that exemplify male aggression. In the establishing scenes, dozens of street boys (no females) are chasing a small, scruffy dog that they believe to be Western and want to kill it. Elsewhere, groups of men and boys (no females) crowd into a courtyard to incite dogs to fight. The children protagonists of the film find a night's refuge in boxcars run by homeless boys. The children are told that girls are banned, as men come at night to abduct them. The new guards of the woman's prison tell the boy that his mother is a whore, and the woman's husband denounces her and condemns her to death.

NONTRADITIONAL GENDER ATTRIBUTES

The young boy in the film stands apart from the other, more feral boys. His compassion for others is evident in his saving of the dog from death and his protectiveness toward his younger sister. He is persistent in his attempts to stay with their mother at night. He protects his sister from the cold as best as he can. He shares what food he has. He cries with remorse when his father refuses to pardon his mother.

ZINA OFFENSES AND HADD AND TA'ZIR PUNISHMENTS

Sexual intercourse outside of marriage is considered a zina offense and is prohibited in countries operating under Islamic Sharia law. Zina offenses are punishable by fines, lashings, imprisonment, or death. The severity of the punishment is a function of whether adultery occurred (if the offenders were married) or fornication (if the offenders were unmarried). According to An-Na'im,[13] the *hadd* punishment (mandated by God) for a married person convicted of zina is stoning to death, and the *hadd* punishment for an unmarried person found guilty of zina is one hundred lashes in a public place. The application of *hadd* punishments for zina requires a rigorous standard of proof. If the accused confesses or if there are four Muslim male eye-witnesses to the actual act of penetration, the *hadd* penalty may be applied. If these evidentiary requirements are not met, *ta'zir* punishments may be applied, which are more lenient. *Ta'zir* punishments can consist of imprisonment for up to ten years, thirty lashes, and a fine. In contemporary times, there are very few convictions for adultery due to the high evidentiary requirements that Sharia requires.[14]

In Afghanistan, it has been estimated that more than half of all female inmates in Afghan prisons are imprisoned for zina crimes, and women who have been raped have been criminally prosecuted for zina.[15] According to Human Rights Watch, the Afghan government is currently drafting a new penal code that would end the criminalization of consensual sex between adults.[16]

Wajma, an Afghan Love Story

Year: 2013; *Director:* Barmak Akram; *Cast:* Wajma (Wajma Bahar)—woman in her 20s; Mustafa (Mustafa Abdulsatar)—man in his 20s; *Length:* 85 minutes; *Setting:* large urban city (Kabul) in Afghanistan; lower middle class

SYNOPSIS

Wajma is a young woman with ambitions of becoming a lawyer. She finds herself caught between two Afghanistans. One is modern and reflects the permissiveness of Western values. In this Afghanistan, young people wear jeans, socialize with their cell phones, go on dates, and grapple with decisions about sex. The other Afghanistan retains the social restrictions imposed by a society that favors patriarchy and is religiously conservative. As the story unfolds, Wajma is excited, as she has just been accepted to law school, and she boasts about her accomplishment to Mustafa, her boyfriend. Mustafa is not so achievement oriented and spends his days working as a waiter in a tea shop and his nights pressuring Wajma to have sex. Mustafa is nothing if not persistent. Wajma is aware of the Islamic Afghanistan that prohibits premarital sex, but she is attracted to the more liberal Western stance that allows sexual interactions between consenting adults. Wajma is ultimately seduced by Mustafa, who professes his enduring love and hints at marriage.

But *Wajma, an Afghan Love Story* is not, in fact, a love story. Wajma discovers that she is pregnant and a shocked Mustafa denies responsibility, asserting that since she did not "bleed" after their intercourse, she must have had sexual relations with other men. Wajma is devastated, and her parents soon discover her pregnancy. Her father is enraged and brutally beats Wajma and locks her in a frigid storeroom for hours. He alternately blames his wife (she was an overly permissive mother) and his son (he was derelict in his duty to protect his sister's honor) and ultimately tracks down Mustafa. He pleads with the young man to marry his daughter, as it is the right thing to do. But Mustafa is not interested in marriage and refuses, resulting in a beating from the father. The father's consultation with a legal authority clarifies that he cannot legally kill the young man, as he didn't catch him in the act.

There is no happy conclusion in *Wajma, an Afghan Love Story*. At the end, Wajma is sent to India for an abortion, a family is destroyed, a young woman's ambition is crushed, and a young man has realized an important truth about himself—that he is a coward.

Patriarchal Traditions and Religious Laws

Islamic Sharia law prohibits sexual relationships outside of the marriage, as such acts dishonor the sanctity of marriage and the family. Penalties are severe for those who engage in premarital sex (even between consensual adults) and can range from imprisonment to death. Wajma is unmarried and pregnant. Her father seeks legal advice as to whether he can legally kill Mustafa, the young man who impregnated his daughter. He is informed that if a close relative catches a couple while fornicating and subsequently kills one or even both of them, he would not be liable to criminal prosecution for murder. But in this case, since he did not catch them in flagrante delicto, he has no legal right to kill Mustafa. If he were to do so, he would be tried for murder and punished with life in prison or death.

TRADITIONAL GENDER STEREOTYPES

Wajma illustrates the authority and dominance of males in both the public and the private spheres. Wajma's father has the final authority over the women in his family, including his wife, his mother, and Wajma. The father is the family breadwinner and head of household, and it is he who ultimately decides Wajma's punishment and her fate. She has no say.

Male dominance is also depicted by Wajma's boyfriend. He evades his responsibility to Wajma and the unborn child by asserting that she was not a virgin when they had sexual relations and therefore the baby could be anyone's. He refuses to marry her, and abortion is not an option in Afghanistan, as abortion is illegal. Instead of doing what he knows is right, he denies his responsibility and exercises his male prerogative to do so, choosing the coward's way out.

Although Wajma and her mother have a strong presence in the film, they are women and thus subordinate. In the end, Wajma has no choice but to conform to rules of patriarchy and Islam, in which premarital sex is a sin and punishable at the very least by social ostracism and loss of familial honor.

Males in patriarchal societies have the liberty to engage in violence toward women who have disgraced their family honor. Wajma's father is enraged on discovering her sexual indiscretion. He beats her with a belt, slaps her repeatedly, and pulls her by the hair, calling her a slut who has dishonored the family. He even orders his wife to fetch the gas so he can kill her. The father's rage also extends to other family members. He beats his son for his negligence in not protecting his sister and beats his wife for her indulgence toward Wajma. "You can mourn your death, bitch. You've drowned me in shame!" he roars.

Mustafa illustrates male aggressiveness in his treatment of Wajma and her pregnancy. He claims that she was not a virgin because her hymen did not tear. Even though his employer explains that this is not a definitive sign of prior sexual involvement, Mustafa will not listen: "I won't marry a girl who is not a virgin. Listen, if the child is mine, then why was there no blood the first time we did it!? You think I'm stupid?"

3

Algeria

COUNTRY PROFILE

BACKGROUND[1]

The People's Democratic Republic of Algeria is located in Northern Africa and borders the Mediterranean Sea. Algeria is currently a member state of the Arab League. The official language of Algeria is Arabic, and the official religion is Islam (under Sharia law of the Maliki school). The form of government is a presidential republic. Almost all (99 percent) Algerians are Muslim, and the majority (77 percent) of the population resides in urban areas.

SOCIOPOLITICAL AND RELIGIOUS ISSUES RELATED TO GENDER

Efforts have been made to ensure that the information presented here reflects current law and policies. However, many Muslim-majority countries are currently contending with challenges to their civil and criminal laws that stem from competing constituencies of those favoring greater freedoms for women and those espousing conservative Islamic principles. As such, governmental policies are continually evolving, and laws relevant to gender issues may be added, deleted, or amended in subsequent years.

Law

Algeria's amended its constitution in 2016.[2] Provisions of the 1984 Family Code (revised 2005) remained largely intact in the 2016 constitution. Many

41

of these positions are based on Sharia law. Algeria ratified CEDAW in 1996, with reservations to Articles 2, 15:4, 19, and 29.

Some key points of the revised Family Code (2005) with reference to gender are as follows:

- The minimum age of marriage is 19 for both sexes
- Women are under the legal guardianship of a husband or male relative; women cannot marry without the presence of their (male) guardians, though women may choose their guardians
- Women may ensure and protect their rights through the provision of stipulations in the marriage contract. Such stipulations might include the right to education or to work outside the home, the right to divorce, and the right to prohibit a second wife
- In 2015, amendments to the penal code were adopted criminalizing both some forms of domestic violence and sexual harassment in public places
- Women are no longer obligated to obey their husbands
- Polygyny is allowed (up to 4 wives) with the consent of all wives and validation by a local court (rarely practiced)
- Men have the right to divorce without any justification; women can obtain a divorce under certain limited conditions (e.g., permanent disagreement between spouses); women can also initiate a divorce through *khul'*, paying the husband a sum of money
- Women typically receive custody of children after divorce up to age 10 for boys and 18 for girls; if a woman remarries, she loses custody of her children; if a divorced man remarries, he does not lose custody
- A woman is entitled to inherit half of her brother's or other male relative's share
- Women have rights to travel freely and obtain their own passport; they can leave the country but not with their children unless the husband authorizes doing so
- Rape and sexual harassment are criminal offenses
- Abortion is permitted to save the life of the woman, to preserve physical health, and to preserve mental health; it is prohibited in cases of rape (unless the woman is raped by a terrorist) or incest or for reasons of fetal impairment

Laws Regulating Homosexuality

The 2016 report on sexual orientation laws compiled by the International Lesbian, Gay, Bisexual, Trans and Intersex Association identified the following items in Algerian penal law:

A breach of decency punished by two months or two years in prison and a fine of 500 to 2000 Algerian dinar. The punishment for those convicted of "abnormal sexual acts" is six months to three years in prison and a fine of 1,000 to 10,000 Algerian dinars.[3]

Additional Issues

In 1989, Algeria allowed independent political parties to form. During the national elections in 1992, the Islamic Salvation Front (FIS), a fundamentalist party, was in position to win. FIS pushed for a strong application of Sharia law. As reported by Meredeth Turshen, the hostility of FIS toward women was demonstrated through attacks on women workers (women should not be employed), female students (women should receive only religious instruction), and mothers living alone (women need the protection of a male relative or husband). With reference to gender issues, the FIS platform claimed that women did not have the right to work outside the home, to hold political office, or to participate in sports. Further, women should wear hijab and should not "wear make-up, perfume, [or] fitted clothes, or mingle with men in public."[4] In response to the FIS threat, the Algerian government cancelled the elections and banned the FIS, which culminated in a civil war between Islamist extremists and the government. The war lasted almost a decade, claiming an estimated 100,000–200,000 lives.

Although the FIS was outlawed in 1992, many Algerian women currently adhere to conservative Islamic tenets, including wearing the veil in public. Social pressures, harassment from religious extremist groups, and freedom of movement in the public sphere all affect women's choice to follow a certain dress code, which may include just a head scarf or total veiling.[5]

FILMS

Daughter of Keltoum (La fille de Keltoum)

Year: 2001; *Director:* Mehdi Charef; *Cast:* Rallia (Cylia Malki)—woman in her 20s; Nedjma (Baya Belal)—woman in her 40s; *Length:* 106 minutes; *Setting:* Rural village in Berber region of Algeria; impoverished community

Synopsis

Rallia has left her home in Europe and traveled to the mountainous region of northern Algeria in search of the mother who abandoned her when she was a baby. She locates her mother's family—her grandfather and aunt, Nedjma—

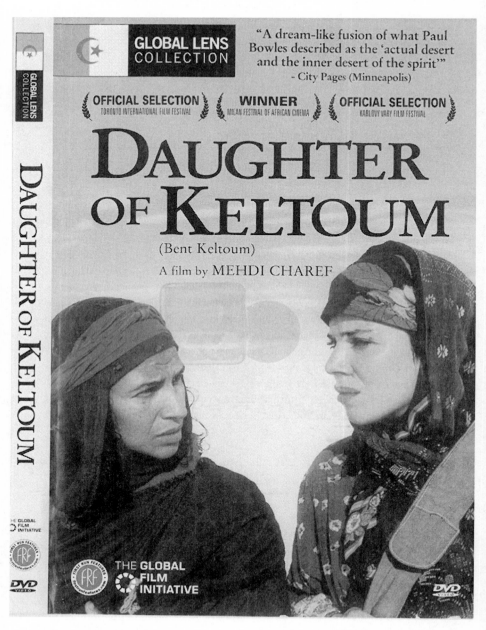

Rallia (Cylia Malki), raised in the West, returns to place of her birth in the Bedouin region of rural Algeria in search of her mother, who abandoned her as an infant. Her Algerian aunt, Nedjma (Baya Belal), accompanies her on a journey to locate her mother (*Daughter of Keltoum* DVD cover—released in 2001).

but her mother is not there. The family lives in poverty in a collection of huts sitting on a hilly, sunbaked plateau. The important activity of each day is finding water, as it is a scarce resource, and the villagers depend on Nedjma to collect it. Nedjma is a strange woman whose eccentric movements and speech lead the other villagers to think she is mad, though they gladly accept her services.

Rallia is informed that her mother, Keltoum, works as a maid at a luxury hotel in another city. Rallia is intent on finding her mother and enlists Nedjma's help. The two set off through the wastelands of Algeria to find Keltoum. In their journey, they encounter the primitive realities of the Algerian desert. A woman they meet recounts how her husband deserted her for younger wife. Another woman is seen tethered to a horse outside a café while her husband drinks inside.

Rallia and Nedjma eventually find the woman whom Rallia believes is her mother, and Rallia learns the truth about her abandonment as an infant. Keltoum casually tells Rallia that she was infertile and her family was starving and desperate for water. Realizing that babies could be sold on the black market for considerable sums, she arranged for soldiers to rape Nedjma, her younger sister, in hopes that a pregnancy would result. As it turns out, Rallia is actually Nedjma's daughter, and when Rallia was born, she was sold for a mule that would transport water. *Daughter of Keltoum* is ultimately a film about relationships between mothers and their daughters, and it examines the practice of child abandonment in cultures of poverty and patriarchy.

Traditional Gender Stereotypes

In rural Algeria, males' dominance over women is complete, and females are powerless to assert any independence. The women portrayed in *Daughter of Keltoum* are nothing more than chattel to be disposed of when no longer useful to men. In the village where Rallia finds her family, it is women who engage in the drudgery of daily life, hauling water and finding food. When Rallia arrives, she notes the village patriarch seated in his hut. Women serve him tea, bring him water, cook his meals and wash his feet. One woman speaks of her past relationship with her husband. She says, "I washed my husband's feet since I was 16. I gave him some lovely children that he has kept.... He said I no longer obeyed him. It's not true. He wants to marry younger women." This woman was ultimately abandoned and left to live in abject poverty.

The domination-subordination gendered binary is illustrated at another point in the narrative. Nearing a desert outpost, a man on horseback pulls his wife by a rope attached to her waist. He stops at the outpost and ties her to the horse while he enters the café for his refreshment. On his return, he unties her, gives her money, and states that he has divorced her. He then rides away, leaving her abandoned at the café.

The male characters in this film are aggressive and misogynistic. A shop owner threatens women who do not wear the veil. A woman is accused of staring at a man, who violently shoves her head into a bus window while raging, "Be silent, woman! You're bareheaded with makeup. You want to perturb me? This isn't Europe. Where are you from? Show some respect to a man!" Another woman is murdered for recognizing her son's friend, who is now a militant. A man on a horse leads his beleaguered wife by a rope with the intention of divorcing and abandoning her. As he leaves her alone in the desert, she attempts to follow him, but he orders her to stop and swats her with a stick. On their journey to find Keltoum, Rallia and Nedjma are caught helping thieves steal grain from a truck driver. Saying that the two women are going to pay, the truck driver punches Rallia in the face and attempts to rape both of the women.

Nontraditional Gender Attributes

Rallia defies patriarchal norms that insist on female obedience and passivity, refusing to be subjugated by men. She challenges rules about female modesty by purposefully entering a café frequented by men and removing her head scarf. The owner orders her to cover her head, but she refuses and is chased out of the café. She likewise challenges a truck driver who has been robbed of his grain by a group of starving men. He orders Nedjma and Rallia to fetch the grain after he has shot one man in the leg. The women do indeed retrieve the grain, but they will not obey him; they run from the driver and give the grain to the men instead. Rallia and Nedjma then rescue each other from the aggressions of the driver, who at one point attempts to rape Nedjma. Rallia prevents the rape by stealing the driver's truck, leaving him stranded in the desert. Nedjma, at the film's conclusion, overcomes her obsequiousness to protect Rallia.

Enough! (Bakarat!)

Year: 2006; *Director:* Djamila Sahraoui; *Cast:* Amel (Rachida Brakni)—woman in her 20s; Khadidja (Fattouma Ousliha Bouamari)—woman in her 40s; *Length:* 95 minutes; *Setting:* urban city and countryside Algeria; middle class

Amel (Rachida Brakni) is searching for her journalist husband, who has been abducted by Algerian terrorists. She receives unexpected help from an old man (Zahir Bouzerar) who is also searching for a missing loved one (*Enough!* DVD cover—released in 2006).

Synopsis

In modern-day Algeria, Amel, a young doctor, returns home one evening to discover that her journalist husband has disappeared. She is informed that Islamic militants have abducted him for the crime of writing subversive materials. Amel learns that he may have been taken to a mountain hideout, and, determined to find her husband, she sets out for the hidden camp. She reluctantly allows Khadidja, an older woman and a co-worker, to join her. Khadidja, after all, was a resistance fighter in the war for Algerian independence from France and could be helpful in the current situation.

On their journey, the two women have an uneasy relationship, mostly because Amel finds it difficult to get close to/trust anyone, let alone an older woman whom she doesn't particularly like. The two women locate the terrorists' camp but find that Amel's husband is not there. They are captured and are to be executed. But Khadidja encounters a camp superior who was a fellow resistance fighter. He owes her a favor and allows the two to be released.

Khadidja and Amel then begin an arduous journey on foot back to their home. They are shoeless, and the journey is slow and painful. An elderly man encounters them and helps them reach their destination by providing a ride in his horse-drawn cart. He, too, is searching—for his son, who never returned from war. The three make their way to the city, and as they do, they share hidden truths. At the end of the film, each in their own way is transformed as they learn to trust each other and themselves.

Traditional Gender Stereotypes

Amel and Khadidja, the two female protagonists, encounter aggressive men throughout their journey to locate Amel's husband. At the beginning of the journey, Amel and Khadidja drive along a deserted Algerian country road to a terrorist camp where the husband is said to be imprisoned. Neither woman is wearing a head scarf. A car pulls ahead of them, and the male driver rages at them that respectable women would be veiled and would not be driving. He calls them "bitches" and "sluts" as he drives away. As it turns out, Amel's husband is not in the terrorist camp, and armed men hold the two women captive with plans to execute them. Though eventually released, Amel and Khadidja are forced to trudge miles in bare feet through unforgiving terrain. The men clearly enjoy the torment that these women will experience. On streets and in cafés, the women are subjected to the hostility of men who sexually harass them.

Nontraditional Gender Attributes

Enough! is a female-centered film about the persistence of two women in searching for a man abducted by terrorists. The women are independent and strong. In their journey through war-torn Algeria, they are undeterred by the abuses of violent men. Armed men have held them captive, sadistic guards force them to trudge miles in their bare feet, and all sorts of men sexually harass them on streets and in cafés. However, the women refuse to comply with feminine gender-based dictates to be silent, invisible, and cowed. In one telling scene in a restaurant populated with male customers, Amel is harassed by men who ogle her and make sexual gestures. One leering man at a nearby table smirks, "Nice merchandise." Amel has clearly had enough. She tells him angrily, "Take a look, then!" As he approaches, she pulls out a gun and watches his hasty retreat with satisfaction.

Additional Issue

Amel embodies a tough masculinity throughout the film. She takes charge in emergency situations; she is resolved to find her husband and travels through the dangerous countryside, knowing that her own life is in danger. She aggressively confronts the men on the street who harass her. She is not afraid to use her father's gun. Amel, however, must be cast as a normal woman. So she weeps at times, and she seeks nurturance and comfort from Khadidja. Did the filmmaker need to soften Amel's toughness to reassure the viewer that underneath the masculine façade there lies a feminine sensibility? If so, then her agency was undermined. Feminine agency was also undermined in the last scenes of *Enough!* The two women are the protagonists of the film. They are in control of the action. Yet at the end it is a man who decides that it is enough as he throws the gun into the sea. Apparently it requires the competent voice of masculinity to be decisive.

Masquerades

Year: 2008; *Director:* Lyes Salem; *Cast:* Mounir (Lyes Salem)—man in his 30s; Rym (Sarah Reguieg)—teenage girl; Habiba (Rym Takoucht)—woman in her 30s; *Length:* 92 minutes; *Setting:* small village in Algeria; working class

Synopsis

In this romantic comedy set in a rural community of Algeria, village gossips have concluded that Rym, the winsome younger sister of Mounir, will never marry due to her "condition." Rym is afflicted by narcolepsy, a disease that renders her unable to stay awake even during the most exciting of times. In fact, it is exciting times that most trigger her sleep attacks. Mounir, as the head of household, is responsible for marrying his sister to a suitable husband, and he becomes easily provoked when the villagers taunt him about Rym and her unmarried status. In a moment of drunken weakness, Mounir fabricates a story that Rym is soon to marry "William Vancooten," a wealthy businessman from the West. The villagers, intrigued by a Western lifestyle that promises ready wealth, treat Mounir as a hero who will bring new wealth and recognition to their village. Rym goes along with the lie only to encourage her secret boyfriend of four years to propose marriage. This boyfriend happens to be Mounir's best friend, and Mounir would not approve of his friend courting his sister. Mounir's own marriage is also experiencing difficulties. His wife is disgusted by the whole scheme of the pretend marriage and promises to expose him and his lies. Mounir in turn faults his wife for her lack of wifely support. The film, however, concludes with happy ending for all. Mounir announces to the village that the marriage is not to be (for some mysterious reason), he and his wife reach a more accepting understanding in their marriage, and Rym marries her boyfriend.

Patriarchal Traditions and Religious Laws

Males are valued in patriarchies, and the older brother in a family is responsible for his younger sisters. Sibling care can entail physical care and protection of sisters, or it can entail as serving as a guide and a mentor. The oldest son is often charged with caring for his sisters' safety and security, which is particularly important in societies where the public sphere enforces restrictions on women. Sisters, for their part, are obligated to obey their brothers and seek their permission to engage in activities that might compromise honor. In *Masquerades*, Mounir understands his obligation to his sister. His chief concern is that she marry a man of worth.

Nontraditional Gender Attributes

The female characters in *Masquerades* are in control of the narrative. Mounir's wife and sister are dominant characters. Mounir's wife serves as a foil to the foolish antics of her husband. She makes many demands of her husband, commands him to stop reprimanding their son and interrogates him about the fabricated marriage that he arranged for his sister. In one scene, she attacks him with a pillow when he attempts to assert control over his family. Mounir's sister, Rym, likewise controls her boyfriend, a hapless, love-struck young man who works at a record store. Various male characters in the film are caricatured as buffoons, milksops, and sycophants. Mounir himself is a well-intentioned but clueless man. He is befuddled by women's concerns and emotions. He swaggers about with his male companions, but in reality both he and they know that his wife is in control. It is interesting that in *Masquerades* these dominant women with agency and these insecure men dominated by women are likeable, as both are good hearted and well intentioned. In other films, the dominance in females would be labeled as shrewish and manipulative, and insecurity in males would be labeled as weak and contemptible.

Additional Issue

Other than dialogue in French and a setting in the desert with the distinctive architecture of the Maghreb villages, the narrative and characters of *Masquerades* could easily be set anywhere in the world. All the standard tropes are there: women pitted against men, the poor against the rich, the theme that love conquers all, a young man coming to his senses and marrying the women he loves, a husband and wife rekindling their passion for each other, and everyone realizing that family is all that is important. It is the basic story of the befuddled man who is clueless about gender relationships (or women) and the no-nonsense wife who essentially runs the show.

Rachida

Year: 2002; *Director:* Yamina Bachir; *Cast:* Rachida (Ibtissem Djouadi)—woman in her 20s; *Length:* 100 minutes; *Setting:* small rural village in Algeria; working class

Synopsis

Rachida relates the story of a victim of the decade-long civil war that occurred in Algeria during the 1990s. This war, called the "black decade," was waged between Islamic fundamentalists and Algerian government forces and ultimately claimed an estimated 200,000 lives. In the film's opening scenes, Rachida, a young modern teacher, is on her way to work in Algiers when she is accosted by extremists who demand that she carry explosives to her school. She refuses and is shot and left to bleed to death on a busy street.

Rachida (Ibtissem Djouadi) is a victim of terrorism in Algeria and struggles to make sense of the seemingly random destruction that she encounters (*Rachida* DVD cover—released in 2002).

Rachida survives, however, and she and her divorced mother flee to a remote village in Algeria to escape the violence.

Rachida recovers physically from her wounds but is damaged psychologically. She sees terror everywhere. She suffers nightmares and panic attacks and isolates herself with her mother inside her home. In time, she slowly adapts to the quiet rituals of community life and agrees to teach the village children. She even joins the other women in preparing for the wedding of a young woman. But this quietude is short lived.

A young girl stumbles into the village, dazed and bruised, her clothing torn. She was kidnapped by religious extremists several weeks earlier and has managed to escape. The girl announces that extremists are close by. Villagers have gathered to celebrate a marriage, unaware that Islamic militants have infiltrated the village with the intent of engaging in murder and rape. Rachida escapes to the underbrush and bears witness to the senseless slaughter. She sees shadowy figures with guns, looking for women to kill or capture. A terrorist shouts amid the sounds of gunfire, "Save the prettier ones, they are for booty."

In the aftermath, the devastation is complete, as wedding gifts, a bridal veil, sheet-covered corpses, and a box of mewling motherless kittens are found strewn about. Rachida is re-traumatized and catatonic, and she rocks back and forth against the wall of her home as her mother packs their belongings to return to the city. Yet Rachida, in moment of clarity, realizes that she controls her fate and the choice is hers. She is defiant and resolute as she rises, grasps her school satchel, and slowly walks through the rubble to return to the school.

One by one, children emerge and take their seats at the school. "Where are all the others?" she asks. But the children are silent, ready to resume their lesson. At the end, Rachida writes on the chalkboard, "Today's Lesson," and stares off into the distance. The conclusion of the film is ambiguous regarding whether there is to be any hope.

Patriarchal Traditions and Religious Laws

Gender Segregation

Patriarchal tradition governs gender interactions, and these are illustrated in *Rachida*. Genders are segregated during wedding preparations and during funerals and burial rites. A young woman and her fiancé are shown anticipating their marriage in joyous ceremonies held in separate rooms. Genders are also segregated during visitations at the village cemetery. Men are shown first, gathered around burial stones, with veiled women surrounding the burial ground perimeter. The women are only allowed to enter the burial area after the men have left.

Female Chastity

The importance of sexual purity for a daughter and the father's duty to protect her purity, and therefore protect his and his family's honor, is a tradition dramatized in this film. In Rachida's village, a young girl staggers into the village square disheveled, with torn clothes and scratches on her face and body. She had been kidnapped by terrorists and held captive. It is understood that she has been raped and hence dishonored herself, her father and her family. Her father tells those around him and his daughter, "She is not my daughter. I don't want her. I'd rather she be dead! She has humiliated us in front of the neighbors, in front of the family. She has dishonored us; I don't want anything to do with her." She is damaged goods and repudiated by her father. The girl's nephew comes to her rescue, but in the name of masculine chauvinism he is brutally attacked by the other children. It is only the village women who, in solidarity, come to her rescue, covering her with their veils.

Algeria's Civil War and Terrorism

Terrorists commit atrocious acts in *Rachida*: they coerce citizens into carrying explosives; they kidnap and rape young girls; they murder innocent villagers attending a wedding ceremony. Who were these terrorists? The film does not identify the terrorist organization, though it relates events from the decade-long Algerian civil war in which the forces of a radical fundamentalist Islamic (FIS) movement were pitted against the national military. During the war, thousands of women were abducted and raped by Islamic extremists. Most of the victims were killed, but some survived. Many of the survivors were pregnant, and, similar to the young rape victim in *Rachida*, families rejected these women, considering them a disgrace to the family honor.[6]

Viva Laldjérie

Year: 2004; *Director:* Nadir Moknèche; *Cast:* Goucem (Lubna Azabal)—woman aged 27; Papicha (Biyouna)—woman in her 50s; Fifi (Nadia Kaci)—woman in her 20s; *Length:* 113 minutes; *Setting:* large urban city (Algiers) in Algeria; working class

Synopsis

Viva Laldjérie chronicles the lives of three female protagonists, each of whom faces problematic personal situations and makes choices that impact their fate. Goucem, Papicha, and Fifi are neighbors, living in a rather run-down residential hotel in modern-day Algiers. Goucem, an unmarried young woman, is the mistress of a much older man, a doctor who is married. The affair has gone on for three years, and Goucem is frustrated with waiting for her lover to divorce his wife and marry her. Other than the occasional tryst with him, she spends her days working as a photographer's assistant and her nights going to clubs to drink, dance, and pick up men for sex. Goucem's mother is Papicha, an aging former cabaret entertainer who spends much of her time in her one-room apartment reminiscing about her past as a dancer and singer of some repute. Papicha's life is lonely, and she is still afraid of the Islamic fundamentalists who threatened the lives of entertainers such as herself during Algeria's civil war. She is reminded by her daughter that these threats are still real. Fifi is a young prostitute who lives life in the moment, content to serve her customers.

It seems that the lives of these three women have little purpose or meaning, and their future appears bleak due to the choices they have made in a male-dominated world. At the end, Fifi is dead, killed by a client. Goucem, with an awareness that her lover will never marry her, is last seen in a public park, attempting to reconnect with a young man whom she had previously spurned. Papicha returns to sing in a nightclub that is a paean to the past. None of the women seem authentic, and there is no transformation of character within the film's narrative arc.

TRADITIONAL GENDER STEREOTYPES

It is the sexuality of the three female protagonists that grants them visibility in a male-dominated world. Papicha lives in her memories as a chanteuse, where her sexual allure was assured in a world of appreciative men. Without male attention, she is unmoored and lonely. In a telling scene, Papicha attempts to obtain city records about a building in Algiers. The first two male officials she approaches are condescending and unhelpful—after all, she is just a woman. She devises a different plan for the third official: using her feminine wiles and hints of sexual favors, Papicha obtains the information she needs. She becomes visible only because of her sexuality. Goucem is defined through her sexual encounters with her married lover and with strangers she picks up in clubs. Following her lover's betrayal and abandonment, she is lost and searches for another man and another sexual attachment. Fifi, as a prostitute, serves as nothing more than an object for male sexual gratification.

Algeria is a traditional patriarchal country and males have the prerogative to assert their dominance through aggression directed at females. One of Fifi's clients is a police officer, and after a tryst, he finds that he is missing his gun. He is sure that she has taken it, and he asserts the ultimate act of dominance when he kills her. Goucem's lover, a married doctor, demonstrates aggression in a more subtle fashion. He has carried on the affair for more than three years, and Goucem is led to believe that he will divorce his wife and marry her. The doctor, however, presumably has no intention of marrying her. He does obtain a divorce but marries another woman with whom he was involved while still in a relationship with Goucem. A subplot of this film involves a young man who is homosexual and engages in sex with other men. These men become quite aggressive with the young man after these sexual encounters and physically assault him.

NONTRADITIONAL GENDER ATTRIBUTES

All three women are autonomous and independent. They negotiate life on their own terms, without the need of a man to provide protection or assistance. Goucem is a strong presence in the film. She places demands on her married lover to divorce his wife. When he stalls, she realizes that he will never marry her, and she makes the choice to leave him. A man on the street harasses her, but she protects herself quite capably against his advances. Goucem is in control of her sexuality, and she selects her partners for the one-night trysts. Papicha has a strong voice as well. She learns that the Copacabana, a nightclub where she performed in the past, is being turned into a mosque. She then takes action to reopen the club despite her fear of Islamic terrorists' threats.

4

Bangladesh

COUNTRY PROFILE

BACKGROUND[1]

The People's Republic of Bangladesh, located in South Asia and bordering the Bay of Bengal, became a nation following the secession of East Pakistan in 1971. The majority (89 percent) of the population is Muslim, and about one-third (34.3 percent) of the population lives in urban areas. The form of government is a parliamentary republic, and the state language is Bangla. There are numerous ethnic groups in Bangladesh, with estimates ranging from 27 to 75.

SOCIOPOLITICAL AND RELIGIOUS ISSUES RELATED TO GENDER

Efforts have been made to ensure that the information presented here reflects current law and policies. However, it must be noted that many Muslim-majority countries are currently contending with challenges to their civil and criminal laws that stem from competing constituencies of those favoring greater freedoms for women and those espousing conservative Islamic principles. As such, governmental policies are continually evolving, and laws relevant to gender issues may be added, deleted, or amended in subsequent years.

Law

The constitution of Bangladesh,[2] established in 1972, guarantees gender equality in public spheres. Bangladesh is classified as having a mixed system of law, with Islamic Sharia law (Hanafi school of thought) applied to Muslim family law and secular laws to other issues. Family laws based on Sharia pertain only to Muslim citizens. Bangladesh ratified CEDAW in 1984, with reservations to Articles 2 and 16. (As stated earlier, Article 16 calls for "the elimination of discrimination in all matters relating to marriage, divorce, and family relations.") Concerns about contradicting Sharia law in family matters prompted the reservations.

Key points of the Muslim family law ordinances with reference to gender are as follows:

- The minimum age of marriage is 18 for women and 19 for men (a proposal has been submitted to the parliament to allow marriage for females at age 16 under special circumstances—if it is their parents' wish, for example, or if a girl becomes pregnant)
- Husbands have unilateral right to divorce their wives at any time they choose with or without cause; women do not have this right but are allowed *khul'* (a woman can divorce but forfeits her dowry)
- Polygyny is allowed with consent of other wives
- Mother is entitled to the custody of her male child until the age of seven years and of her female child until she has attained puberty; upon remarriage, custody of the children belongs to the father
- Women are entitled to some portion of an inheritance, but always less than a man; however, mechanisms exist for families to agree on more equitable distributions if they so desire
- Dowry violence, acid attacks, stalking, and sexual harassment (eve teasing) are criminal offenses
- Abortion is only allowed to save the life of the mother, but there is a loophole with "menstrual regulation" services that are available until eight weeks after the last menstrual period. Menstrual regulation involves flushing the menstrual lining out of the uterus, which is viewed as a family planning method and not an abortion procedure. It is difficult to prosecute the offense of abortion since the use of menstrual regulation makes it impossible to obtain documentation of the pregnancy.[3] The law prohibiting abortion was temporarily waived in 1972 for women who were raped during the war that created the nation of Bangladesh.

Laws Regulating Homosexuality

The 2016 report on sexual orientation laws compiled by the International Lesbian, Gay, Bisexual, Trans and Intersex Association identified the following items in Bangladesh penal law: "Whoever voluntarily has carnal intercourse against the order of nature with man, woman, or animal, shall be punished with imprisonment for life, or imprisonment of either description for a term which may extend to 10 years, and shall also be liable to fine."[4]

Additional Issues

According to the United Nations Children's Fund (2014), Bangladesh currently has one of the highest rates of child marriage (marriage before age 15) in the world.[5] Although national law sets the minimum marriage age for females at 18, it is difficult to enforce the law in rural areas where tribal laws permitting early marriage take precedence over national law. Females are especially disadvantaged in child marriage, as they face a disproportionate risk of death, abuse, and deprivation.[6]

Bangladesh also has the highest world incidence of acid violence, with women predominantly victims.[7] Acid violence involves the deliberate throwing of acid on the body of a person with the intention of causing physical damage through disfigurement, maiming, or death. In 2002, Bangladesh introduced the death penalty for acid attacks. Laws are in effect that seek to control the sale, use, storage, and international trade of acids. Enforcement of these laws, however, is problematic due to ineffective policing and societal tolerance.[8]

According to Nathaniel Adams in his report on women's empowerment, Bangladesh is making progress in its legislative efforts to protect women's safety and rights. The following are recent landmark laws[9]:

1980	Dowry Prohibition Act
2000	Prevention of Women and Children Repression Act
2002	Acid Crime Control Act
2006	Bangladesh Labour Act
2009	Citizen Amendment Act
2010	Domestic Violence Act
2011	National Development Policy on Women and Children
2012	Hindu Marriage Registration Act
2012	Human Trafficking Deterrence and Suppression Act

FILMS

On the Wings of a Dream (Swopnodanay)

Year: 2007; *Director:* Golam Rabbany Biplob; *Cast:* Fazlu (Mahmuduzzaman Babu)—man in his 30s; Matka (Rokeya Prachy)—woman in her 30s; *Length:* 84 minutes; *Setting:* small rural village; working class

SYNOPSIS

Fazlu is a poor man who lives in a rural village of Bangladesh with his wife and two young children. He works as a peddler of various goods, and his wife, Matka, tends to the numerous household chores. The two live a simple and contented life. At the local market, Fazlu buys a pair of pants and gives them to his wife to wash. She discovers that the pants contain a large amount of paper money. The money is foreign, and they are unsure of its worth. Fazlu, however, is convinced that because the money is foreign, and because there is such a large quantity of it, he is now rich. Fazlu is a simple man who has lived in his small village for all of his life. He has very little knowledge about the modern world of banking and commerce. He therefore approaches an acquaintance, more worldly than he, to help ascertain the money's worth.

As Fazlu waits for authentication of the money, his greed takes its toll. He becomes arrogant and remote. He jealously guards the money and becomes suspicious of neighbors and friends. He neglects his family and rejects his wife's pleas to use the money for an operation for their crippled daughter. Fazlu also takes an interest in a seductive neighboring woman and considers taking her as his second wife. Matka notes these changes in Fazlu and confronts him. He responds to her with indifference. In a moment of despair, she contemplates destroying the money and then killing herself. But she cannot do so.

In the end, Fazlu finds out that the money has no value and he returns to his family, realizing his folly. Redemption for him is allowed through his wife's grace. Matka forgives him and accepts his flaws. He is repentent and returns to his family.

TRADITIONAL GENDER STEREOTYPES

Fazlu and his wife are in opposition with each other regarding how to spend their newfound money. She wants the money for medical help for their crippled daughter, and he wants the money to improve his status in the community and attract a second wife. In this patriarchal society, his desires have dominance. There is little Matka can say or do, as her status as a wife is subordinate to his control. Fazlu ultimately decides to use the money out of greed.

Matka is unhappy about the choices Fazlu is making, which will negatively affect their family. He has turned into a brooding, paranoid man. He plans to take a second wife and will not fund an operation for his daughter.

Matka feels that she is powerless to change the desperate situation in which she finds herself. Her only option, she believes, is to kill herself, and she goes so far as to put a noose around her neck while standing on a chair. Yet she realizes the futility of her action and steps down, resigned.

A strict division of labor is depicted in *On the Wings of a Dream*. The mother and daughter in Fazlu's family perform the necessary domestic chores of washing, cooking, and cleaning. Fazlu does not help the women with their chores, instead ordering them to tend to his needs. Fazlu's young son also does not participate in domestic chores, as he spends his time playing in the yard. Fazlu is the breadwinner, and he and his son sell goods in the local market, which is populated by males. Only men are seen working at government buildings and at a bank.

Television

Director: Mostofa Sarwar Farooki; *Year:* 2012; *Cast:* Chairman Amin (Shahir Kazi Huda)—man in his late 50s; Solaiman (Chanchal Chowdhury)—man in his mid–30s; Kohinoor (Nusrat Imroz Tisha)—woman in her early 20s; *Length:* 106 minutes; *Setting:* rural village in Bangladesh; working class

SYNOPSIS

As the autocratic, though benevolent, leader of a small village in rural Bangladesh, Chairman Amin bans every kind of image—television, cell phones, and even imagination—as such things are forbidden for devout Muslims. But the traditions of his faith are in direct opposition with encroaching modernity and its associated technological wonders. *Television* is a seriocomedic film about Amin and his attempt to not only enforce his village technology ban but also participate in the Hajj, the obligation of every pious Muslim to journey to Mecca. However, there are problems. The villagers have discovered the marvels of technology and devise all sorts of clever ruses to overturn Amin's image prohibitions. Amin's submissive wife, his intimidated but devious son, his son's rebellious fiancée, and an assortment of eccentric Muslim and Hindu villagers all conspire to find ways to access technology.

As Chairman Amin seeks to journey to Mecca, he discovers that traveling requires a passport with photo identification, and his ban on images applies to photos. Despite his moral misgivings, Amin devises a means of obtaining the necessary photo, but, en route to the airport, he is robbed of his passport. His pilgrimage has failed, and he retreats to his hotel in a profound depression. While lying forlornly in on his hotel cot, he hears a great commotion outside the window and discovers that the Hajj is being captured live on a large-screen television. With an epiphany of sorts, he gains the understanding that television, once maligned, could be used to fulfill his holy obligation. Perhaps, he muses, it is not the image itself that is meant to be vilified.

TRADITIONAL GENDER STEREOTYPES

Chairman Amin is the head of the village. He is the religious authority whom the villagers consult on matters concerning morality, commerce, and other topics of governance. Amin reaffirms the patriarchal regulations that have been long established, and his interpretation of Islamic principles sets restrictions on the roles of women. Among other things, women are not allowed to attend governmental meetings. However, while the men in *Television* have a visible presence, it is really the women—placed in the background—who are in control. Giving men the illusion that they have power is a traditional feminine attribute and suggests subordination. The woman's agency must be covert so as not to give the appearance that the man's authority is undermined.

Amin's wife is silent during the interaction between Amin and his son, Solaiman, when he forbids his son to buy a cell phone. His wife then takes Solaiman aside and tells him to go ahead and buy one. Solaiman is confused: "How can I go against my father? ... It is him who forbids me to buy one." "Just go and buy one," she says, "because I asked you to." Solaiman in turn believes himself to be in control of his relationship with his girlfriend, Kohinoor; yet she is the dominant one. She actually purchases the forbidden phone and chastises him for his obedience to his father. She gives him an ultimatum: "If he wants to marry me, he will have to stand against his father. He will have to buy a television and come straight to my house. Together, we will watch it. The entire village will watch. Then I will marry him."

NONTRADITIONAL GENDER ATTRIBUTES

The people in this rural Bangladesh community are an emotional people, especially in response to sad situations. The traditional stereotype that males should be stoic in response to adversity is not supported in this film. The males cry a lot: Solaiman cries when he apologizes to his father, Chairman Amin, for his many sins. Chairman Amin also cries, as he cannot forgive his son. Solaiman cries throughout the film because he misses his girlfriend. Both Solaiman and his best friend cry when they reminisce about the past. Chairman Amin sobs in response to his failed trip to Mecca.

Additional Issue

Chairman Amin has prohibited images, as they are un–Islamic. His beliefs are aniconistic, which in Islam refers to proscriptions against the creation by humans of images of living beings. Images of God, the Prophet Muhammad, and the relatives of Muhammad are forbidden by the hadith; depictions of humans and animals are likewise discouraged. Aniconism is also found in other religions and cultures, particularly in the monotheistic Abrahamic religions such as Judaism and Christianity.

Third Person Singular Number

Year: 2009; *Director:* Mostofa Sarwar Farooki; *Cast:* Ruba (Nusrat Imroz Tisha)— woman in her early 20s; Topu (as himself)—man in his mid–20s; *Length:* 123 minutes; *Setting:* urban city in Bangladesh; working class and upper class

SYNOPSIS

Ruba is an attractive woman in her early 20s who at the beginning of the film is homeless. Her husband has been imprisoned, and she has been ordered by her in-laws to leave their home. She has no place to stay and must find both a place to live and a job. But this proves difficult. Home owners will not rent to a single woman due to the impropriety of a woman without a male guardian, and employers will not hire her unless she agrees to have sex with them. But Ruba is clever and uses the men who would use her. She accepts the living arrangements of a lecherous older man who offers her a "love-nest" apartment rent free, but she has no intention of having sex with him. She derisively calls him "uncle" and taunts him by threatening to tell his wife of his propositions.

As the film progresses, Ruba continues to experience challenges. She is a single woman and a distraction to the men of the neighborhood, and she is ultimately evicted. Ruba eventually contacts a childhood friend, Topu, who is now a popular musician. (Topu plays himself and is in real life a pop star.) He rents an apartment for her, and the two live together. Ruba is falling in love with him, but her husband is released and the three live together, an arrangement that is not too realistic in conservative Bangladesh. The film concludes with Ruba in a quandary. She must make decisions about her life and the love triangle in which she finds herself embedded.

TRADITIONAL GENDER STEREOTYPES

The stigma placed on young women who choose to live independently without the protection of marriage is a topic of *Third Person Singular Number*. Although the male and female characters engage in similar activities, females encounter gender-based restrictions. Ruba, as a single woman, faces restrictions as to where she can live. No one will rent a home to her. She is a single woman and therefore morally questionable. Muslim clerics complain about the impropriety of a young woman living on her own in the neighborhood and force her to leave. Ruba cannot enter the cemetery where her mother is buried because she is a female (though females are allowed inside if they're dead!). Men, by contrast, face few restrictions on their activities. They can travel freely at night without assumptions being made about their character, and, as in the case of Topu, men can rent apartments without being subject to scrutiny about their morality.

Sex is a commodity in *Third Person Singular Number*. Females are portrayed as nothing more than objects for males' sexual pleasure. Ruba walks alone at night on city streets. A woman alone at night on a public street is assumed to be sexually available, and various men take advantage of her presence. As Ruba passes a fenced-in park, several young men grab at her. Another man sinisterly follows her down an alley, stopping only when she runs into a lighted street. At one point, she has paused at a bridge, looking over a river. A car stops and a man shouts, "How much? Come on. Come. Come. Come with me. Hey, come with me. I'll take you to a good hotel. Hey ... come with me. Why so much attitude?" A woman alone at night must be a prostitute, and she is fair game to the men who roam the streets.

Ruba has left home and is seeking both a place to live and a job. But both goals present challenges. Since she is unmarried and on her own, she must be morally corrupt (or corruptible), as no chaste woman of marriageable age would seek an independent life over duty to her family and husband. As a consequence, she is offered opportunities for housing and employment by men who make it clear that sex is part of the deal. An older married man offers Ruba an apartment and will pay her rent, but on one condition: that she exchange sex for rent. Another man offers her a job as long as she understands that sex will be one of her job duties.

In this film, men are also censorious about female sexuality. Muslim clerics take it upon themselves to decide what to do about Ruba's living arrangement as a female tenant living on her own. One cleric blames her for the social ills of the world and demands that she relocate:

> A single woman is like a piece of pie. Wherever you keep it ants will come in droves. Renting the house to this woman has brought a crowd of young folks to the front of the house. Even the curfew can't move them away. When I go for the first prayer I see young boys are standing there. And when I come back home after the last prayer I see they still are standing there. The neighborhood is being spoiled. Youth education is being disturbed. The rate of education is decreasing. So kick this woman out.

NONTRADITIONAL GENDER ATTRIBUTES

Despite the barriers imposed on females by a patriarchal social system, Ruba, the female protagonist in *Third Person Singular Number*, projects a strong, assertive presence. Faced with gender-based restrictions that limit her freedom, Ruba is unafraid to challenge those who enforce compliance. She admonishes the police who question her about being out alone at night and the male guards who refuse to let women enter a cemetery. She aggressively manipulates the men who offer housing and employment in exchange for sex. And she is at once amused and offended by the lecherous men who proposition her. All this is not to suggest, however, that Ruba is a paragon of the liberated woman. Though brave in her defiance of patriarchal strictures, she is not very likeable. Ruba is vain, immature, shallow, and conniving. She cannot depend on herself, instead depending on men to rescue her—first her husband, then the various men she uses to obtain shelter and jobs, and finally the rock star who rescues her over and over and over again.

5

Egypt

COUNTRY PROFILE

BACKGROUND[1]

Egypt, located in Northern Africa and bordering the Mediterranean Sea, is a member state of the Arab League. Egypt's official language is Arabic, and the official religion is Islam. The form of government is a presidential republic. Egyptians constitute the largest ethnic group in the country. Slightly more than half of the country is rural, and the majority (90 percent) of the population is Muslim.

SOCIOPOLITICAL AND RELIGIOUS ISSUES RELATED TO GENDER

Efforts have been made to ensure that the information presented here reflects current law and policies. However, many Muslim-majority countries are currently contending with challenges to their civil and criminal laws that stem from competing constituencies of those favoring greater freedoms for women and those espousing conservative Islamic principles. As such, governmental policies are continually evolving, and laws relevant to gender issues may be added, deleted, or amended in subsequent years.

Law

Egypt's 2014 constitution declares the principles of Islamic Sharia law (Hanafi school of thought) to be the main source of law.[2] Egyptian family law reflects recent sociopolitical issues that have affected post-revolutionary Egypt (the period between 2011 and 2013). Both during this period and afterward, proposed amendments to family law revealed several points of contention, which included the rights of women to obtain a divorce through *khul'* (in which a woman can divorce if she compensates her husband with money) and the rights of women to maintain custody of their children following divorce. Egypt ratified the CEDAW in 1981, recording reservations with regard to Articles 2, 9, and 16. The reservation to Article 16 (equality in marriage and family life) was based on the provisions of Islamic law, under which husbands and wives have different rights and duties. In general, there is compliance with CEDAW articles as long as they do not conflict with Sharia law and principles.

The following lists key points of the Personal Status Law (with 2005 amendments) with reference to gender. It is important to note that due to Egypt's evolving sociopolitical environment, many of these points may be amended in the future.

- The minimum age to marry is 18 for females and males
- Polygyny is allowed (up to 4 wives); a wife can ask for a divorce only if she can prove that her husband did not do justice to her
- Women may enter into the marriage contract stipulations to protect their marital rights; such stipulations might include the right to education or to work outside the home, to divorce, and to prohibit a second wife
- Men have the right to unilateral divorce without resort to legal proceedings (verbal repudiation, or *talaq*)
- Women have the right to seek a divorce provided certain conditions are met; however, in order to receive alimony, the woman must prove damage; women can also seek a divorce by claiming *khul'* (without the burden of evidence), in which case they must return the dowry
- Divorced women may raise their children until they reach the age of 15, with child support from the father
- The father is the guardian of the children and is responsible for the children's financial maintenance
- Women have the right to inherit, but the share of the woman's inheritance will be half of the man's
- Abortion is prohibited in all circumstances unless there are grounds of necessity (e.g., the mother's life is in danger)
- Women do not need the permission of their husbands or fathers to travel and obtain a passport
- As of 2008, female genital mutilation/cutting (FGM/C) is prohibited by law

Laws Regulating Homosexuality

The 2016 report on sexual orientation laws as conducted by the International Lesbian, Gay, Bisexual, Trans and Intersex Association identified the following items in Egyptian penal law: "Sexual relations between consenting adult persons of the same sex in private are not prohibited as such. However, the Law on the Combating of Prostitution, and the law against debauchery have been used to imprison gay men in recent years."

Article 9 refers to debauchery laws:

> Punishment by imprisonment for a period not less than three months and not exceeding three years and a fine … or one of these two punishments applies in the following cases:
> (a) Whoever lets or offers in whatever fashion a residence or place run for the purpose of debauchery or prostitution, or for the purpose of housing one or more persons, if they are to his knowledge practicing debauchery or prostitution.
> (b) Whoever owns or manages a furnished residence or furnished rooms or premises open to the public and who facilitates the practice of debauchery or prostitution, either by admitting persons so engaged or by allowing on his premises incitement to debauchery or prostitution.
> (c) Whoever habitually engages in debauchery or prostitution.[3]

Additional Issues

Patriarchal traditions are strong in Egypt, especially in rural areas (e.g., Upper Egypt). Child marriages, FGM, and honor killings are frequently practiced despite laws prohibiting them. In a recent survey on Muslim political beliefs, the majority of Egyptians felt that laws should adhere strictly to the Quran. For example, the majority (82 percent) agreed with the punishment of stoning for zina (adultery) offenses.[4]

FILMS

A Girl's Secret (Asrar el-banaat)

Year: 2001; *Director:* Magdy Ahmed Aly; *Cast:* Yasmine (Maya Sheiha)—16-year-old girl; Nadia (Sawsan Badr)—woman in her 30s; Awatef (Dalal Abdel Aziz)—woman in her late 30s; *Length:* 91 minutes; *Setting:* large urban city in Egypt; upper middle class

SYNOPSIS

In the opening scenes of *A Girl's Secret*, Yasmine, an unmarried 16-year-old, sits apart while her female cousin and other family members are celebrating a birthday. She complains of not feeling well, and it is arranged for her to stay overnight at her cousin's home. She wakes during the night and rushes to the bathroom, where she sits on the toilet, her face contorted with pain and moaning loud enough to awaken the family. As the moans continue, her aunt and uncle break down the locked door and discover a semi-conscious Yasmine slumped on the floor with a blood-streaked newborn baby by her side. Yasmine and the infant are rushed to the hospital, with Yasmine undergoing surgery for childbirth complications. Both the relatives and Yasmine's own parents are shocked, as her pregnancy had been successfully hidden.

The reactions of both families to Yasmine's childbirth represent differences between conservative and moderate Muslims in Egyptian society. Yasmine's parents are conservative. Her mother, Awatef, wears the veil and presents herself as a pious woman. She is conflicted. She loves her daughter and is torn between desire to protect her and desire to protect the honor of the family. Awatef admonishes her daughter for her shame. She shakes her and slaps her in the face: "Who did this ... huh? Were you abducted and feared to hell? Answer me!" Yasmine's father reacts with deep despair. He simply doesn't know what to do with the situation other than offer the pretense that Yasmine has a husband who is abroad. Yasmine's aunt, Nadia, adopts a more moderate voice. She is more sure-footed about her moral duty to her niece, protecting Yasmine from the hysteria of her mother and raging against the doctor who takes it upon himself to circumcise Yasmine during surgery. But in the end, both moderate and conservative voices agree that Yasmine must marry her boyfriend, and that is what happens. At the conclusion, the baby dies of birth complications, Yasmine and her boyfriend divorce, and Yasmine's father is seen fitting new locks on the door of her bedroom.

In *A Girl's Secret*, each of the principal characters must struggle with their own moral and religious judgments about the topics of premarital sex, female genital mutilation/cutting, abortion, suicide attempts, forced marriage and family honor.

PATRIARCHAL TRADITIONS AND RELIGIOUS LAWS

Female Genital Mutilation/Cutting (FGM/C)

Of the several rationales posited for FGM/C (see commentary for the film *Dunia*), the safeguarding of female respectability through the curtailment

أسرار البنات

A Girl's Secrets

Yasmine is 16, and her family typifies conservative Egyptian middle-class Muslim values. She and her boyfriend, Shady (Sherif Ramzy), have engaged in an illicit sexual encounter that results in tragic consequences (*A Girl's Secret* DVD cover—released in 2001).

of sexual pleasure is frequently cited. As open expressions of sexuality threaten female honor, the ultimate restraint is imposed—that of clitoral excision and consequent prevention of female orgasm. In *A Girl's Secret*, Yasmine has been brought in for emergency surgery for some unknown childbirth complication. The two surgeons have finished the operation, but, in a startling scene, one of them grabs a scalpel and circumcises the still anesthetized Yasmine (although not detailed in the film, it is assumed that a clitorectomy was performed). After the surgery, a colleague angrily confronts him: "She's only a child from a decent family, probably a virgin. So her tough luck made her go through this experience. And you destroy her.... How, where's the approval of her parents? You decided and acted. It's a crime. Sorry, doctor, I'm reporting." The offending physician rationalizes his behavior as follows: "I did what my conscience dictates for a Muslim doctor.... And is she not a criminal? A kid of 16 years, ill-bred, pregnant and having a child. What I did may help her control herself. Circumcision is important, doctor."

Premarital Sex

According to the Egyptian legal code based on Islamic Sharia, all sexual relationships outside of marriage are forbidden, and such relationships, if they occur, are punishable criminal acts. Yasmine's father confronts Shady's parents about his sin: "We are here to discuss Yasmine and Shady. Yasmine was pregnant and delivered in hospital. We learned your son is the father. The girl is hardly 17, so she's a minor. Tests are being carried out to prove his paternity to the child. Of course he could be jailed and have his life wasted." In *A Girl's Secret*, Yasmine gives birth and swears to her mother that she didn't have sex. Her examining doctor states that her hymen is intact. How can that be? Yasmine and her boyfriend are shown in her bedroom partially undressed and in a "compromising position." It is possible that there was no penile penetration and her boyfriend ejaculated outside her vagina, resulting in one of those rare, but possible, pregnancies.

NONTRADITIONAL GENDER ATTRIBUTES

The moderate, progressive Muslim woman as personified by Yasmine's aunt and the conservative Muslim woman as personified by Yasmine's mother are juxtaposed and illustrate differences in reactions to unjust events. Yasmine's mother did not know that she was pregnant, and she learns from her sister that Yasmine has given birth and is in the hospital. She faints, bites her ring, hangs her head in despair, and later lectures Yasmine about the great shame she has brought on her family. When the mother learns that the surgeon has circumcised Yasmine without parental permission, she is dismayed but silent about the matter. Yasmine's aunt, by contrast, is infuriated and confronts the doctor: "How can a decent, educated doctor do that to a decent girl? ... I'll go to the syndicate, the court, I won't let it go.... Our prophet never circumcised his daughters. She's a kid. We should teach them decently, not butcher them. It's a crime."

Asmaa

Year: 2011; *Director:* Amr Salama; *Cast:* Asmaa (Hend Sabry)—woman in her 40s; Mohsen El Seesy (Maged El Kedwany)—man in his 50s; *Length:* 96 minutes; *Setting:* large urban city (Cairo) in Egypt; working class

SYNOPSIS

Asmaa is about to undergo surgery for gallstone inflammation, a painful, life-threatening condition that causes her considerable pain. While on the operating table, and prior to receiving anesthesia, she divulges that she is HIV positive. As a consequence, the surgeon refuses to operate. Asmaa contracted HIV years ago from her now-deceased husband. She has hidden her HIV status from her family and from her employer and co-workers.

Asmaa's story shifts from the present to her past with the portrayal of a young woman who lives quite simply and contentedly with her father in a small village. The young Asmaa is high spirited and independent, and she attracts the attention of Mosaad, a young landowner; the two fall in love and marry. They dream of conceiving a son to ensure the inheritance of his family land and protect his lineage. But their plans are interrupted when Mosaad is imprisoned for killing a man who has insulted his wife (and his honor). Upon his release, Mosaad reveals that he has contracted AIDS and refuses to have sex with Asmaa. Asmaa, aware of her dying husband's desire for a male heir, requests a blood test at a local clinic to ascertain her own HIV status. With assurances that a child thus conceived would be at minimum risk of contracting HIV, and fully aware of her own high risk of contagion, she lies to Mosaad and claims that she, too, is HIV positive. A child is conceived, but Mosaad dies before his daughter is born.

Asmaa is now middle aged and living in Cairo. She is the sole support of her teenage daughter, and she has a choice to make. She needs surgery but cannot find a hospital willing to treat an HIV-positive person. She is given an opportunity to tell her story on a television exposé program but will risk loss of employment, rebuke by her daughter, and ostracism from society. Eventually she yields to the persuasive arguments of Mohsen, the host of the

TV program, but only if she does not have to reveal her face or name. Asmaa appears on the program shrouded in a head scarf, long gloves, and a blue smock, and she eventually decides to reveal her identity as she tells her story.

The film ends ambiguously. Her daughter praises her for her courage, but Asmaa loses her job. Mohsen has found a donor (himself) who will fund her surgery abroad. But social ostracism prevails. A suitor has abandoned her, and she is shunned by passers-by on the streets of Cairo.

PATRIARCHAL TRADITIONS AND RELIGIOUS LAWS

Inheritance

The importance of a male heir and his inheritance rights to land is a patriarchal tradition that ensures patrilineality will continue through generations. In this film, the issue of inheritance is key, as decisions made by Asmaa and her husband will change the course of her life. Mosaad, aware that he will soon die, is in anguish about the lack of a male heir. His own brother is sterile, and if he doesn't have a son, "this land will die with us." Asmaa is pregnant when Mosaad dies of AIDS complications, and it is understood that if a boy is born, she will give him to Mosaad's family to continue his family's lineage.

TRADITIONAL GENDER STEREOTYPES

One traditional feminine stereotype involves the virtue of sacrificing one's individual needs to nurture others at the expense of self. Throughout the narrative of the film, Asmaa is willing to make the ultimate sacrifice— her life in exchange for fulfilling her husband's final wish. Her husband is dying of AIDS and refuses to have sex with Asmaa out of fear that she will contract the disease. Asmaa, aware of his desire for a male heir, lies to him and claims she is HIV positive. The message thus conveyed is that a female's sacrifice of herself is the good and virtuous thing to do, as it sustains relationships and family. But, in actuality, who will be helped and who will be harmed as a consequence of the sacrifice? Obviously Asmaa herself is harmed, as she will live out her days in excruciating pain, as well as Asmaa's daughter, who was placed at risk of contracting HIV prenatally and who is now at risk of losing her mother. It is debatable that this is a story about the nobility of a strong woman who sacrifices herself for love, for family, for honor. A different reading might question how noble it was for Asmaa to sacrifice her life in seeking to provide a male heir to perpetuate a family lineage.

Asmaa is clearly a victim in this film and males are portrayed as her rescuers. Early in her story she is victimized by the patriarchal insistence on producing a male heir to inherit the properties of her dying husband. Later, she is a victim of society's ignorance and prejudice toward those infected with HIV and, perhaps, a victim of herself in her martyrdom. Though she chooses at the end of the film to step forward and publicly reveal her HIV status, it is ultimately the man, the TV talk show host, who rescues her. Males have agency to rescue, if they so desire, those who are victimized within patriarchal structures. Mohsen is a well-known TV persona, and he chooses to rescue Asmaa, first, by persuading her to tell her story on national TV and, second, by providing funds for her surgery. He controls her fate. *Asmaa* ultimately sends a message that women are vulnerable and in need of protection from men.

Females are either chaste or impure in *Asmaa* and this sexualized binary is illustrated by Asmaa's interactions with a doctor from a charitable organization. He has agreed to conduct her surgery on the condition that she will tell him how she contracted HIV. He must assure himself and his patrons that Asmaa did not contract the disease through immoral behavior: "I need to know that the charity goes to those who deserve it. But I must ask you a question to be reassured. How did you contract the virus? I'm sure it was from a blood transfusion or from your husband. But I want to hear it from you, to be reassured." It is implied that if HIV is contracted by a woman through less than virtuous means, she would not be worthy of an operation.

Asmaa is angered by this question. She confirms that she was not infected while committing a sin or adultery, but she also refuses to explain how she contracted the virus. "No one," she says before walking out, "has the right to ask how I got this disease. No one. It's no one's business how I got this disease. No one should ask me to prove my virtue."

NONTRADITIONAL GENDER ATTRIBUTES

Asmaa, as both a young woman newly married and a middle-aged woman with HIV, has strong opinions about her life and is not afraid to assert herself despite the restrictions placed on women's voices in patriarchal societies. Asmaa sells her rugs at the village market. The marketplace is male dominated, with men having the implicit prerogative to insult women. Asmaa incurs disparaging remarks from a male competitor jealous of her sales: "Won't you stop causing problems? Reject the devil, stay at home, serve your husband ... swear to God you won't make a living here, girl. If you don't leave, I'll burn your carpets and you along with them." Asmaa spits in his face and angrily retorts, "Didn't I tell you not to call me girl?"

The young Asmaa is different from other women in her village. She wants to work outside the home and to be independent. Her husband questions her about her discontent at home:

"Why don't you stay home and sell carpets from home? People can come here to buy them, like the other village women."
"You knew when you married me that I wasn't like other village women. You'll hate me if I became like them. I'd hate myself, if you don't.... If you're worried about me, don't bury me alive."
"Staying at home is like being buried alive?"
"Yes, if I am forced to do something against my will. Eating, sleeping, afraid of gossip, and doing nothing? Please let me live."

As a middle-aged mother, Asmaa is equally assertive. She has no difficulty presenting her demands to the television crew prior to her interview. She likewise rebukes the doctor who is willing to perform her surgery for his hypocrisy, knowing that in so doing she will lose her opportunity to be well.

Cairo 678

Year: 2010; *Director:* Mohamed Diab; *Cast:* Fayza (Bushra)—woman in her 20s; Seba (Nelly Karim)—woman in her 20s; Nelly (Nahed El Sebai)—woman in her 20s; *Length:* 100 minutes; *Setting:* Large urban city (Cairo) in Egypt; middle class

SYNOPSIS

In *Cairo 678*, the binary of woman as victim and woman as empowered is explored as three women, all victims of sexual harassment, struggle with issues of misogyny and their role and responsibility in addressing sexual harassment. The serious problem of sexual harassment in Egypt is dramatized through the narratives of Seba, Fayza, and Nelly, each of whom has been sexually victimized and each of whom deals with this victimization in different ways.

Seba is an upper-class modern woman who mentors those who have been sexually assaulted. She herself was a victim of sexual molestation in an attack by a group of men on a crowded public street. Her husband, though present, was unable to defend her. After the attack, he avoided her, as he could not deal with the shame of her abuse and his failure to protect her. His emotional abandonment ultimately led to their divorce. Seba encounters Fayza, a working-class woman who dresses conservatively in full hijab. Fayza relates her daily experience with sexual harassment that takes the form of sexual taunts and gropings that occur on crowded city buses and streets. Fayza states that she has had enough. She takes vengeance against the harassers by stabbing them in the groin with her scarf pin and then escaping into the crowds.

Intertwined with the stories of Seba and Fayza is the story of Nelly, a middle-class woman who works in a call center. She experiences continual sexual harassment from telephone callers and, like Fayza, she has had enough. Upon returning to her home from work one day, a male driver grabs her, steals her bag, and mocks her with sexual gestures. Nelly chases him and has him arrested. She then decides to initiate a sexual harassment lawsuit against him—Egypt's first. Despite opposition from her family and her soon-to-be in-laws, she follows through with the lawsuit and wins; her harasser is sentenced to three years in prison. The film concludes with the message that legislation has been passed in Egypt to criminalize sexual harassment. To date, cases remain rare.

TRADITIONAL GENDER STEREOTYPES

Female victims of sexual harassment are often silent. Seba, who provides self-defense lessons to women, encourages them to be open about the sexual harassment they have endured. All they need to do, she counsels, is answer three questions: "Have you been sexually harassed? How many times? How did you react?"

The women remain silent out of shame. Seba vents her frustration: "And sexual harassment is not shameful. Only the scumbag who harasses you has reason for shame. Not you. Express yourself. Say it. Say it, 'I was sexually harassed.'" Yet Seba's own mother warns her against openly discussing her sexual harassment, stating that Seba's father's job cannot withstand a scandal of this type. As seen in many films with themes of female oppression, women are often complicit with men's efforts to silence the protests of female victims.

As reported in Egypt and many other countries, male sexual harassment of women is endemic. In *Cairo 678*, males are shown harassing women verbally, physically, and by gesture on public streets, on public transportation, and over the telephone. For these women, misogynistic experiences are quotidian (see Eve Teasing below).

Men, too, are victims of a patriarchal society that dictates that sexual violations against women are shameful and should not be publicized. Men who fail to protect a female's honor are dishonored themselves and suffer the consequences. In the story of Nelly, men react strongly and in opposition to Nelly's plan to bring suit against her harasser. A public lawsuit would bring dishonor to Nelly, to her family, and to her fiancé and his family. The police officer who arrested Nelly's street harasser readily agrees to file assault charges but refuses to file sex harassment charges for fear of a scandal: "I'm writing a solid assault report. I'm trying to get you justice.... Why sexual harassment? I'm going to destroy him for you.... The penalty for assault is more severe. Or do we want a scandal?" At a family meal, Nelly's prospective in-laws urge her to drop the lawsuit, claiming that she couldn't possibly know what is in her best interest. All that should matter is her reputation and that of her fiancé. Already, she is told, people are gossiping that she must be part of a conspiracy to ruin Egypt's reputation. Nelly ruefully replies, "I choose between shutting up or tainting Egypt's reputation?" Seba's husband also cannot deal with his shame in reaction to his wife's sexual victimization by a group of men. He can barely look at her, much less stay with her in their home. "Seba," he explains, "this would have been tough for any man. I wanted to protect you." Though in love with Seba, his shame leads to divorce and isolation in a life without her.

NONTRADITIONAL GENDER ATTRIBUTES

Two of the male characters in *Cairo 678* are sympathetic to the plight of women who are sexually harassed. The police detective's duty is to find the perpetrators of the stabbing attacks against various men, and he ultimately finds the three women. But he is sensitive to their circumstances and lets them go. Fayza has turned vigilante and begins attacking men who harass by stabbing them. She turns herself in, but the detective, much to her astonishment, lets her go as well. Nelly's fiancé, Omar, is at the beginning unsure about his support of Nelly in face of his family's opposition to her lawsuit. He cites the sacrifices he's made in order for them to marry. Why shouldn't she do the same and sacrifice her desire for justice to protect his family name? Yet, in the final scene, Nelly and Omar are in attendance in the crowded courtroom where Nelly must decide whether to withdraw or pursue her case. The judge asks if she will drop the charge. Omar, somewhat melodramatically, stands and shouts, "No, she won't." The case proceeds and Nelly is vindicated.

Cairo 678 imparts a strong message that contemporary women in Egypt have power and presence and will fight for their rights. The three women protagonists confront those who wish to oppress them and, by doing so, question the fairness of the patriarchal rules that create women's oppression. The women have a strong voice and are not afraid to confront men whom they perceive as abusive. Fayza dramatically and publicly challenges a school principal about his punishment of her children for her delay in paying tuition. Fayza also finds that her husband is sexually harassing women on a bus. Angrily, she shouts, "Why do you do this? You could have taken a second wife. Or divorce me. But never lay a finger on a woman against her will." Nelly presses her case against sexual harassment on public television, incurring the outrage of male viewers who claim that she probably provoked her attacks by wearing seductive clothing. At the end, Nelly refuses to drop the lawsuit against her harasser. Seba tells her husband to divorce her; she cannot forgive him for his shame, lack of support, and masculine pride after her attack.

The women in *Cairo 678* demonstrate agency in seeking vengeance against men who violate them. Fayza is angry: "Every day I ride the bus. Every day shit happens to me. Every single day. And you expect me to be sane. They deserve what they get. If he knew someone did this to his sister, daughter or wife, he would say it was well deserved." She has had enough when a man fondles her on the street, and she jabs him in the hand with her scarf pin. "Next time I'll cut your hand off." And then again, on a crowded bus, she stabs a groping man in his groin.

Nelly is victimized as well. While crossing a busy street, she is followed by a man in a car who suddenly reaches out and grabs her purse, making sexually suggestive comments. He pulls on her shirt and drags her while the car is in gear. Nelly reacts with fury, hitting his car and ordering him to get out. She has him arrested but is later faced with a moral dilemma: Do people (women) have the moral legitimacy to take retribution on those who violate them?

The three female characters are conflicted about their decisions to confront the men who harass them. Issues about responsibility for one's actions are raised in this film. If men brought up in a patriarchal society are emasculated as a consequence of economic deprivation, how culpable are they for their harassment of women? If women choose to dress and behave "seductively" in the public sphere, how culpable are they for their own sexual victimization? Fayza raises this issue when she confronts Seba about guilt for their actions. "I have no guilt," she says, "but what about your guilt?" She accuses Seba of sexually objectifying herself with her choice to expose her unveiled hair and body to men while in public. Nelly is clear, however, about the issue of guilt: men are indeed responsible for their actions, and women as victims are not to be blamed for their objectification. These women ultimately have to deal with the constructions of femininity and masculinity in an urbanized society that is transitioning from rigid patriarchal norms to modernity.

EVE TEASING/SEXUAL HARASSMENT

Eve teasing refers to sexual harassment of females by males in public venues. Eve teasing (also termed street harassment) consists of verbal abuse, physical abuse, or sexual gestures. Recent survey data of men living in Cairo revealed that almost two-thirds of male respondents reported committing some form of street harassment aimed at females, and 13 percent admitted to physical harassment.[5] In a United Nations–sponsored 2013 survey of sexual harassment in Egypt, 99.3 percent of Egyptian women reported being sexually harassed in one way or another, with high rates of physical and verbal harassment.[6]

Eve teasing is a significant problem not only in Egypt but also in other parts of the world. Bangladesh, for example, reports one of the highest rates of street sexual harassment in the world, where, it is theorized, such factors as the patriarchal social system, lack of education, negative attitudes toward women, unemployment, and abuse of political power contribute to the high rates. In one study of Bangladesh females, more than three-fourths reported verbal teasing (suggestive comments and whistling) when outside their home and physical teasing when they traveled to the market, cinema, or school or on public transportation. The female respondents reported frequent unnecessary touching such as pushing, pinching parts of their bodies, and blocking. Females were also subject to nonverbal teasing of suggestive gestures or looks, licking lips, staring or leering.[7]

Despite a name that sounds trivialized, eve teasing is a serious offense that can inflict psychological and physical damage in victims. Reports of young women committing suicide following street sexual harassment are not uncommon. Many countries have enacted laws prohibiting public and private sexual harassment, and punishments can be severe.

Social scientists contend that the dramatic increases in street harassment that are observed and reported are due to dual forces of rising unemployment rates among males and the lessening of patriarchal influences in the family. Stagnating economies in many of the countries that report high rates of harassment are associated with massive unemployment of young men. According to Fatima Mareah Peoples, unemployment is considered one of the main factors undermining the masculine norm of providing for one's family. As males are no longer in a position to fulfill the traditional masculine role of breadwinner, stress is experienced, with resulting aggression taking the form of sexual harassment of women.[8] Why do men who are demasculinized displace their aggression onto women? The simple answer is because they can. In cultures where women are viewed as passive and weak and the police response is slow or nonexistent, women are vulnerable targets.

Dunia: Kiss Me Not on the Eyes
(Dunia)

Year: 2005; *Director:* Jocelyne Sa'ab; *Cast:* Dunia (Hanan Turk); *Length:* 112 minutes; *Setting:* large urban city (Cairo) in Egypt; middle class

SYNOPSIS

Dunia relates the story of its eponymous protagonist, a young woman living in a modest apartment in modern Cairo. She is an aspiring dancer who seeks to perfect her art through emulating her mother, a once-celebrated Egyptian belly dancer. Dunia is lively and exotic. She dresses in brilliant reds and wears her long black hair uncovered. Her dances are graceful and sensuous. Yet Dunia struggles with emotional expressivity in her dance. Her instructor critiques her difficulty in truly experiencing the raw emotions of dance.

Dunia also struggles in her marriage. As a child, Dunia underwent genital cutting ("excision"), and now she is unable to experience sexual pleasure with her husband, who is perplexed by her coldness toward him. "Mahmoud," she tells a friend, "calls me cold. I feel like it, I try, but my body says no." Her bitterness is reflected in her poetry:

> Whose hand cuts the rose?
> Cuts the bird's wing?
> Why this tear on my cheek?
> Who tears away the light of day?
> Whose hand delights in blood?
> This forever bleeding wound?
> Whose hand delights in blood?
> This forever bleeding wound?
> Whose hand cuts the rose?
> Cuts the bird's wing?

For Dunia, her body is her art, her prime mode of expression; yet she is alienated from a core part of herself. Her essence as a sexual being has been denied through the practice of female genital mutilation/cutting. Dunia now takes it upon herself to protect a friend's young daughter from the practice but finds herself caught in an intergenerational conflict between a mother and her daughter regarding the continuation of a patriarchal custom.

At the film's end, Dunia's fate is ambiguous. She dances with an older man who has engaged her intellectually and spiritually. The dance is sensuous, her face ecstatic. Has she found her own sexual agency through accepting the entirety of herself? Perhaps so, as her last dance suggests.

PATRIARCHAL TRADITIONS AND RELIGIOUS LAWS

Female Genital Mutilation

According to many religious and historical scholars, there is no recognized mainstream Islamic authority that requires the practice of FGM/C.[9]

Dunia (Hanan Turk) is a young woman in contemporary Egypt who aspires to be a famous dancer. Conflicts in her marriage and her increasing attraction to Beshir (Mohamed Mounir), an intellectual many years her senior, cause her to examine her true identity (*Dunia* DVD cover—released in 2005).

Rather, FGM/C is believed to reflect pre–Islamic patriarchal traditions that have continued into contemporary times (see below). In Egypt, a country that reports one of the highest rates of FGM/C in the world, Islamic authorities have declared that FGM/C is prohibited:

> Al-Azhar Supreme Council of Islamic Research, the highest religious authority in Egypt, issued a statement saying FGM/C has no basis in core Islamic law or any of its partial provisions and that it is harmful and should not be practiced.[10]

In 2007, the Egyptian government permanently banned FGM/C throughout the country. *Dunia* offers insight into the practice of FGM/C in Egypt and illustrates its psychological and physiological consequences. At the conclusion of *Dunia*, the following text slide is presented:

> Despite a ban in many countries, including Egypt, up to 130 million women have undergone female circumcision or female genital mutilation (FGM), as it is also known, and 6,000 girls are subjected to it every day.

TRADITIONAL GENDER STEREOTYPES

In *Dunia*, women are defined through their sexuality—they are either virgin or whore. Women are morally virtuous if chaste or if faithful in their marriages, or women are immoral and wicked if they are not a virgin before marriage or if they choose not to marry. Two ideologies are at work here: the danger of female sexuality to men and the preservation of female purity and consequent masculine honor. As open expressions of sexuality threaten males, the ultimate restraint is imposed: excising the organ (clitoris) that gives sexual pleasure. In *Dunia*, a grandmother exhorts her young granddaughter to undergo a procedure (implying a clitorectomy) that will make her "a real woman, respectable." "Don't be scared," she says. "It's just a small wound to be clean."

Young girls in societies where FGM/C procedures are commonplace have no say in the matter. Just as generations of females before them have had the procedure, so will the current generation. Rituals are difficult to challenge, particularly when one perceives there is no choice. In *Dunia*, the grandmother has invited a local daya to her apartment to excise her granddaughter, who is cowering in the corner. Her grandmother drags her to the daya, who is brandishing a razor blade: "We're going to remove a good for nothing piece of skin. It will only do you good. So you will grow up to be beautiful." Her grandmother pinions her arms and spreads the young girl's legs apart. Screams echo throughout the building. Dunia rushes into the apartment and finds the girl unconscious, lying in blood-soaked towels. Enraged and horrified at what she sees, she castigates the grandmother for her cruelty and carries the girl to her home.

NONTRADITIONAL GENDER ATTRIBUTES

Dunia is outspoken and unafraid to challenge patriarchal convention. She attempts to protect the granddaughter from FGM/C and is vocal in her disapproval of the practice. But Dunia cannot save her from the procedure. Discovering that the girl has just undergone a clitorectomy, Dunia rages at the grandmother: "You've put her out ... her cooking will remain cold ... no matter how hot the fire. All the world's spices won't help. You've butchered her." To her husband, she does not pretend that she feels any sexual desire: "You want my body? Take it. But I can't kiss you. [She points to her head.] I'll look for my pleasure here. Anybody can fill this bed.... But here? [Points to her head] No!"

FEMALE GENITAL MUTILATION/CUTTING (FGM/C)

The practice of FGM/C is concentrated among 29 countries spanning Africa and the Middle East.[11] Of these, 26 countries have prohibited FGM/C by law or constitutional decree (notable exceptions are South Africa and Zambia). The 1979 Convention on the Elimination of All Forms of Discrimination Against Women (CEDAW) denounced the practice of FGM/C. Despite the law, however, the practice of FGM/C continues, largely in rural areas where people are misinformed and policing is nonexistent. In addition, as researchers have noted, in many regions village authorities believe FGM/C to be religiously mandated, including "many Islamic clerics in northern Iraq Kurdistan who advise women to practice FGM."[12]

Types of FGM/C

The World Health Organization[13] has identified four different types of FGM/C. Type I involves excising the prepuce (hood of the clitoris), with or without excision of part or all of the clitoris. Type II involves excising the clitoris, with partial or total excision of the labia minora. Type III involves excising part or all of the external genitalia and infibulation (stitching/narrowing of the vaginal opening). Type IV, which is the most invasive, is unclassified, involving any number of different procedures, such as pricking or piercing the clitoris, stretching the clitoris, or cutting the vagina. Different regions of the world practice different forms of FGM/C. Regardless of the type, the procedures are irreversible and their effects last a lifetime.

Rationale for the Practice of FGM/C

Reasons for the continued practice of FGM/C can be categorized under cultural, religious, and mythological concerns. The United Nations Population Fund provides the following five reasons for modern-day practice of FGM/C:

> Psychosexual reasons: FGM is carried out as a way to control women's sexuality, which is sometimes said to be insatiable if parts of the genitalia, especially the clitoris, are not removed. It is thought to ensure virginity before marriage and fidelity afterward, and to increase male sexual pleasure.
>
> Sociological and cultural reasons: FGM is seen as part of a girl's initiation into womanhood and as an intrinsic part of a community's cultural heritage. Sometimes myths about female genitalia (e.g., that an uncut clitoris will grow to the size of a penis, or that FGM will enhance fertility or promote child survival) perpetuate the practice.
>
> Hygiene and aesthetic reasons: In some communities, the external female genitalia are considered dirty and ugly and are removed, ostensibly to promote hygiene and aesthetic appeal.
>
> Religious reasons: Although FGM is not endorsed by either Islam or by Christianity, supposed religious doctrine is often used to justify the practice.
>
> Socio-economic factors: In many communities, FGM is a prerequisite for marriage. Where women are largely dependent on men, economic necessity can be a major driver of the procedure. FGM sometimes is a prerequisite for the right to inherit. It may also be a major income source for practitioners.[14]

Islam and FGM/C

FGM/C occurs in many Muslim-majority countries (though not in all, and it is not limited to Muslim countries), and a question that is frequently raised regards the position of Islam on the issue of FGM/C. Islamic scholars disagree about Islamic prescriptions that obligate females to undergo FGM/C. Some religious scholars say that there are no rules in religious writings about female circumcision, and since female circumcision practices existed before Islam, this practice appears to have been incorporated into Islamic practice by local tradition.[15] Other scholars cite the hadith that mentions female circumcision as an honorable (though not obligatory) act. According to Sami Aldeeb, the most frequently cited passage regarding female circumcision concerns the following debate between the Prophet and a woman known to perform "excisions" on female slaves:

> Having seen her, Muhammad asked her if she kept practicing her profession. She answered affirmatively, adding: "unless it is forbidden, and you order me to stop doing

it." Muhammad replied: "Yes, it is allowed. Come closer so I can teach you: if you cut, do not overdo it, because it brings more radiance to the face, and it is more pleasant for the husband.[16]

FGM/C Incidence, Ages, and Beliefs

As cited by Fatma El-Zanty and Ann Way, the 2000 Demographic Health Survey conducted on Egyptian women found that 97 percent of married women experienced FGM/C. The age at which female genital mutilation is carried out varies and can range from infancy to children between 6 and 10 years of age, to adolescence, and occasionally to adult years. In Egypt, trained medical personnel perform the majority of circumcisions, though dayas (traditional birth attendants) perform many in rural areas. According to recent survey data, two-thirds of married women felt that the practice of circumcision should continue, with more than half of the women believing that female circumcision is a religious (Islamic) requirement.[17]

Scheherazade, Tell Me a Story (Ehky ya Scheherazade)

Year: 2009; *Director:* Yousry Nasrallah; *Cast:* Hebba (Mona Zakki)—woman in her 30s; Karim (Hassan El Raddad)—man in his 30s; Amany (Sawsan Badr)—woman in her 40s; Safaa (Rehab El Gamal)—woman in her 40s; Nahed (Sanaa Akroud)—woman in her 30s; *Length:* 134 minutes; *Setting:* large urban city (Cairo) in Egypt; upper class

SYNOPSIS

Hebba and Karim are a wealthy young married couple living in Cairo. Both have high-profile careers. Hebba is a popular television talk show host, and Karim is a journalist aiming to become the next editor-in-chief of a state-run newspaper. The editors of Karim's newspaper are not happy with his wife's politicization of current Egyptian events, and Karim asks her to soften her approach (at least until he gets his promotion). Hebba reluctantly agrees and changes the focus of her show to the apolitical—the lives and loves of ordinary women. But, as it turns out, the three women she chooses to interview on live television have anything but ordinary narratives. Their stories reveal dysfunctional male-female relationships formed in part by a sociopolitical system that subordinates and oppresses women. The apolitical has now become political.

Hebba's first interviewee discloses what occurs when a woman seeks a marriage based on love. Amany has preserved her virginity, waiting for the ideal man, but now she is middle-aged and has given up, realizing that a marriage based on mutual respect cannot exist in a patriarchal society where women are objectified.

Hebba's second interviewee is Safaa, who has recently been released from prison for murder. Safaa and her two sisters inherited their father's hardware shop some years ago. The sisters soon realized that they would need the involvement of a man to help them negotiate with the male-dominated world of business. They enlisted the services of a young man who had been their father's apprentice, and they raised the possibility that one of them should marry him to secure the business. The young man, however, took it upon himself to secretly seduce and marry each sister, an act of treachery that resulted in his murder at the hands of Safaa.

Hebba's show has now captured the attention of the country, and her third interviewee has an equally troubling story. Nahed, a young dentist from a wealthy family, was courted by one of her patients, an older man from an upper-class background and prominent in the government. He was romantic, attentive, and chivalrous, and she fell in love. Nahed agreed to marry him but refused to have sex prior to marriage, as it was important to her to preserve her virginity. However, on one occasion, she yielded to him and conceived a child. They married soon after, and she informed him of her pregnancy. At this point, Nahed discovered that the man she had married was a conniving scam artist. Her husband claimed (falsely) to be infertile and accused her of adultery, as the baby could not possibly be his. His plan all along was to extort money from her family in exchange for his silence about her alleged adultery and the attendant shame that it would bring to her family. Nahed is angry, distraught, and desperate. She divorces her husband and chooses to terminate the pregnancy.

Hebba herself has a story that she relates to the television audience: Her husband was rejected for the promotion that he had thought was his. He blamed Hebba and her show for his loss, accusing her of raising political issues about gender relationships that had given Egypt a black mark. Further, his masculinity had been undermined, as he was told to control his wife and clearly did not. He physically attacked her, leaving Hebba with a damaged face.

TRADITIONAL GENDER STEREOTYPES

The male characters in *Scheherazade, Tell Me a Story* display aggression toward women, albeit in different ways. At first, Hebba's husband displays subtle aggression toward his wife, as he blames her for his failures. Later, his aggression becomes more direct in his physical assault of her. Hebba's first interviewee, Amany, encounters male aggression in the form of contempt for women, which her suitor displays in his callous disregard of her needs and desires. And lastly, Nahed's husband's aggression is demonstrated through his cold and calculating demeanor as he manipulates her emotions for his own gain.

NONTRADITIONAL GENDER ATTRIBUTES

There are strong female characters in *Scheherazade, Tell Me a Story*. They are assertive, emphatic, and, at times, aggressive. Amany, the first to tell her story on television, is shown in a flashback listening to an older man's marriage proposal. He has introduced his "rules of their eventual partnership" and provides the following stipulations:

Managing the household is your inalienable right. But I decide the policies to be followed ... I have to be informed of every single detail. Even if you decide to buy a pound of potatoes.... As for our salaries, we put them in a joint account. I'll decide how we spend it.... You'll wear the veil. Gasoline is settled as well. We live under one roof. One car is enough. You sell your car, I sell mine and we buy a new one. I'll drive you to work and I'll pick you up. Driving is dangerous for women.

Amany is incredulous at his demands. She replies that she will go along with the proposal provided that he answer one question correctly: "What do I get in return?" He responds rather smugly that she will get a husband. Amany is incensed: "You mean you sleep with me. You fuck me. You are an idiot. I swear you are. You veil me, take my money, impose your conditions and your mother's! If marriage just means having sex, I'll pass on you! Dumb ass!"

Safaa, who has just been released from prison for murder, relates her history of abuse at the hands of a man. In a flashback, Safaa's uncle brings a man to the home that she shares with her two sisters and states that he has arranged for one of them to marry this man in exchange for money to support his opium habit. Safaa is enraged and forcibly removes her uncle and the man from her house and threatens to alert the police to his drug activities. Safaa later confronts the man, who has lied about his marriage. She savagely attacks him, leaving him semi-conscious in a building that she then sets on fire.

When Nahed informs her husband, a prominent government official, that she is two months pregnant, he denies that the child is his and attempts to blackmail her for her family's money. She will not pay; she wants justice and seeks her revenge by publicly humiliating him.

Hebba is not afraid to confront her husband when he rages about her "disgusting, repulsive and depraved" television show and her "stubbornness, stupidity and selfishness," which caused him to lose a promotion. Hebba responds angrily: "I offended Auntie by talking to a woman who fell into the abyss and survived? Who salvaged her humanity? She paid her debt to society and to herself. Listen, Karim, never, ever speak to me like that again.... You are not as great an ass-licker as you thought. Grow up! Try to be a man, baby."

The women in *Scheherazade, Tell Me a Story* are agentic, as each in their own way exacts revenge on the men who betrayed them. Are there consequences for feminine agency? At first glance, there are indeed consequences, and these seem quite dire. One woman now resides in a psychiatric hospital, one has just been released from prison, one suffered an abortion, and one was battered by her husband. Yet these women made choices, and their decisions garnered self-respect, agency, and liberation of self. The authentic self, the self that is realized and stripped of illusion, comes at great cost.

Closed Doors (Al abwab al Moghlaka)

Year: 2000; *Director:* Atef Hetata; *Cast:* Mohammad (Ahmed Azmi)—teenage boy; Fatma (Sawsan Badr)—woman in her 30s; *Length:* 107 minutes; *Setting:* large urban city (Cairo) in Egypt; working class

Synopsis

Mohammad is a solemn and lonely adolescent boy who is struggling with incipient sexual feelings. He covertly watches girls at his school and lusts after an older female friend of his mother. Fatma, Mohammad's mother, is a single parent who barely ekes out a living working as a maid. She is a strong-minded, independent, and attractive woman. Her life revolves around Mohammad, and she is involved (perhaps over-involved) with her son and his future.

Mohammad's sexual thoughts are becoming increasingly obsessive and confusing. He notes with distress that his devoted mother is also a sexual being, as she accepts the attentions of a man who is courting her. Mohammad also has conflicted feelings about his mother's female friend, who trades sex for money. He enjoys her affection and kindliness toward him, yet judges her as impure for the sins of prostitution.

Typecast Releasing Presents

The Closed Doors

Mohammad (Ahmed Azmi) is an Egyptian teenage boy conflicted about his emergent sexuality and the teachings of a religiously conservative society that punishes sexual activity outside the confines of marriage (*Closed Doors* DVD cover—released in 2000).

In a search of moral guidance, Mohammad turns to the local mosque and its imam, a kindly mentor who espouses a fundamentalist Islamic ideology. The imam provides lessons about morality, sin, virtue, and the role of women. A woman, he instructs, can be either chaste or impure, good or evil. Further, a woman's identity is her husband and her family, and her place is in her home serving the needs of her family. The imam takes an interest in Mohammad and offers himself as a father figure (and even offers his own young daughter in marriage). But first, Mohammad is instructed to get his own household in order, a challenge for a youth with a headstrong mother. Over time, Mohammad's struggle to reconcile the dual personas of his mother as a devoted and loving maternal figure with that of his mother as a sexual being with needs of her own is resolved with disastrous results.

TRADITIONAL GENDER STEREOTYPES

The predominant theme of *Closed Doors* concerns male sexuality and the sexualized binary of the chaste (and therefore good) woman and the impure (therefore bad) woman (virgin-whore). In *Closed Doors*, the imam reassures Mohammad that his sexual yearnings are normal but cautions that sexual expression is good only within marriage. His concern about Mohammad and his sexual needs is so solicitous that he offers his daughter in marriage to Mohammad. The imam lectures Mohammad about the danger that female sexuality poses to men. "Female anatomy," he says, "stimulates the sexual cells in man's brain. He becomes terribly tense, he behaves in ways that endanger his life ... he may be driven to adultery." Female sexuality is dangerous and, as such, needs restraints to ensure the purity of womanhood. Mohammad is told that, as the man of his household, it is his duty to transform his mother from a wanton, independent woman who works outside the home to a "proper" and chaste woman who accepts traditional feminine roles.

Cultural norms in patriarchal societies dictate that women need male protection from predatory males. Purdah (seclusion in the home), marriage, and veiling are necessary to protect women from the sexual predation of men and the potential of dishonoring themselves and their family. The imam in *Closed Doors* intones to the young Mohammad, "In my opinion, your mother should marry and her husband will look after you. Tell your mother to stay inside and to wear the veil if she must go out." Mohammad, now fully indoctrinated, reproaches his mother: "May God show you the way ... unveiled women will burn in hell, hanging by their hair.... You need the veil. Woman, thou shalt remain in thy home."

The imam is concerned about the irreligious and immoral environment that Mohammad must return to after he leaves the mosque. He takes it upon himself to meet with Fatma, Mohammad's mother, and relate to her that he has arranged for her to marry a pious man selected by him. Fatma learns that the man already has a wife and complains. The imam is surprised at her concern: "Sheik Assiz is married. So what? God allows us to marry two, three, or four women. You'll never have to leave home, he'll visit you here."

NONTRADITIONAL GENDER ATTRIBUTES

If the traditional role of women is one of chastity and submission, as the imam and his followers dictate, Fatwa is an exception to tradition. She does not fit into the binary of woman as either virgin or whore—she is a complex character. She is both the good mother who provides for and protects her son at all costs and a woman who is a sexual being with her own needs.

The Yacoubian Building

Year: 2006; *Director:* Marwan Hamed; *Cast:* Zaki Pasha El Dessouki (Adel Imam)—man in his 60s; Buthayna El Sayed (Hend Sabry)—woman in her 20s; Haj Assan (Nour El-Sherif)—man in his 50s; Hatim Rasheed (Khaled El Sawy)— man in his 40s; *Length:* 161 minutes; *Setting:* large urban city (Cairo) in Egypt; upper class and working class

SYNOPSIS

This film relates the interconnected stories of residents of the Yacoubian Building, an actual building that was home to Cairo's elite in the 1930s and 1940s. Residents in this dramatization are divided by class: there are the bourgeoisie, who live below in spacious, well-appointed apartments, and the "rooftop dwellers," people who live on the roof in crowded, impoverished conditions. On occasion, the two classes encounter in intertwining stories.

Representing the bourgeoisie are Zaki, Haj, and Hatim. Zaki is a wealthy older man whose dissolute lifestyle causes conflicts with the women in his life. Haj is a self-made wealthy business owner whose ambitions include obtaining a seat in the Egyptian parliament; his social status provides him with the license to use people as he desires. Hatim, a wealthy middle-aged newspaper editor, is homosexual and engages rather openly in homosexual behavior. Crossing paths with these characters is Buthayna, a pretty young woman who is the sole support of her family, who are residents of the rooftop.

Matters of sexuality infuse the narratives of *The Yacoubian Building* with

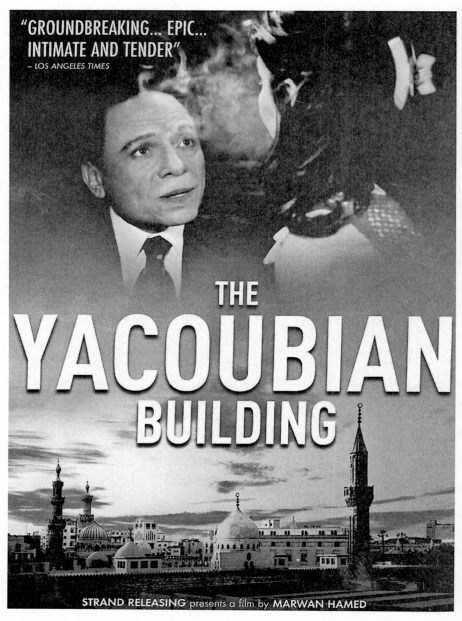

The Yacoubian Building relates the intertwining stories of Egypt's privileged class and poor and working class. Pictured are Zaki Pasha El Dessouki (Adel Imam), a member of Egypt's aristocracy, and Buthayna El Sayed (Hend Sabry), an impoverished shop clerk (*The Yacoubian Building* DVD cover—released in 2006).

issues of female prostitution; male homosexuality; male sodomy; frotteuristic fetishism; marital rape; arranged marriage; polygyny; and forced abortion. Scenes in the film alternate between amoral decadence and the moral certitude of fundamentalist Islam.

PATRIARCHAL TRADITIONS AND RELIGIOUS LAWS

Polygyny

Egyptian law based on Islamic law (Sharia) permits the practice of polygyny, in which a man may marry up to four wives at the same time. In *Yacoubian Building*, Haj is a wealthy man who has been married for many years. He has a problem: he is sexually frustrated and seeks counsel with the sheik at a mosque. Haj relates the discomfort he experiences due to lack of sexual activity with his wife. "Imagine," he says, "still having wet dreams at my age!" To which the sheik replies, "How wonderful. Allah has granted you good health." "But here's the problem," Haj complains. "My wife is no longer interested in such things. If I get close, she says behave yourself. Even if she agrees, she's my age and gets tired easily." The sheik provides a solution to Haj's dilemma and advises him to take a second wife: "It's your right to marry four women so as not to give in to Satan.... What religion allows can't be disputed by anyone. It's God's law."

Homosexuality

Sexual relations between consenting adult persons of the same sex in private are not prohibited as such in Egypt; however, according to the International Lesbian, Gay, Bisexual, Trans and Intersex Association, Egypt has laws against debauchery, and these laws have reportedly been used to imprison gay men in recent years.[18] To Hatim, the middle-aged editor, the laws that might affect him for engaging in homosexual acts matter little to him, as he engages rather openly in homosexual behavior. Hatim makes advances to a young soldier he spots on the street. The soldier, married and a new father, angrily refuses the overtures, declaring them improper and irreligious. Hatim is undeterred and takes him to his home, where the soldier, plied with plentiful alcohol and pornographic videos, is seduced. The soldier is remorseful the next morning and bemoans what he has done. But Hatim explains, "Do you know what the most sacrilegious act is? Adultery. Sleeping with a woman who isn't your wife. It harms the lineage. If a lover's child is declared as her husband's or if a baby is gotten rid of, that's very wrong. But if a man loves another man, what's the problem? Men don't get pregnant."

TRADITIONAL GENDER STEREOTYPES

The women in this film are portrayed as victims of a patriarchal system that reinforces male objectification of females, who are "things" to be used for male sexual pleasure. Buthayna is an attractive young woman who adopts a modern lifestyle. Her interactions with the various men in her life are characterized as sexual harassment. At one point she quits her job, explaining angrily to her distraught mother that her boss had wandering hands—he was groping her. She asks her mother if she wanted her to lose her honor, to which her mother replies that a clever girl knows how to protect her honor without upsetting anyone. At her next job, as a low-level shop girl, she must endure the advances of the owner. Her co-worker explains what awaits her: "We were in the storeroom—we were doing it … with our clothes on … he rubs against me till he shudders and quivers, and that's all. We're all the same; it'll be your turn soon." And indeed it does become Buthayna's turn, as she submits to the shop owner's sexual advances. Zaki is an aging wealthy and jaded man who does little more with his life than womanize. Eventually he enters into a love relationship with Buthayna, whom he marks as a vulnerable woman in need of his guidance and protection; she sees him as a means of escape from a life of tedium and harassment. The men in *The Yacoubian Building* are portrayed as entitled and users of others for their own narcissistic gain. The consequences of their actions mean little.

In this film, sex is used as an expression of male dominance. Abdo, the soldier who enters into a homosexual relationship with a wealthy patron, is chastised by his wife for spending too much time with his lover and away from her. Abdo responds with rage to her criticism and rapes her, claiming his right to her body under male prerogative. Marital rape does not exist.

Sex is also a commodity exchanged for the protection of marriage that is needed to survive. Haj's slick moral preening and his social status provide him with the ability to use people as he pleases. Although married, Haj enters into a legal marriage contract with an impoverished widow and mother of a young boy. He offers her a substantial amount of money to become his second wife and in return requests that she send her child to live with relatives and to be sexually available to him. The marriage contract is negotiated between Haj and the widow's older brother, who must provide his approval. The widow is forced into marriage by her poverty and ultimately is made to undergo an abortion and a divorce. She is a victim of a male-dominated society that allows men to use others for their own personal gratification.

Buthayna, the young woman who lives on the roof, is also victimized by the men she encounters. Her aging lover is guided by male fantasy and the need to construct himself as her protector. He uses her to satisfy his own ego needs. Other men are sexual predators and use her to satisfy their lust. None of these men see her as an individual with her own identity. She exists only to serve as an object of masculine fantasy.

6

Iran

COUNTRY PROFILE

BACKGROUND[1]

Iran is located in Central Asia and is officially known as the Islamic Republic of Iran (one of five countries in the world with the title of "Islamic Republic"). Iran is a multi-ethnic/multicultural country with large Kurdish and Turk (Turkmen) minorities. Iran is not an Arab country; rather, it is Persian, and the official language is Farsi/Persian. Most of the population is Muslim Shia (90–95 percent), with a minority Sunni population (5–10 percent). The official religion is Islamic Shi'ism. The majority (73.4 percent) of Iranians live in urban areas. The form of government is a theocratic republic.

IRAN KURDISTAN

The Kurdish people of Iran reside in the mountainous areas of western Iran. They constitute Iran's largest ethnic group, and the majority of Kurds are Sunni Muslims. Currently, Iran recognizes an autonomous Kurdish regional government. As Devrim Kilic reports on his website, KurdishMedia.com (December 26, 2005):

> The Kurds constitute approximately 10 percent of the Iranian population, numbering around 6 million. Although there is a province called Kurdistan in western Iran, it cannot be said that there is no tension between the Kurds and the Iranian state. Although Iran does not deny the existence of Kurdish culture and language, it does not allow any Kurdish "nationalist" movement to take seed within its borders. Iranians and Kurds have been accepted as "relative nations" by many historians. For this reason, the Kurds are often mistaken as being Iranian or Persian by the international community. In fact,

96

there are more similarities between Kurdish culture and Iranian culture than between Turkish and Kurdish culture, but still Kurdish and Iranian cultures are very different.

SOCIOPOLITICAL AND RELIGIOUS ISSUES RELATED TO GENDER

Efforts have been made to ensure that the information presented here reflects current law and policies. However, it must be noted that many Muslim-majority countries are currently contending with challenges to their civil and criminal laws that stem from competing constituencies of those favoring greater freedoms for women and those espousing conservative Islamic principles. As such, governmental policies are continually evolving, and laws relevant to gender issues may be added, deleted, or amended in subsequent years.

Law

Iran's constitution (1979; amended 1989)[2] and Family Protection Law (1979) are based on conservative understandings of Islam (Sharia law of the Ja'fari school of thought). A conservative-dominated Guardian Council monitors proposed legal changes for compliance with Sharia and has the power to block any measures that may have already been accepted by the Iranian parliament. As an example, the Iranian parliament agreed to join the CEDAW (Convention on the Elimination of All Forms of Discrimination Against Women) treaty in 2003, but this action was rejected by the Guardian Council, as certain provisions of the CEDAW violated Islamic principles.

Some key points of the revised Family Protection Law with reference to gender are as follows:

- The minimum age of marriage is 13 for girls, 15 for boys
- Women may conclude their own marriage contracts
- Polygyny is allowed (up to 4 wives); currently, the requirement of the first wife's permission is contentious and under review[3]
- Men have the right to divorce without any justification; women can obtain a divorce only under certain conditions (e.g., abandonment, intolerable difficulty, and hardship)
- Divorce occurs only through the courts (a husband cannot divorce his wife through *talaq*, or verbal announcement/repudiation)
- Women receive custody of children after divorce up to age 7; if a woman remarries, she loses custody of her children, but if a divorced man remarries, he does not lose custody

- Women are entitled to inherit half of a brother's or other male relative's share
- Abortion is forbidden

Laws Regulating Homosexuality

The 2016 report on sexual orientation laws compiled by the International Lesbian, Gay, Bisexual, Trans and Intersex Association identified the following items in Iranian penal law:

Part 2: Punishment for Sodomy
Chapter 1: Definition of Sodomy
Article 108: Sodomy is sexual intercourse with a male.
Article 109: In case of sodomy both the active and the passive persons will be condemned to its punishment.
Article 110: Punishment for sodomy is killing; the Sharia judge decides on how to carry out the killing.
Article 111: Sodomy involves killing if both the active and passive persons are mature, of sound mind and have free will.
Article 112: If a mature man of sound mind commits sexual intercourse with an immature person, the doer will be killed and the passive one will be subject to Ta'azir of 74 lashes if not under duress.
Article 113: If an immature person commits sexual intercourse with another immature person, both of them will be subject to Ta'azir of 74 lashes unless one of them was under duress....

Part 3: Lesbianism
Article 127: Mosaheqeh (lesbianism) is homosexuality of women by genitals.
Article 128: The ways of proving lesbianism in court are the same by which the homosexuality (of men) is proved.
Article 129: Punishment for lesbianism is hundred (100) lashes for each party.
Article 130: Punishment for lesbianism will be established vis-à-vis someone who is mature, of sound mind, has free will and intention.
Note: In the punishment for lesbianism there will be no distinction between the doer and the subject as well as a Muslim or non-Muslim.
Article 131: If the act of lesbianism is repeated three lashes and punishment is enforced each time, [SIC] death sentence will be issued fourth time.
Article 132: If a lesbian repents before the giving of testimony by the witnesses, the punishment will be quashed; if she does so after the giving of testimony, the punishment will not be quashed.
Article 133: If the act of lesbianism is proved by the confession of the doer and she repents accordingly, the Sharia judge may request the leader (ValieAmr) to pardon her.
Article 134: If two women not related by consanguinity stand naked under one cover without necessity, they will be punished to less than hundred (100) lashes (Ta'azir). In case of its repetition as well as repetition of punishment, hundred (100) lashes will be hit the third time."[4]

Additional Issues

Marriage

Muslim marriage is a civil contract. This is important for a woman, as she may enter stipulations into the contract to protect her marital rights. Such stipulations might include the right to education or to work outside the home, to divorce, and to prohibit a second wife. These marriage contracts are often registered in pre-printed booklets that deal with the stipulated conditions, and each person can sign those conditions to which they are amenable.

Iran, as a Shi'ite state, recognizes temporary marriages (*mut'a*). A Muslim man can contract an unlimited number of temporary marriages for a fixed time period, in addition to his permanent marriages. Only an unmarried woman can engage in a temporary marriage. This type of marriage is not permitted by Sunni Islam.

Inheritance

The inheritance of a male is twice that of a female, and there are several specific points in the Iranian Civil Code that refer to the rights of children and the wife:

> "If the deceased leaves no parents, but has one or more children … [i]f there are several children, some being boy(s) and some girl(s), each son takes twice as much as each daughter." … When a husband dies, if he has at least one child, his wife may only inherit one-eighth of the assets; otherwise she is only entitled to a quarter…. "If there is more than one wife, one-fourth or one-eighth part of the assets, which belongs to the wife, will be divided equally among them."

Furthermore, a wife may never inherit more than a quarter of the assets of her deceased husband, even when there is no child or other inheritors. In fact, if there is no other inheritor, while a husband inherits all the assets of his deceased wife, a surviving wife may only inherit a quarter of the assets and the rest belongs to the State.

> "If a husband or wife is the sole inheritor, the husband takes the whole of the assets of his deceased wife; but the wife takes only her share [half], and the rest of the assets of the husband shall be considered as the estate of an heirless, and will be dealt with in accordance with Article 866."[5]{/ext}

Criminal Behavior

With reference to gender issues, the Iranian Penal Code (2013) is specific as to types of crimes penalized and the corresponding punishments. The following articles reference punishments for acts of moral turpitude:

> Article 637—When a man and a woman who are not married to each other, commit indecent acts other than *zina*, such as kissing or sleeping next to one another, they

shall be sentenced to up to ninety-nine lashes; and if the act is committed by force only the one who has used force shall be punished as *ta'zir*.

Article 638—Anyone in public places and roads who openly commits a *harām* (sinful) act, in addition to the punishment provided for the act, shall be sentenced to two months' imprisonment or up to 74 lashes; and if they commit an act that is not punishable but violates public prudency, they shall only be sentenced to ten days to two months' imprisonment or up to 74 lashes.

Note—Women, who appear in public places and roads without wearing an Islamic *hijab*, shall be sentenced to ten days to two months' imprisonment or a fine of fifty thousand to five hundred Rials.[6]

Punishments

Crimes are punishable by *hudud*, *qisas*, and *ta'zir*. Mohammad Hossein Nayyeri, an attorney with expertise in Iranian law, explains the distinctions among these terms:

Crimes punishable by *hudud* (i.e. the limits, or the limits prescribed by God; singular: *hadd*) are those with fixed and severe punishments in Islamic sources [such as illicit (out of marriage) sex (*zina*), sodomy and homosexual acts between men (*livat*), homosexual acts between women (*mosahaqa*), procuring (*qavvadi*), etc.]....

Crimes punishable by *qisas* (retaliation) are a category of crimes under Islamic criminal law, in which, homicide and bodily harm are punishable by the same harm (i.e., the death penalty for murder and inflicting the same injury for bodily harm)....

Crimes punishable by *ta'zir* are less serious crimes [for which] punishments are not fixed and left at the discretion of a *Shari'a* judge. In principle, all forbidden or sinful acts, that do not constitute *hadd* offences, homicide or bodily harm, are punishable under this category. The Islamic judges may, at their discretion, impose punishments on those who have committed such acts. However, most of the *ta'zir* crimes are dealt with in the Penal Code and the judge applies the punishments stipulated in the Code.[7]

FILMS

A Separation (Jodaeiye Nader az Simin)

Year: 2011; *Director:* Asghar Farhadi; *Cast:* Nader (Peyman Moaadi)—man in his early 40s; Simin (Leila Hatami)—woman in her early 40s; Rezieh (Sareh Bayat)—woman in her 30s; Hojjat (Shahab Hosseini)—man in his 30s; *Length:* 123 minutes; *Setting:* large urban city (Tehran) in Iran; upper middle and working class

SYNOPSIS

Nader and Simin, a well-to-do married couple and parents to a 11-year-old daughter, go to court to explain why Simin wants a divorce. Simin wants her family to emigrate to America, but Nader refuses, as his elderly father, suffering from late-stage Alzheimer's, relies on him for caretaking. While Nader agrees to both the divorce and Simin's emigration, he does not agree to let his daughter leave the country. Simin decides to move out of the family home, and Nader, who works full-time, must find a domestic worker to care for his bedridden father while he is at work. He employs Rezieh, a young woman in dire need of money, as her husband is unemployed. Rezieh is a pious Muslim and thus conflicted, as some of the work responsibilities might go against her faith.

Unbeknownst to Nader, Rezieh is pregnant and is forced one day to leave her caretaking duties in an emergency visit to a doctor. Nader confronts her about her job dereliction, fires her, and (perhaps) pushes her out the door of his home. She falls down the stairs and suffers a miscarriage. Upon the urging of her religiously conservative husband, Hojjat, she files a lawsuit against Nader, accusing him of murdering the unborn child. All three appear in court to contest or confirm the charges. Nader is unsure if he actually touched Rezieh, and Rezieh is unsure of when she miscarried. But everybody lies in this confusing case, which drags out to a conclusion that provides more questions than answers.

PATRIARCHAL TRADITIONS AND RELIGIOUS LAWS

Child Custody and Guardianship

A Separation illustrates several of Iran's civil laws, which are based on Sharia. The rules of custody and guardianship are exemplified. Regardless of who has custody of their daughter, the father remains the guardian of his children. Nader has agreed to the divorce, but, as the law provides, he will not allow his daughter to accompany his wife if she emigrates to the United States. Their daughter must remain with him if Simin leaves. Iranian law allows children of a certain age to choose the custodial parent, and, at the end of the film, the judge requests that Nader and Simin's daughter choose the parent with whom she wants to live.

Criminal Abortion

Rezieh accuses Nader of pushing her and ultimately causing her to miscarry. She files a lawsuit against Nader, accusing him of murder. The jurist

A well-to-do married couple appear in Iranian court requesting a divorce and cus-todial care of their 11-year-old daughter. Simin (Leila Hatami) plans to emigrate to America with her daughter, but Nader (Peyman Moaadi), under Iranian law, is the child's guardian and refuses to allow his daughter to leave the country (*A Separation* DVD cover—released in 2011).

in charge of the case explains that the charge of murder is warranted, as Rezieh was four and a half months pregnant. A fetus at 19 weeks, he reasons, is a full human. But Nader's alleged crime is more appropriately classified as criminal abortion under Iran's penal code. According to Article 622 of Iran's penal code, "Anyone who intentionally and by hitting, beating, and bothering a pregnant woman causes an abortion, should pay blood money. Plus he/she would face one to three years in prison"[8] (see below).

TRADITIONAL GENDER STEREOTYPES

A Separation provides contrasting portrayals of female and male characters who embody both traditional and nontraditional gender stereotypes and attributes. The character of Hojjat illustrates masculine dominance and privilege that is sanctioned by Islam and by patriarchal societies. Nader, by contrast, illustrates that males need not always conform to masculine stereotypes. Two different women are juxtaposed in the portrayals of Simin and Rezieh. Simin, as the divorced wife with her own agency in the world, is contrasted with Rezieh, the traditional and conservative wife who lives her life according to the precepts of Islam.

Hojjat represents the traditional male whose fundamentalist Islamic beliefs guide his behavior toward his family. In one scene, he angrily challenges Nader, who hired his wife as a housekeeper without asking for the husband's permission first. At another point in the film, Hojjat's rage about what he perceives to be an unfair legal system is displaced onto his wife, whose piety he questions. He states that he could sue her for divorce since she has worked for a man of whom he had not approved.

Rezieh, as a traditional Muslim wife, is respectful of traditional Islamic principles dictating that wives are to be obedient to their husbands and that women should not interact with men who are not their husbands or relations. Rezieh is conflicted: she wants to earn money to help her husband pay off his debts by working as Nader's housekeeper, but she is afraid of her husband's anger if she even requests permission to work outside the home. She does agree to assist Nader in looking after his father, who has dementia. She then encounters a problem: the father has wet his pants and is unable to clean himself. As a pious Muslim woman, she is not allowed to touch a man not in her family. She calls a religious hotline for guidance and asks the advisor if it is a sin to change the pants of a senile elderly man. Apparently she is allowed to do so as long as she wears kitchen gloves.

NONTRADITIONAL GENDER ATTRIBUTES

Males are depicted in a nuturing role in *A Separation*. Nader is the head of household and the primary caregiver for his daughter and bedridden father. He bathes his father, changes his clothes, and kisses him on the forehead. He helps his child with her studies, plays games with her, and drives her to school. He also does the household laundry and the cooking. Nader is not adverse to displays of emotion; he shows considerable affection toward his father and his daughter.

Simin is a modern woman. She is employed outside the home, and she is quite capable of living on her own following her divorce from Nader. In courtroom scenes, she is not afraid to argue with the judge to stand up for her rights. Rezieh likewise has moments of agency. Although she is employed by Nader, she argues with him about his father's care. And although she is an obedient wife, she seeks employment without her husband's permission and refuses to be complicit in her husband's lies.

ADDITIONAL POINT

A *Separation* features the lives of ordinary Iranians who deal with challenges experienced by people worldwide. As with most families of the world, aging parents, single parenting, and child custody are issues that affect Iranian families. In many of the scenes that take place in private homes or in the judicial system, an Iranian society that tolerates both traditionalist and moderate Islamic voices is depicted. A *Separation* was awarded the Academy Award for Best Foreign Language Film in 2011.

CRIMINAL ABORTION AND BLOOD MONEY

As stated earlier, according to Iran's penal code, "Anyone who intentionally and by hitting, beating, and bothering a pregnant woman causes an abortion, should pay blood money. Plus he/she would face one to three years in prison." In a review of A *Separation* in the *New Yorker* magazine, Rollo Romig provides an interview with Sanaz Alasti, an Iranian lawyer and professor of criminal justice, who clarifies the code. Professor Alasti, as cited by Romig, explains that blood money refers to a fine that a person must pay to his or her victim. In the cases of criminal abortion, the amount of blood money is a function of the age and sex of the fetus. If the fetus is older than two months, it is considered "infused with life," and the perpetrator would be fined. If the fetus were a boy, blood money is paid in full. If a girl, half is paid, and if the gender is unknown, three quarters. Criminal abortion in Iranian law is considered a crime against individuals and, as such, can be pardoned or have punishments mitigated. These crimes are in contrast to crimes against God, which are non-pardonable. Adultery is an example of a crime against God.

According to Professor Alasti, Nader should have been charged with the criminal abortion, not murder.[9]

A report conducted by the United Nations Population Division, Department of Economic and Social Affairs, provides an analysis of Iran's abortion laws in place after the 1979 revolution and cites Iran's penal code:

> Under the Penal Code of 1991, which is based on Islamic law, abortion is categorized as a lesser crime involving bodily injury (*oisas*), which is punishable by the payment of blood money or compensation (*diyah*). Compensation is paid to the victim or, in the case of the victim's death, to the victim's relatives. In the case of abortion, the amount of compensation paid depends on the stage of the pregnancy when the abortion is performed. It is 20 dinars if semen is established in the uterus; 40 dinars if the embryo has formed a blood clot; 60 dinars if the embryo has attained the shape of flesh; 80 dinars for a foetus that has attained the shape of bone upon which the flesh has not yet grown; 100 dinars for a foetus in which bones and flesh are completely bound, but there is no spirit; and the full diyah payable for a human if the foetus is ensouled. Before ensoulment, the compensation is the same regardless of sex. After ensoulment, half of the full diyah is payable in the case of a woman, or, if the sex of the foetus is indeterminate, three-quarters of the full diyah. If the pregnant woman aborts her own child, she is not to receive any part of the compensation. The amount of full diyah is set by the Code at 1,000 unadulterated or unalloyed gold dinars, 10,000 unadulterated or unalloyed silver dirhams, or certain numbers of camels, cows, sheep or garments. Although the abortion provisions of the Code do not express any exceptions to the prohibition against abortion, other sections of the Code exempt from criminal punishment persons who perform criminal acts in order to save the life of another person. Presumably these would justify the performance of an abortion to save the life of a pregnant woman.[10]

A Thousand Women Like Me (Hezaran zan mesle man)

Year: 2000; *Director:* Reza Mirkarimi (as Seyyed Reza Mir-Karimi); *Cast:* Sharzad (Niki Karimi)—woman in her 30s; Hesam (Fariborz Arabnia)—man in his 30s; *Length:* 108 minutes; *Setting:* large urban city (Tehran) in Iran; upper middle class

SYNOPSIS

Sharzad is a lawyer in Tehran who has divorced Hesam, a successful businessman. As a consequence, and as the law dictates, the courts have awarded Hesam custody of their seven-year-old son and allowed Sharzad once-weekly visiting rights. Hesam is a loving father but inattentive to the special needs of his son, who is diabetic. At one point, the boy collapses at school due his father's failure to administer the appropriate amount of insulin.

Sharzad is concerned about her son's health and wants custody of him.

"... [a] solid, pro cast... but as Sharzad, Karimi occasionally finds deeper moments as a mother torn...." -Robert Koehler, VARIETY

A Thousand Women Like Me
a Film by Reza Karimi

Iranian law dictates that, in divorce, fathers typically receive custody of their sons once they reach the age of seven. Pictured here is Sharzad (Niki Karimi), a divorced attorney, who has lost custody of her son to her ex-husband (*A Thousand Women Like Me* DVD cover—released in 2000).

But Hesam, aggrieved by the shame of her divorcing him, refuses and instead offers to remarry her. Sharzad does not love him and petitions the court for custody on the grounds that Hesam is a neglectful father. The petition is unsuccessful, and Sharzad, frustrated, angry and fearful for her son, kidnaps him.

On the run for several days and aware that the police are looking for her, she eventually realizes that she must contact her ex-husband about the boy's future. Desperate to get his son back, Hesam tells Sharzad that if she returns the boy, he will allow her to have custody. But he has lied, and he cruelly chastises Sharzad: "A mother who commits such a horrible thing just to possess her child does not deserve to raise him. I'll never give him to you." Sharzad understands that she will never have her son and, in anguish, runs blindly down a busy city street only to be struck by a car. In the bleak and unforgiving final scene, Hesam and his son are seen on the grounds of an institution walking slowly toward a remote figure. It is Sharzad, now confined to a wheelchair. Her son rushes to her and they embrace as Hesam looks on sympathetically.

Patriarchal Traditions and Religious Laws

Child Custody

The issue of child custody in the situation of divorce is a key theme of this film. Iranian family law based on Sharia dictates that mothers are awarded custody of children up to age seven, after which fathers are given custody (see below). A mother can regain custody if paternal incompetence can be demonstrated to the satisfaction of the court. In *A Thousand Women Like Me*, Sharzad is a lawyer whose legal practice involves assisting mothers in custody cases. She complains about the Iranian legal system, which is based on gender inequality, favoring males over females in custody cases.

Sharzad herself experiences the judiciary privileges that men receive in child custody cases. At age seven, her son was transferred to her ex-husband's care. His parenting is inconsistent at best. He is negligent about providing his son's diabetes medicine in a timely manner, and she fears that her son's health could be in danger. Sharzad returns to court and petitions for custody of her son. However, her petition is considered without merit, and the case dismissed.

Nontraditional Gender Attributes

Sharzad is a strong presence in *A Thousand Women Like Me*. In asking for a divorce, she is aware that women who want a divorce (or who refuse to marry in the first place) undermine Islam's prioritization of marriage as the foundation of a civil society. Despite the strong likelihood that she will lose custodial rights to her son, she cannot tolerate living with a man she doesn't love or respect. In divorcing her husband, she also transgresses the patriarchal norm that a woman's primary and only duty is to be a wife and mother. Sharzad's strong presence is depicted in court scenes with her forceful arguments before the judge, arguing for the rights of a mother who seeks custody. The judge has ruled that there is no strong evidence in the case to prove that the father in this case is incompetent. Sharzad retorts, "No strong evidence? He doesn't give a damn about his son." Sharzad also shows agency (or foolishness?) in kidnapping her son. She is defying a legal system that perpetuates gender inequality in child custodial rights. Are there consequences to her challenge and to her refusal to remain in a loveless marriage for the sake of her own autonomy? It appears so. Not only has she lost her son, but she also loses the autonomy of mobility.

CUSTODY LAWS

Muslim-majority nations differ in their application of Islamic laws related to custody following a divorce or death of a spouse. In nations that base their laws on Sharia, the specific school of thought (e.g., the Hanafi or Ja'fari school) informs policy on guardianship, custodial parent, age of child in changing custodians, visitation rights in cases of divorce, and similar issues. Regardless of the school, those who have custody of the children are obligated to raise them as good Muslims.

The custody laws of many Muslim countries have been amended through the years, but generally the mother is awarded custody of children up to a certain age, after which the father assumes custody. Often a gender distinction is in place, with fathers assuming custody of boys at earlier ages than girls. According to Central-Mosque, a website that provides information on Islamic judicial interpretations, the rationale for custodial decisions and differential age criteria are based on the premise that young children (both boys and girls) need to remain with their mothers to receive their love and care. Boys, however, by age seven are considered by some schools of thought to be at the "age of understanding" and are transferred to their fathers to receive masculine socialization. Girls, upon reaching puberty, are transferred to their fathers for paternal protection. In some Sharia schools (e.g., Hanafi), boys, upon reaching puberty, are allowed to choose the custodial parent. A girl remains with their father until her marriage.

As to guardianship of children, many Muslim-majority nations distinguish between custody and guardianship and a priori grant guardianship to fathers. For example, the Iranian Civil Code notes that even when custody of children is with the mother, "natural" guardianship remains with the father (or paternal grandfather).[11]

Baran

Year: 2001; *Director:* Majid Majidi; *Cast:* Lateef (Hossein Abedini)—boy in late teens; Rahmat/Baran (Zahra Bahrami)—girl in mid-teens; *Length:* 94 minutes; *Setting:* large urban city in Iran; working class

Synopsis

Baran is a love story set within an urban area of Iran adjacent to the Afghanistan border. At a large construction site, dozens of workers are seen carrying heavy cement bags, tearing down walls, and building scaffolding. Most of these workers are Afghan refugees who are in the country illegally, struggling to survive on what little wages they earn. One Afghan worker has injured himself and sent his teenage daughter, Rahmat, to replace him. Rahmat is disguised as a boy, as only males are allowed at the construction site. She struggles to do the heavy lifting that is required and is admonished by Lateef, a young Iranian man who is employed at the site as a cook, tea server and all-around errand-boy. Lateef is mercurial and hot-headed, and he is easily provoked to fist fights when he perceives that his masculine pride is threatened.

As the story unfolds, Lateef engages in one fight too many and loses his somewhat undemanding job; he is then relegated to construction work. To make matters worse, Rahmat assumes his old job and proves popular with the other workers. Lateef is jealous, yet intrigued with Rahmat, who is efficient, obsequious, and totally silent. He spends time covertly watching her and discovers her true identity as a girl. As he continues watching her, Lateef becomes enamored with Rahmat. He finds himself in a role that is new to him, that of protector, and takes it upon himself to shield Rahmat's true identity from the others.

Iranian inspectors arrive at the site to search for illegal workers, and Rahmat (who is illegal) disappears. Lateef searches for her and discovers her working in hellish conditions, excavating heavy stones from frigid waters. Her family needs her wages to allow them to return to Afghanistan. Lateef knows he must help her, and he arranges (through great personal sacrifice) to provide enough money for the family and to free Rahmat from her labor.

Throughout this love story, Lateef and Rahmat never touch, never exchange words of affection (in fact, she never speaks at all). It is only at the end, through the slightest of gestures, that their mutual affection is revealed.

As the family prepares to return to their home country, Lateef must see Rahmat one last time. He has arranged to be present when the family departs. Rahmat is now clad in a burqa, with only her eyes unmasked. As she passes Lateef, she drops a basket of fruit. Both stoop to gather the fruit, careful not to let their hands touch. She is called to leave and at the last moment lowers her facial scarf, allowing him to see her face. They stare at one another, and she provides a slight smile. It is enough.

TRADITIONAL GENDER STEREOTYPES

Lateef finds himself in many situations where he protects Rahmat. On the construction site, a worker criticizes Rahmat for a failed errand. Lateef then confronts the construction worker, which ends in another physical altercation. Later, building inspectors are searching for illegal workers and spot Rahmat. She runs away, with the inspectors close behind. Lateef in turn chases the inspectors and prevents them from arresting Rahmat by fighting them off. Later, Lateef provides one last rescue that will save Rahmat from a life of arduous physical labor. Rahmat's family desires to return to Afghanistan, but they are too poor to afford transportation. Lateef wants to help them but needs to find money. He sells his valuable ID card on the black market and gathers his years of saved wages to give to the family.

NONTRADITIONAL GENDER ATTRIBUTES

Baran is a story about Lateef and his transformation. At the beginning of the film, Lateef is superficial, aggressive, and self-serving. He is mercurial, joking with the other construction workers one moment and then quick to anger when he perceives an insult. Later in the film, he begins to care deeply about another person. He sees Rahmat suffering, and he suffers for her. Lateef's gift of money to Rahmat and her family is anonymous and selfless— he has no desire for reciprocity. It is enough to see her freed from her difficult labor and her family financially able to return to their homeland. His transformation is complete.

In many films set in strict patriarchal societies, men are portrayed as in control and powerful, as patriarchy has emboldened the masculine privileges of dominance, agency, and, all too frequently, aggression toward women. In *Baran*, however, the privileged masculinity is honorable and nurturing. A message of this film is that men do not need to be bound to the rules of patriarchy and need not yield to masculinity norms. It has been suggested that men's violence stems from fear of the female and the need to negate the feminine qualities within them. By extension, perhaps men's charity and nurturance stem from acceptance and welcoming of the feminine.

Border Café (Café Transit)

Year: 2005; *Director:* Kambuzia Partovi; *Cast:* Reyhan (Fereshteh Sadre Orafaiy)—woman in her 30s; Nasser (Parviz Parastui)—man in his 40s; *Length:* 105 minutes; *Setting:* A modern, moderate-sized urban city in Iran; middle class

SYNOPSIS

Reyhan is a newly widowed mother of two children. According to patriarchal custom, a deceased man's male relative is honor bound to marry his widow, even if he is already married. Nasser, the brother of Reyhan's husband, duly proposes marriage; however, contrary to social custom, Reyhan refuses his offer, preferring to stay unwed. To support her family, Reyhan reopens her deceased husband's café, which is located on a busy highway. She is a skilled cook and the café turns out to be a great success, much to the consternation of Nasser and his family, who believe that it is dishonorable for a woman to own or run a business. Throughout the film, this strong, independent woman meets with considerable challenges from a social structure that espouses patriarchal traditions.

PATRIARCHAL TRADITIONS AND RELIGIOUS LAWS

Levirate Marriage

One patriarchal tradition dramatized in this film involves a type of marriage called a Levirate marriage, in which the widow is obligated (forced) to marry the brother (or another male relative) of her deceased husband, even if the other man already has a wife. This tradition underscores the principle that women are regarded as the property of family groups and ensures that any of the widow's inheritance is kept in the family. The practice of Levirate marriage dates to ancient times and is found today in some highly patriarchal Islamic and Judaic communities. However, this practice is contrary to Islamic Sharia law, which mandates that consent is a prerequisite for any marriage. In *Border Café*, Reyhan rejects this tradition, as she does not wish to marry her brother-in-law. Her in-laws support the tradition and attempt to persuade her to reconsider. In one scene, the female relatives of Nasser visit Reyhan with gifts and plead on Nasser's behalf for her to accept his marriage proposal.

The women assert that Reyhan must remarry to protect the honor of both her dead husband and Nasser. The women attempt to shame Reyhan and remind her that she is lucky to have her deceased husband's brother to protect her: "Things are different here. You can't do anything you want. A woman has never run a restaurant around here."

Inheritance

Iranian law governs the inheritance of assets following the death of a spouse and is based on Sharia law. Male children of the deceased typically receive twice as much as female children (see below), and widows can never receive more than one-fourth of the inheritance. In *Border Café*, a judge (male) explains to Reyhan her inheritance rights if no will was established: "According to Islamic law, if there is no will, a widow is entitled to one-eighth of her husband's estate and any children are given inheritance before the mother."

TRADITIONAL GENDER STEREOTYPES

There is a clear gendered division of labor in *Border Café* with females expected to fulfill caregiving responsibilities and males expected to fulfill roles as provider for the family. In this film, men work outside the home as business entrepreneurs, truck and bus drivers, and construction workers. Women work within the household, taking care of children, preparing meals, washing dishes, and weaving. This gender tradition is depicted in Nasser's own home, where female members of the household are restricted to the confines of the house and to caregiving responsibilities.

Patriarchal tradition holds that it is improper for women to independently own or run a business, as they lack the competence required to do so. The sterotype that only men are competent is evident in *Border Café*. Nasser and his associates continually tell Reyhan that women are inept and useless in dealing with the outside world. Attempts are made to shame her when she insists on running the café that was owned by her late husband. At several points, her independence is challenged by her in-laws, who exhort her to close the restaurant and marry Nasser.

Men in this film are portrayed as active participants in society in their roles as judges, police, truck drivers, and business owners. Women (with the notable exception of Reyhan) are portrayed as mere onlookers to the events that will affect their lives. As an example, Nasser's wife is passive and compliant. During a meeting to persuade Reyhan to marry Nasser, she appears unhappy at the prospect of a second wife joining the family but says nothing to object. Later, Reyhan visits the home of Nasser, and Nasser orders his wife to greet Reyhan and serve tea to both himself and Reyhan. His wife obeys with passive acceptance.

NONTRADITIONAL GENDER ATTRIBUTES

In a patriarchal-dominant society, the greatest virtue for a woman is to embrace domesticity in the role of wife and mother. A woman who rejects this role and chooses to remain unmarried poses a threat to the masculine presumptions that only males are capable of being breadwinners and that only males can provide protection. Reyhan is the exception to the traditional stereotype that women are without agency and thus threatens the status quo.

Reyhan has a voice throughout the narrative. Despite admonitions about her "shameful" behavior, she rejects proposals of marriage, establishes a successful business, and raises her children without male involvement. To the village women who insist that she remarry to protect the honor of the men, she replies that she is quite capable of protecting her deceased husband's honor. But Reyhan is also pragmatic and aware of restrictions placed on women in patriarchal societies. She cooks for the patrons but conceals her gender by working in a walled-off kitchen.

However, Reyhan's independence has consequences. Locals (i.e., Nasser's accomplices) complain about her business and want it shut down. Nasser claims that the café is corrupting Reyhan, and he ultimately forces her business to be closed. In many Iranian films, when women step out of the traditional role, there are dire consequences. But not in this film. In the final scene, Reyhan finds another location for her café and Nasser looks on in silence.

INHERITANCE RIGHTS

Under Iranian law (Sharia), women and men have equal rights to ownership. However, with regard to inheritance, the constitution, as based on Quranic text, stipulates that males are entitled to twice as much as females. Hence, if the deceased has several children, all sons are granted twice as much as each daughter. If the deceased were a married man, the wife inherits one-fourth, and if he had at least one child, the wife inherits one-eighth. To complicate matters further, if the deceased husband had more than one wife, either one-fourth or one-eighth of the assets are divided among the wives. In any event, a wife's inheritance is limited to a maximum of one-fourth of the deceased husband's assets, and if there are no other inheritors, the remaining assets belong to the government. By contrast, a husband inherits all the assets of his deceased wife. Article 949 of the Iranian constitution states that:

> If a husband or wife is the sole inheritor, the husband takes the whole of the assets of his deceased wife; but the wife takes only her share [half], and the rest of the assets of the husband shall be considered as the estate of an heirless, and will be dealt with in accordance with Article 866.[12]

In many Muslim-majority countries that adhere to Sharia law, certain Islamic premises or tenets that are considered discriminatory toward females have undergone amendment or are under discussion regarding amendment. For example, the minimum age of marriage has been raised in many countries, and conditions required for divorce are becoming more egalitarian. However, Mohammad Hossein Nayyeri offers the legal opinion that the inheritance rules favoring males are incontrovertible:

> The main problem which prevents these rules to be modernized and amended fundamentally to accord with gender equality is that, the Islamic Shari'a rules for the inheritance of women is considered eternal. In fact, because the shares of the inheritors are dealt with in the Quran (mainly in *Sura al-Nisa* 4:11–12) it is taken as unchangeable by Islamic jurists; and even shifts and developments in the modern world cannot make them change their minds.[13]

Born Under Libra
(Motevalede mahe mehr)

Year: 2001; *Director:* Ahmadreza Darvish; *Cast:* Mahtab (Mitra Hajjar)—woman in her 20s; Daniel (Mohammad Reza Foroutan)—man in his 20s; Peyman (Mahmud Azizi)—man in his 50s; *Length:* 94 minutes; *Setting:* large urban city (Tehran) in Iran; upper middle class

SYNOPSIS

Mahtab and Daniel are a young couple in love but find it difficult to sustain their relationship due to Mahtab's father's disapproval of Daniel. The two are university students and find themselves on opposing sides of a political controversy involving compulsory gender segregation in the classrooms of their university. Daniel favors the conservative Islamic position that would mandate gender segregation, while Mahtab advocates for the reformist position of gender integration. She is the leader of the reformist students and speaks assertively to school administrators and fellow students about her position. At one of the political meetings, a love letter from Daniel to Mahtab is made public and the attendant shame forces Daniel to leave the university and return to his hometown in a rural area of Iran. Mahtab realizes that she cannot lose him and travels to his village to be with him. They decide to return to Tehran but have a traffic accident along the way and end up in a deserted war zone filled with abandoned military machinery and hidden mine traps. Daniel and Mahtab must navigate a perilous terrain to return home. But Daniel dies from stepping on live ammunition, and in the last scene, Mahtab is staring off into the distance as a train passes by.

TRADITIONAL GENDER STEREOTYPES

The stereotype that males are dominant and females are subordinate is evident in *Born Under Libra*. Peyman, Mahtab's father, represents the dominant and controlling masculine voice in this film. He is the patriarch of the family and makes the important decisions about family life. He demonstrates his authority by berating his wife for interrupting him at the breakfast table. He tells her to shut up and to mind her own business—which she does. He lectures his adult daughter about immodesty and orders her to cover her hair when only a few wisps are showing from under her scarf. At a police station where his daughter and her fiancé are being held after their involvement in an auto accident, the police are concerned that an unrelated male and female were alone together in a car. Peyman states that he will punish both of them; he slaps Daniel in the face and later slaps Mahtab for what he sees as her insolence.

Mahtab, like her mother, displays traditional feminine traits. She conforms to the Iranian dress code of hijab while in the public sphere (she really doesn't have much of a choice, as it's the law). Regarding the patriarchal custom of needing her father's approval before marriage, Mahtab is aware that, without his approval, her engagement to Daniel would be considered "illegal." But she doesn't dare assert herself to her father and approaches her mother to intercede on her behalf. Her mother, true to traditional femininity, refuses, saying she doesn't meddle in her husband's affairs.

The stereotype that females are victims in need of rescue and that males are rescuers is evident in the relationship betwen Mahtab and Daniel. Mahtab is a study in contrasts. On the one hand, she is strong and tenacious, but, on other hand, she finds herself in situations where men must rescue her. At the university, she and her fellow female students find themselves stuck in an

BORN UNDER LIBRA

A film by Ahmadreza Darvish

Human Rights Award
Nominee
POLITICAL FILM SOCIETY

DVD
VIDEO

The relationship between Mahtab (Mitra Hajjar) and Daniel (Mohammad Reza Foroutan) is complicated. They are university students on opposite sides of Iranian political issues but are in love and wish to be married (*Born Under Libra* DVD cover—released in 2001).

elevator, only to be rescued by male students. Daniel, her fiancé, is ever present to rescue her from some peril or other. He fixes her flat tire, stops a thief who has stolen her purse, and defends her from other students who question her commitment to the cause. During their escape through the minefields of a former war zone, Mahtab falls into a stream (twice!), and Daniel saves her from drowning. When Mahtab panics on discovering a human skeleton, Daniel heroically disposes of it.

NONTRADITIONAL GENDER ATTRIBUTES

Many women in *Born Under Libra* are portrayed as outspoken, with a mind of their own. Female university students engage in heated political debates to which other students, both male and female, respectfully and thoughtfully listen. A judiciary council of university administrators that includes an outspoken female administrator engages in debate about school policy issues. Mahtab heads one of political factions and is outspoken about her political positions. Mahtab also rebels against patriarchal tradition that subordinates females, leading the student protestors and challenging university administrators. At one point, an administrator demands that Mahtab and her fellow students leave a classroom, and she shouts back that they will not abide by his senseless regulations. Ignoring rules that prohibit public interactions with unrelated men, she drives Daniel around town in her car, and, in the ultimate transgression against patriarchy, she runs away to join Daniel.

But Mahtab can't be portrayed as too tough—too masculine—as it would disturb the natural gender order that characterizes patriarchal societies. So she must be softened. She has her weepy moments, she shrieks with feminine appropriateness when discovering skeletal remains in the minefield (Daniel, of course, disposes of said skeleton with hardly a tinge of queasiness), and even her search for Daniel is motivated by romantic (feminine) love. Daniel, for his part, is continually coming to her aid, which only highlights his inherent masculine prowess and her inherent feminine weakness.

This film imparts a message and a moral lesson. The message? No matter how tough and independent a woman appears, she is at heart weak and morally vulnerable. The moral? Transgressions of patriarchal-dictated gender norms don't bode well for the transgressors. Daniel dies, and Mahtab is alone.

Education in Iran

Education for both sexes is a priority in Iran. According to Islamic doctrine, the pursuit of knowledge is an obligation of every Muslim, regardless of gender. Following the 1979 revolution, gender segregation was enforced in all Iranian elementary and secondary schools. Typically, in these schools, girls have female teachers and boys have male teachers. At the university level, classes remained co-ed, with professors of either gender, but, per demands from the post-revolutionary conservatives, gender segregation was enforced through seating arrangements in which men sat on one side and women sat on the other. Conservative Islamists continue to argue for gender-segregated universities, maintaining that the mixing of genders distracts from scholarship and leads to inappropriate relationships between women and men.

Children of Heaven (Bacheha-Ye aseman)

Year: 1999; *Director:* Majid Majidi; *Cast:* Ali (Amir Farrokh Hashemian)—boy, age 9; Zahra (Bahare Seddiqi)—girl, age 7; *Length:* 89 minutes; *Setting:* large urban city (Tehran) in Iran; working class

Synopsis

Children of Heaven is an Iranian film about family relationships, moral responsibilities, and the value of compassion. Two siblings, Ali and his younger sister Zahra, live with their parents in a modest one-room home. Zahra's shoes are worn out and in need of repair. Even though she covets the pretty new shoes with a bow that she saw in the market, her family is too poor to buy them. Ali is entrusted with finding a merchant in town to repair his sister's shoes, but he loses them. The family cannot afford to buy another pair of shoes, and the children must find a way to deal with the loss without telling their parents or teachers. The two, of course, must wear shoes to school, and since Ali's school begins earlier than Zahra's, they trade off the one pair that they have. So Ali must race to meet Zahra for the exchange, and she then rushes to school wearing his shoes. This goes on for days, with both children becoming fast runners.

At Ali's school, a running competition for boys is announced, and Ali learns that he can win a pair of new sneakers, but only if he wins third place. He is determined to win these shoes and enters the competition. He wins the contest and receives a trophy and all sorts of accolades—but no shoes. Ali returns home in tears: he has failed his little sister. Unbeknownst to him, though, his father has earned some extra money, and, as a surprise for Zahra, he purchases the pair of shoes that she so coveted.

Issues associated with gender relationships are important in this film.

Ali (Amir Farrokh Hashemian) and Zahra (Bahare Seddiqi) are a brother and sister in contemporary Iran. Ali has lost his sister's shoes and, in shame, cannot tell his family, as they are too poor to buy another pair. In order to go to school, the two must alternately share Ali's shoes (*Children of Heaven* DVD cover—released in 1999).

Children of Heaven is a heartfelt film that shows the everyday lives of ordinary Iranians in their homes, at work, and at school.

PATRIARCHAL TRADITIONS AND RELIGIOUS LAWS

There is a clear gendered division of labor in *Children of Heaven*, in which men work outside the home and (with the exception of teachers) women work within the household. The children's mother and Zahra work in the household, preparing meals, washing clothes and dishes, and caring for a baby. The men in the film work in the city in a variety of businesses— shoe repair, bakery, teaching, grocery, and lawn care. Interestingly, in both the household and the workplace, males serve tea.

Schools for young children are gender segregated. There is a dress code for the girls, who all wear a white head scarf and blue gown. Female teachers wear a head scarf and chador. By contrast, boys and male teachers wear diverse contemporary clothing.

TRADITIONAL GENDER STEREOTYPES

While at school, boys engage in active recreation during recess periods, with opportunities provided for competitive games such as soccer. The school principal announces that boys will be able to compete in a long-distance race, and at the end of the film many boys are seen competing. Girls are not provided with a similar competition. Girls, during their recess, either huddle together and chat or jump rope. Boys and adult males also interact with the outside world. They purchase groceries and other goods at the local market. Girls and adult females engage in passive activities and are not shown interacting in any setting other than school or home.

NONTRADITIONAL GENDER ROLES

Ali does not evince the traditional masculine attributes that boys show at very young ages. Rather, he is a sensitive child who puts his sister's and his family's needs above his own. At several points, he cries with remorse about losing his sister's shoes. He passively accepts an unfair punishment at his school, and he sacrifices his own comfort by sharing his shoes with his sister. Ali's demeanor stands in contrast to that of his father, who demonstrates traditional masculine traits. He is the breadwinner, and he accepts the responsibility of his role as head of his family. He is a stern authoritarian parent who, while caring deeply about his family's welfare, stoically deals with the challenges of their financial burdens.

Daughters of the Sun (Dokhtaran Khorshid)

Year: 2000; *Director:* Maryam Shahriar; *Cast:* Amangol (Altinay Ghelich Taghani); *Length:* 92 minutes; *Setting:* small rural village in Iran; impoverished community

SYNOPSIS

In the countryside of rural Iran, Amangol, an adolescent girl, is standing motionless as her father cuts off her long hair. A single tear falling down her face indicates the sorrow she is experiencing about her fate. She is being transformed into a boy and will be indentured to a local carpet merchant to earn money for her impoverished family. The father, perhaps aware that males receive more compensation than females, dresses his daughter in male garb and renames her Aman. Aman's job is to weave carpets and, as "he" is the only male, to supervise the work of three young women who also weave.

It is evident that the carpet merchant is a cruel and greedy man. He does not allow Aman to leave the small stone weaving hut, locking her in at night. The merchant beats his female workers for even the smallest infractions but beats Aman more brutally for not supervising the girls properly. All this Aman accepts stoically and silently, for she is trapped with no way out.

As the days wear on, Belghies, one of the weavers, develops a romantic attachment to Aman. She fantasizes about a future with Aman and asks Aman to marry her. It is not clear if she knows Aman's true identity, but Aman allows the fantasy and agrees to the marriage. That imagined future is soon disrupted, however, when Belghies kills herself after her uncle arranges her marriage to a man many years her senior.

Daughters of the Sun is a bleak and despairing film. The oppression of women has resulted in Aman's enslavement and Belghies' suicide. Yet, at the end of the film, there is a glimmer of hope. Aman has broken her silence. She learns of the merchant's deceit in not giving her a letter informing her of her mother's illness and eventual death. Aman exacts her revenge and chooses her own fate.

TRADITIONAL GENDER STEREOTYPES

Daughters of the Sun takes place in rural Iran, a region governed by entrenched patriarchal traditions. The females in this film are subjected to

Amangol (Altinay Ghelich Taghani) is a teenage girl and an expert weaver. Her impoverished family forces her to cut her hair and wear boy's clothing to be indentured to a rug merchant seeking a male weaver. Amangol, now renamed Aman, endures enslavement and isolation until she is forced to make a choice (*Daughters of the Sun* DVD cover—released in 2000).

male dominance, personified by Aman's father and employer. Aman is nothing more than property to be used, first by her father, and then by the carpet merchant. Her father cuts her long hair to transform her into a boy. She silently endures, as it is evident that she has no say in the matter. She accepts without protest her father's decision to send her away to the carpet merchant along with her new identity as a boy. The carpet merchant has assigned Aman responsibilities to weave and supervise the other workers. He does not allow her to leave during the day and locks her in at night. He has assumed control of her life, and she acquiesces.

The girls who also work in the weaving hut similarly suffer under patriarchy. Belghies, a young girl with an attachment to Aman, discloses her family's financial problems. Her uncle is commanding her to marry a much older man in exchange for money to pay off his debts. Her despair is evident as she commits suicide to avoid this fate.

NONTRADITIONAL GENDER ATTRIBUTES

Aman is a transformational character. In the beginning, she personifies traditional feminine stereotypes. She is passive, obedient, and voiceless. She accepts her father's command to become the financial provider for her family. She has a steep price to pay—the loss of her identity as a female—and she accepts that in silence. She likewise accepts the cruelty of her employer. It appears that there is no way out for her in a patriarchal system that treats females as nothing more than property. But at the end, Aman ends her silence and asserts her ability to choose and to determine her own fate. She dons female clothing, sets fire to the workshop, and, in the last frame, is seen walking slowly down a path leading away from the village. What will happen to her is unknown, though, at the very least, agency is hers.

Donya

Year: 2003; *Director:* Manoucher Mosayeri; *Cast:* Donya (Hediyeh Tehrani)—woman in her mid–30s; Haji Reza Enayat (Mohamad Reza Sharifinia)—man in his late 40s; *Length:* 105 minutes; *Setting:* large urban city (Tehran) in Iran; upper middle class

SYNOPSIS

Donya, the eponymous protagonist, is a divorced woman in a relationship with Haji, a middle-aged married man with two grown children. Donya is independent and financially secure and in control of her life, whereas Haji is a somewhat buffoonish character who, as the ostensibly pious and conservative patriarch of the family, asserts control over his wife and children. Donya has just returned to Tehran from abroad and is seeking to buy a house with the help of Haji, who owns a prosperous real estate business. It turns out that Donya doesn't want to buy just any house—she wants Haji's house. However, Haji's wife and children don't want to move.

Donya has a plan. She flirts with Haji, leading him to believe that she is in love with him. She pretends to be trapped in an elevator so he can rescue her. She teases him about his old-fashioned looks and arranges a kind of "makeover" for him to appear more youthful. Haji, in the throes of a midlife crisis, finds himself falling in love with Donya and arranges an out-of-town vacation for his family, leaving him free to court and propose marriage to Donya. Donya accepts on the condition that his wife approves, to which Haji readily agrees (but in actuality he does not inform his wife). Established in her own apartment, the now-married Donya plots to assume ownership of Haji's house (for reasons revealed at the end). In the end, she gets what she wants. For Haji, however, events do not turn out so well. Not only does he lose his house, but he also loses both his first wife and Donya, who divorces him. Haji is alone.

PATRIARCHAL TRADITIONS AND RELIGIOUS LAWS

Polygyny

Based on Sharia, polygyny is codified as law in Iran, allowing a man to marry up to four wives at the same time. A man who wishes to marry additional wives must attain consent from the court and demonstrate that he is capable of treating all wives equitably (see below). Furthermore, if the second wife was aware of the first wife but married the man without the first wife's consent and the court's permission, she could face criminal charges. (The requirement of the first wife's permission was in effect at the time of the film's production, but this requirement is currently under review.) In *Donya*, both Haji and Donya are cognizant of the law. Donya insists that Haji inform his wife of his intention to take a second wife, though Haji never informs his wife and lies to Donya about his wife giving her consent.

Gender Segregation

In Iran, interactions with unrelated members of the opposite sex are restricted. If rules about gender segregation are strictly observed, a female should seek her male guardian's permission to interact with an unrelated male. Haji is aware that his adult son and his son's girlfriend have been seen together in public; consequently, he labels the girlfriend as immoral and forbids his son's continued contact with her. However, Donya flaunts the gender segregation rules. She arranges a birthday party for a teenage boy and invites a number of similarly aged boys and girls to her apartment. Even though the young people enforce their own gender segregation (the boys sit together in a circle listening to music while the girls stand outside the circle), the morality police are still summoned to disband the party. At another point, Donya, now married to Haji, allows her co-worker, a man, into her apartment. Haji is not pleased and states that she is not allowed to have contact with a man unless she gets his permission. She replies that she will see whoever she wants. He then slaps her in the face—a big mistake, as Donya threatens him with divorce.

NONTRADITIONAL GENDER ATTRIBUTES

In *Donya*, the female protagonist is dominant. Donya runs the show, flaunts the rules, deceives the man in order to marry him, and divorces him when she no longer needs him. Donya turns the tables on traditional gender roles—she is the predator, she manipulates for her own gain, and, in an unusual ending for a contemporary Iranian film, she wins and does not suffer. In this film, the man is the victim. Haji is emasculated and humiliated through the loss of his home, his family, and his manhood. Donya, however, does not represent feminine self-authenticity or moral rectitude. Her victory over Haji is achieved through feminine guile and not through the strength of her moral position or persuasive argument.

POLYGYNY/POLYGAMY

Polygyny is defined as having more than one wife at one time (polygamy is defined as the practice of having more than one spouse at one time). Islamic polygyny laws allow a man to marry as many as four wives at once. Polygyny is legitimatized according to the Quranic text that specifies that multiple marriages are allowed provided the husband treats each wife equally and justly. Muslim-majority countries that base laws on Sharia provide for the practice of polygyny in their family laws. (Turkey and Tunisia are two Muslim countries that have outlawed polygyny.)

According to scholars, the laws allowing polygyny are a point of contention between modernist and traditionalist Muslim voices.[14] Modernists advocate for the abolishment of laws permitting polygyny or, at the very least, stricter judiciary oversight to ensure that just and equal specifications are indeed in force. Hence, they argue, all wives must provide consent and the husband's financial ability to care for all wives and future children must be assured by the courts. Traditionalists, however, maintain that polygyny in Quranic text is immutable and the word of God.

How common is polygyny today in Muslim-majority countries? Black, Esmaeili, and Hosen claim, "The trend across most Muslim nations is away from polygyny.... Prohibition of polygyny is rare although many Muslim nations now restrict the practice, making polygyny a conditional, not absolute, right of the husband."[15] Marriage contracts in many countries (e.g., Egypt) include stipulations against polygyny, and these stipulations are enforceable.

Hemlock (Shokaran)

Year: 2000; *Director:* Behrooz Afkhami; *Cast:* Mahmoud (Fariborz Arabnia)— man in his 30s; Sima (Hediyeh Tehrani)—woman in her 30s; *Length:* 83 minutes; *Setting:* large urban city (Tehran) in Iran; upper middle class

SYNOPSIS

In *Hemlock*, Mahmoud, a married, well-to-do businessman, begins an affair with Sima, a single woman who is a hospital nurse. The two engage in a "temporary marriage" and have several clandestine romantic meetings. However, things get complicated. As Sima becomes increasingly possessive of Mahmoud, he gradually loses interest in her. Sima then discovers that she is pregnant. Mahmoud refuses responsibility for the unborn child and presses her to have an abortion, which she refuses. Mahmoud ends the affair, claiming love for his wife. The ending of the film is bleak. Sima realizes that Mahmoud will not leave his family, and she is killed in an auto accident, an apparent suicide.

PATRIARCHAL TRADITIONS AND RELIGIOUS LAWS

Temporary Marriage

In Iran, the practice of temporary marriage is endorsed by the Islamic regime as being in accord with Islamic tenets. Sima and Mahmoud want to have sexual relations, but their desire is constrained by two problems: one, Iranian law and patriarchal tradition frown on unmarried people (especially women) engaging in sexual relationships, and two, Iranian law based on Sharia prohibits married people engaging in extramarital sex. Indeed, the penalties

Mahmoud (Fariborz Arabnia), a married, successful businessman, enters into an affair with Sima (Hediyeh Tehrani), a single woman. The two engage in an Iranian "temporary marriage," which culminates in tragic consequences (*Hemlock* DVD cover—released in 2000).

for adultery are severe. The practice of temporary marriage obviates these problems, as Mahmoud is now legally allowed to have an affair with a woman who is not his wife, and Sima, an unmarried woman, is legally allowed to have an affair with Mahmoud (see below for more details on temporary marriage).

TRADITIONAL GENDER STEREOTYPES

Hemlock provides a contrast between the traditional stereotype of the passive, subordinate woman (the "good" woman) and the single, independent woman with her own agency (the "bad" woman). Mahmoud's wife is traditional. She wears a black chador (flowing black robe) in all of her scenes. She is a homemaker who cooks, serves refreshments to her husband and grown son, and is not very interesting. While another woman might question her husband's mysterious phone calls and unexplained absences, she does not. Mahmoud's wife is juxtaposed with the "bad," impure woman, Sima, who is having a secret affair with her husband. Sima is unmarried, works outside the home, and, in contrast to the black chador of the wife, wears a head scarf, overcoat, and colorful neck scarves. She is depicted as a seductress who in the beginning takes control of the affair with Mahmoud. Her impurity is portrayed in a number of ways: dressing with colors; wearing full face makeup; engaging in sex outside of the confines of formal marriage; conceiving a child outside of marriage; and meeting with dealers to obtain her father's illicit drugs.

NONTRADITIONAL GENDER ATTRIBUTES

Sima is the exception to traditional feminine stereotypes. She has a career outside the home, she is contentedly single, she is independent, and she knows what she wants. As one example, when Sima arranges a date with Mahmoud, she pays for the tickets for a guitar concert, orders for him at a café, and drives him about town. At another point, Mahmoud tries to cancel his date with Sima, but she orders him to cancel whatever else he had planned. He acquiesces. But there are consequences. In her temporary marriage with Mahmoud, Sima becomes pregnant and is abandoned by both her lover and her only relative—her father. Her father berates her about living in sin, threatens to kill her, and orders her to leave his house. This shame that she brings to herself and to her family is a central theme. She must pay for her dishonorable actions, and she does—with her life. Sima, distraught, drives her car into oncoming traffic and is killed. Mahmoud, on learning about her accident, shows little emotion or ostensible remorse. He has emerged from the affair unscathed.

TEMPORARY MARRIAGE (*MUT'A*)

Iran, as a Shi'ite state, permits temporary marriage, which allows a man and woman to marry for a fixed period of time for the purpose of engaging in sex. A temporary marriage requires the couple to agree to an informal contract that stipulates the length of the relationship and the amount of money to be awarded to the woman. A temporary marriage favors men, as, under Iranian Sharia law, men are allowed multiple wives and women are allowed only one husband. A formally married man entering into a temporary marriage could thus engage in an extramarital relationship and not be charged with adultery. However, a married woman entering into a temporary marriage could be charged with adultery and face severe criminal penalties. The vast majority of Iranians disapprove of the practice of temporary marriage, which they consider equivalent to prostitution.[16] However, proponents, who include some traditionalist Islamic clerics, view temporary marriage as means of controlling prostitution and preventing couples from "living in sin." The practice of temporary marriage is prohibited in countries that follow Sunni Islam (the vast majority of Muslims worldwide are Sunni).

My Tehran for Sale

Year: 2009; *Director:* Granaz Moussavi; *Cast:* Marzieh (Marzieh Vafamehr)—woman in her late 20s; Saman (Amir Chegini)—man in his late 20s; *Length:* 96 minutes; *Setting:* Large urban city (Tehran) in Iran; middle class

SYNOPSIS

In the opening scenes of *My Tehran for Sale*, a rave-type party is being held in a secluded farmhouse outside of Tehran. The twenty or so young men and women are dancing, smoking, drinking, and using drugs. Marzieh, a free-thinking, independent young woman, and Saman, an Iranian-born Australian, have left the party and are witness to a raid by the "morality police," who haul the partygoers in for the obligatory lashings as punishment.

Later, Marzieh and Saman have fallen in love and are living together. They plan to marry and reside in Australia once Marzieh gets her emigration papers. But Marzieh fails the requisite medical exam and finds out that she is HIV positive. She will not be allowed to emigrate. Saman cannot accept Marzieh's condition and abandons her. She has lost her lover, her job and her chance to escape to Australia. Her family has long refused any contact with her, and she has nothing to gain by remaining in Iran, as she has been betrayed by her family, her fiancé, and society. Marzieh arranges an illegal transport to Australia, and she ultimately ends up in an Australian immigration center, seeking asylum. Unfortunately, her arguments for asylum fail to convince, and she is forced to return to Tehran.

The ending of the film is bleak. It is night, and Marzieh wanders aimlessly through the crowded city streets, looking for no one and with nowhere to go.

TRADITIONAL GENDER STEREOTYPES

Males are callous and unsentimental in *My Tehran for Sale*. The men in Marzieh's life typify this gender stereotype. At first, Marzieh's lover encourages her free spirit and unconventionality. He agrees to move in with her (a taboo in Iranian society), he supports her "underground" theater job, and he plans to marry her. But plans change. Upon discovering her HIV status, he calls her a whore and cruelly abandons her. Marzieh's father disowned her years before, as she dishonored her family with her independent lifestyle. Her attempt to reconcile with him is coldly rejected. The (male) immigration official is unfeeling about her reasons for asylum and rejects her plea, forcing her to return to Tehran.

My Tehran for Sale is a "tale of two cities" in its exploration of the different social norms that apply to the public and private spheres of Iranian life. In the public sphere, the Islamic legal codes that govern female dress are in effect. Females, by law, must wear the hijab (head scarf and loose overcoat or full-length black chador) in public or when in presence of unrelated men. Marzieh is careful to don a head scarf in public (though parts of her hair are visible).

In the film, "morality police" (see below) raid a party attended by young people who are dancing, drinking alcohol, and taking drugs. All of this is forbidden, and the police order the males and females to separate. They are especially incensed at the females, who have flaunted the dress code and are not wearing the requisite attire. One rages at the women, "Shame on you! Do you think this is Europe? Men and women apart. Put on your scarf! Fuck. Like a bunch of animals. Shut up! Make yourselves decent!" (It is interesting to note that it is apparently acceptable for young people to consume drugs and alcohol—the evil is the missing headscarves.)

In public, male and females associate with each other freely, but the rules prohibiting cross-sex touching are still observed. In one scene, Marzieh and Saman climb a steep hill; Marzieh, in chador, struggles to keep up with Saman and clearly needs assistance. But he does not put out a hand to help her.

Marzieh (Marzieh Vafamehr) is a feminist in contemporary Iran and rebels against the Iranian regulations that restrict the lives of women (*My Tehran for Sale* DVD cover—released in 2009).

Restrictions on female activities are in place at young ages. A young girl in Marzieh's care asks to be taught to ride a bike and is told that girls can't ride bikes to school. "Well, then," she says, "I'll just dress like a boy." Marzieh's feelings of restriction and confinement in patriarchal Iran are expressed in a song she has composed: "Two wanderers, two lonely souls, traps and enemies waiting before and behind us. Remembering the ones who have gone and the ones who have loved.... Only a miracle might help to join one lonely soul to another. What awaits us, friends? ... I see no green fields of hope in this wasteland."

NONTRADITIONAL GENDER ATTRIBUTES

In the private sphere, however, moral norms shift. Not only has Marzieh's boyfriend moved in with her, but they are also shown in bed together. The two of them attend parties where both men and women smoke (cigarettes and cannabis), drink alcohol, and play and listen to music. Marzieh is an actress but must work in underground theater as an entertainer. Females are free to date who they please: "Marzieh, my friend, I'm going to show you someone. He's just your type. Just flirt with him, and you'll be on." Marzieh retorts, "Here we go again. Another jerk you've found for me."

Additional Issue

Topics raised in this film include abortion, state censorship, premarital sex, HIV, and the display of a woman's uncovered head, all of which contributed to the film's ban by Iranian authorities.

GASHT-E ERSHAD: IRANIAN "MORALITY POLICE"

Since the 1979 Islamic Revolution in Iran, various forms of "morality police" have been in force, but currently the Gasht-e Ershad (the guidance patrol) is the agency responsible for enforcing Iran's code of conduct in public. Gasht-e Ershad is responsible for monitoring people (both sexes) deemed to be immodestly dressed or undermining the dress code, checking male–female fraternization, and prohibiting women from wearing "immodest" amounts of makeup, tight clothing, or short trousers.[17] Females receive the greatest scrutiny for violations of hijab, such as not covering their hair or body with appropriate apparel. The Iranian penal code's Article 683 provides the following:

> Those women that appear in the streets and public places without the Islamic hijab, shall be sentenced from ten days to two months' imprisonment or fined from fifty thousand to five hundred thousand Rials.[18]

In the past, agents had the power to arrest violators, but currently they are only allowed to call the police, who will then determine whether a crime has been committed. The "party-going subculture" of Iranian youth in large cities has attracted the attention of police and the Gasht-e Ershad. As reported by Saeid Golkar, police records in just one year (2013) showed that the Gasht-e Ershad gave more than three million verbal warnings for improper behavior or dress.[19]

Protest (Eteraz)

Year: 2000; *Director:* Masoud Kimiayi; *Cast:* Amir (Dariush Arjmand)—man in his 50s; Reza (Mohammad Reza Foroutan)—man in his late 20s; *Length:* 100 minutes; *Setting:* large urban city (Tehran) in Iran; middle class and working class

SYNOPSIS

In the startling opening scenes of *Protest*, Amir, a rough-looking middle-aged man, is angry. We see only a close-up of his face and hear his threats. The object of his rage is a woman shrouded in black, her face in shadow. She is seated in a chair, motionless. Amir has murdered the woman, who is the wife of his brother Reza, and he is lecturing the dead woman about her affair with another man and the consequent dishonor to his family.

Amir is subsequently imprisoned; after 12 years, he is released to his family. Amir finds that his family is in ruin due to the scandal of his imprisonment and is puzzled, as he considered his killing of the adulterous wife an honorable act. Yet his brother and family are less than appreciative, since they lost their home and Reza cannot find a well-paying job despite his college degrees. Reza also feels he must end his relationship with his fiancée now that Amir is out of prison. As he explains, "He went to prison for me. How can I tell him I'm marrying you now?"

Amir, for his part, falls in love with a woman he meets through a prison contact, but now, in experiencing love for the first time, he feels guilt for the murder of the young woman whose only sin was loving the wrong man. Amir realizes that he cannot marry the woman he loves because of his guilt. In the end, Amir "arranges" his own murder at the hands of the murdered woman's lover, and Reza is free to marry his fiancée.

PATRIARCHAL TRADITIONS AND RELIGIOUS LAWS

Honor killings refer to the practice of a male family member murdering another family member who is perceived to have brought shame to the family

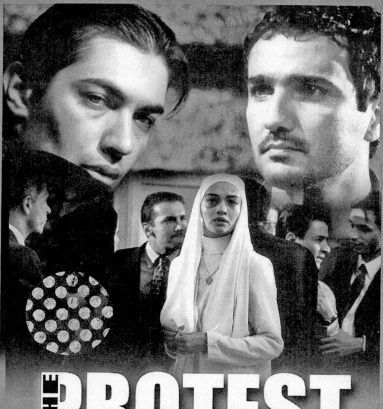

THE PROTEST

A Film by: Masoud Kimiayi

Farsi with English Subtitles

Amir (Dariush Arjmand) and Reza (Mohammad Reza Foroutan) are brothers. Amir has just been released from prison, having served his sentence for the honor killing of Reza's adulterous wife. Reza must now abandon his own plans for remarriage to Ladan (Mitra Hajjar) (*The Protest* DVD cover—released in 2000).

through dishonorable conduct. Typically, the victim is female, and dishonorable conduct could include sexual misconduct (e.g., adultery), refusal of an arranged marriage, or being a victim of rape. The government of Iran forbids the practice of honor killing but does exempt a husband from punishment if he murders his wife and her lover after having caught them *in flagrante delicto* (in the act). Despite the law, in groups or tribes with strict patriarchal norms, honor killings do occur, and it is difficult to prosecute the perpetrators of these killings. It must be noted that honor killings are not justified in Islamic teachings.

In *Protest*, Amir is aware of the law, but, because of his strong patriarchal beliefs, he is willing to sacrifice his liberty for what he deems fair and just in his murder of his brother's adulterous wife. He ominously states to the woman he just killed, "Listen closely—you should just sit quiet and listen. Interrupt me once and you'll regret it for long after you die.... Did you miss out on anything after becoming our bride? I told you privately that as part of our family I would keep an eye on you." Later, on learning that the woman he killed was pregnant, he is unrepentant: "So the sinner was carrying a sin? I am only more proud of my deed."

Reactions to the honor killing are mixed. Though Amir's fellow prisoners honor him for his righteousness, Reza, the wronged brother, agrees that family honor is important but would have approached the infidelity of his wife differently. "Keeping your dignity is good," he states, "but ruining another's life is going too far. She could have left in peace.... The consequences of what you did was our family's real tragedy. The days of such reactions have passed."

NONTRADITIONAL GENDER ATTRIBUTIONS

Protest features the stories of two brothers: Amir, who was just released from prison, and Reza, his younger brother, who delivers pizza for a living. Tradition would have it that sacrificing oneself for one's family is a feminine attribute; yet both Amir and Reza are self-sacrificial, deferring to their family's needs. Amir, as the older brother, chose to work in order for Reza to attend college and obtain a successful career. Amir believed that, had he not killed Reza's adulterous wife, Reza would have been honor bound to do so and Reza would have been imprisoned. In Amir's view, he sacrificed his freedom to allow Reza to continue with his education and his life. For his part, Reza cannot marry his fiancée once Amir is released from prison. To honor his brother, Reza sacrifices his love for his fiancée and his future happiness. At the film's conclusion, Amir is once again self-sacrificial and finally admits his guilt. He atones for his guilt with his life by entreating the murdered woman's lover to kill him: "You and she deserve to spill my blood."

Iranian women in this film are portrayed as strong and independent. They are not afraid to question injustices and confront those who perpetuate said injustices. In *Protest*, female college students assertively discuss the political issues of the day with their male colleagues. They are free to commingle with the men in public places. In another scene, a woman shopkeeper has no compunctions about ordering a man to shut down his noisy motorcycle. She tells him to move the bike, and when he refuses, she pushes it over. Reza's fiancée is distraught that he has broken off their engagement. Now she must marry another man whom she does not love. But she has her own agency and realizes at the last moment that she does not have to marry the other man, and she abandons her engagement party to find Reza.

Secret Ballot (Raye makhfi)

Year: 2001; *Director:* Babak Payami; *Characters:* election agent (Nassim Abdi)—woman in her 30s; soldier (Cyrus Abidi)—man in his 30s; *Length:* 105 minutes; *Setting:* rural area of remote Iranian island; impoverished communities

SYNOPSIS

Secret Ballot is a light-handed film about a female election agent whose job is to collect votes for a national election on a remote, desert Iranian island. She engages a somewhat oafish local soldier as her reluctant driver for the day. The two set off across a sparsely populated countryside, she in a flowing black chador and he sour with a rifle at his side. Numerous people are approached to vote for candidates whose photos are printed on a ballot. The villagers she encourages to vote are apathetic about the election or ignorant about the voting process in general. The soldier is disdainful of her attempts to enthuse the villagers about voting but begrudgingly carries out his duties. In spite of numerous failures to obtain votes, the agent's idealism remains intact. This is the job she was hired to do, and this is the job she will do. In the end, she wins the soldier's admiration.

TRADITIONAL GENDER STEREOTYPES

This binary of gender associated with importance is exemplified in several scenes as the female agent and the soldier travel the countryside. Initially,

An unnamed election clerk (Nassim Abdi) perseveres in her task of gathering ballots for an upcoming national election on a remote Iranian island (*Secret Ballot* DVD cover—released in 2001).

the agent states that the soldier must follow her orders in this voting process. The soldier interprets her statement as a joke and states that "the order is no good" because a woman is giving the orders. She confronts the realities of gender-based traditions at every hut and village she encounters throughout the day. At one point, she encounters an elderly man driving a truck with several female passengers. The driver attempts to cast all of the females' votes himself, but she insists that each female vote individually and comments scornfully, "How is it a young girl of 12, who can marry, cannot vote?" At another village, women refuse to vote without the permission of a male family member, and at another village they refuse because they would have to view photographs of unknown men who are running for office and that is prohibited.

The spaces in the villages she visits are gendered. Men are allowed the public space and women the private (and thus invisible) spaces. The agent approaches a gathering of men at a cemetery to collect their votes but is informed with some vehemence that women are barred from funerals. At another village, only men are allowed outside in the presence of a stranger; a woman, peering out of a door, is ordered to go back inside.

NONTRADITIONAL GENDER ATTRIBUTES

The agent clearly has agency. She is there to get the job done, whatever the cost. She perseveres until the end, even in the face of so many rejections. She has a strong voice and is confident. She argues with villagers about the importance of voting, even though they have never heard of the men up for election. Discussing the inequities of arranged marriages, she tells the soldier that voting might change social courtship laws so that women will be able to choose their own mates. By the film's end, the guard, while dismissive at first, has come to respect her. His is the last vote cast, and he casts it for her.

Purdah

Ensuring that unmarried women are chaste and that married women are faithful is of paramount importance in societies characterized by rigid patriarchal norms. To ensure chastity and fidelity, the practice of purdah, or female seclusion, has been implemented in many regions of the world. This practice restricts women from interacting with unrelated men in the public sphere. Purdah can take the form of veiling in public or confinement to one's home (as seen with many of the female villagers in Secret Ballot). Though purdah has been associated with a conservative Islamic ideology, it is not an explicit Islamic practice. Though the female agent in *Secret Ballot* was prohibited from entering a cemetery, in modern Iran, the practice of barring women from funerals and cemeteries is not observed.

The Circle (Dayereh)

Year: 2000; *Director:* Jafar Panahi; *Cast:* Arezou (Maryiam Parvin Almani)—woman in her 20s; Nargess (Nargess Mamizadeh)—woman in her 20s; Pari (Fereshteh Sadr Orafai)—woman in her 20s; *Length:* 91 minutes; *Setting:* large urban city (Tehran) in Iran; working class

SYNOPSIS

The Circle is about women's oppression and marginalization in a strong patriarchal society. The film depicts a day in the lives of women who, because of circumstance, have been branded by society as outcasts. In the film's opening scene, an unseen woman has just given birth to a girl, and an elderly woman (ostensibly her mother) intones her dread about the anger of in-laws who wanted a boy. Next two women, Arezou and Nargess, are seen as they furtively dart through crowded Tehran streets searching for a means to earn money. These women are on temporary release from prison and are planning an escape to the countryside. A third woman, Pari, has escaped from prison. She is pregnant and seeking help for an abortion from a former inmate who now works as a nurse. Her story intersects with that of another woman who is destitute and abandons her child by a busy restaurant, hoping someone will adopt her. In despair, she walks the streets of Tehran alone at night and is picked up for prostitution. The outcome for each character is bleak as, at the end, all the women are captured and returned to prison. Each woman is trapped in a circle of patriarchal-based laws and traditions, each unable to break out of a never-ending cycle.

PATRIARCHAL TRADITIONS AND RELIGIOUS LAWS

A patriarchal-based law that affects the women in *The Circle* concerns the right to abortion. Currently, Iranian law allows abortion for medical reasons, with permission needed from medical personnel and from the father of the fetus. Pari is pregnant and turns to an acquaintance who is a hospital nurse for help obtaining an abortion. She is told that she needs her father's or her husband's consent. Pari's request is thus denied, as she cannot obtain the required permission: the man who impregnated Pari was executed in prison, and her family has severed relations with her.

From the director of *The White Balloon*

A film by Jafar Panahi

The Circle

Her only crime was being a woman

"★★★★ Shattering!
Panahi weaves a sinuous spell that
knocks you flat by the final scene."
— *Jan Stuart, Newsday*

"Endlessly absorbing.
Truly a masterpiece."
—*Glenn Kenny, Premiere*

WINNER
GOLDEN LION,
BEST FILM
2000 Venice
Film Festival

WINNER
FIPRESCI
GRAND PRIX
Best Film Of
The Year

The Circle portrays women's oppression and marginalization in a rigid patriarchal society. Nargess (Nargess Mamizadeh) is one of three women on temporary release from prison in Iran, and she is planning an escape to the countryside (*The Circle* DVD cover—released in 2000).

TRADITIONAL GENDER STEREOTYPES

The differential valuation of males and females is exemplified in *The Circle*. In the film's opening scene in a hospital maternity ward, an older woman has just been informed that her daughter has given birth to a girl. This woman is terrified that her daughter's in-laws will be furious that the child is not a boy and will insist on a divorce. The woman knows full well that bearing a son is the key to a woman's prestige and power in the family.

The restrictions placed on women's behavior in public places is a salient theme in *The Circle*. In this Iranian society, women cannot travel alone, cannot register for a hotel room unless accompanied by a male, and cannot smoke in public. In public, women are required to be veiled at all times and cannot ride in cars with males to whom they are not related. The women in *The Circle* are furtive, fearful figures. In traditional black chadors, they are shadow-like as they crouch by cars, hide in alleys, and dart from police. These are women who have broken with the traditional female stereotypes of modesty, chastity, and docility. After all, they have broken laws, abandoned children, and engaged in prostitution. They threaten the "natural" order of patriarchy, and, as a consequence, they face even greater restrictions on their behavior.

There are several examples of the restrictions that women encounter. One woman, Nargess, attempts to buy a bus ticket to escape to her hometown. She is interrogated by the male ticket agent, who will not allow her to travel unless she has a student ID or a male escort. Nargess and Arezou are seen throughout the film furtively smoking cigarettes in deserted alleys, as women cannot smoke in public venues. Another woman is not allowed to register for a room at a hotel without a male signing the hotel registry. Another cannot accept a ride from a man lest she be mistaken for a prostitute and arrested. And yet another woman is arrested for prostitution due to having been found sitting in a parked car with an unrelated man. The man expresses remorse for his moral lapse and is let go, but she is sent to jail.

Interpretative Differences About The Circle

A critical analysis of *The Circle* illustrates how one's perspective on gender issues is informed by worldview. As an example, film critics in the West have lauded *The Circle* for bringing to light the oppression of women in a religiously conservative Iranian society. As Deborah Young notes in a September 11, 2000, article in *Variety*, *The Circle* dramatizes discrimination against women in Iran and "both fascinates and horrifies ... about what it means to be a woman under a cruel, institutionalized patriarchy." Kamran Rastegar argues that sentiments such as these provide an example of a biased frame of understanding from a Western perspective that ignores the universality of oppression that limits people within all societies, not just Iran.[20] Indeed, according to Rastegar, the filmmaker of *The Circle* himself interprets his narrative of oppression as including any member of any society, female or male, who feels trapped in a circle with no way out. Furthermore, the emphasis placed on individual rights within a Western perspective may obscure an understanding of more generalized social oppression that occurs in collectivistic social structures. Then again, while circles exist for both men and women, as Gönül Dönmez-Colin puts it in her analysis of the conflicting opinions about the message of *The Circle*, the radius of that circle may be larger for men in patriarchal systems.[21]

The Day I Became a Woman (Roozi ke zan shodam)

Year: 2000; *Director:* Marzieh Makhmalbaf (as Marziyeh Meshkini); *Cast:* Hava (Fatemeh Cherag Akhar)—9-year-old girl; Ahoo (Shabnam Toloui)—woman in her mid–20s; *Length:* 74 minutes; *Setting:* rural Iran; impoverished community

SYNOPSIS

Set in rural Iran in a small village by the sea, Hava is woken early. It is her ninth birthday, and her friend, a young boy, comes to visit. On this occasion, Hava's grandmother pushes him away, telling him that Hava is not a child anymore—she is nine, and she is becoming a woman. She will not play with boys anymore. Later, Hava's mother brings her first chador (black, flowing cape-like garment that covers one's body and hair) and warns Hava not to sin: "You are a woman today. You cannot play with boys anymore. Hide your hair." But Hava wants to play outside with her friend, and she is allowed to do so one last time for only one hour. Then she will be veiled. Hava spends that hour watching boys make a sailboat, buying ice cream for herself and the boy who visited her, and walking along the shore. Hava's story ends when her mother and grandmother, both draped in their chadors, find Hava, dress her in her own chador, and guide her indoors. Hava's world is now one of passivity, obedience, and sexual repression.

In a second story, Ahoo, a woman in her 20s, is competing in a bicycle race with fifty or so other women. They are racing along the edge of the sea, all looking alike, covered in their billowing black chadors. A man on horseback appears and taunts the women about their inability to find husbands: "Why are you all riding, don't you have men?" The man is Ahoo's husband, and he orders her to quit the race. She refuses. He threatens divorce. She is agreeable to that. He leaves and returns with other male riders, one of whom is the local Islamic cleric, who threatens Ahoo with damnation for shirking her wifely duties. She only pedals faster. As was true for Hava, Ahoo is forced to yield to the demands of patriarchal rule. The men surround her and force her off her bike. This film is pessimistic about women's ability to escape patriarchal traditions. There is no way out. Hava must abandon the freedoms allowed for children and enter a world of restrictions. Ahoo's attempt at independence of feminine role constraints is thwarted in a male dominant society.

TRADITIONAL GENDER STEREOTYPES

In the story of Hava, boys and men are outdoors, actively engaged in work and play. Boys build a small sailboat and set off in the sea. Men are busy repairing boats or riding horses along the shore. Women, represented by Hava's mother and grandmother, are seen in full hijab while walking on the grounds near their home or sitting by themselves in their house. The activities in which they engage are cooking and sewing. Hava, once allowed to roam the village, play with boys, and climb on roofs, will now (since she is nine) be forced to comply with the restrictions placed on women in the public sphere. She and her male friend are told that she is now a woman. They are perplexed. What does that mean? She will be largely confined to her home in the company of women who are trained to be passive and docile.

In the story of Ahoo, females and males engage in outdoor activities. Several men ride horses, and groups of young women race in a bicycle competition. The bike riding is causing quite a commotion among the men of the village, as these woman are engaged in competitive physical sports that may not be appropriate for feminine modesty and detract from their duties in the home.

Ahoo's husband and the other male horseback riders represent the male arrogance and aggressiveness that are not only permitted in patriarchal systems but also encouraged. The husband's masculinity is on display: he is bare chested, and his horse is powerful. He taunts the female bicycle riders for their inability to attract men. He threatens Ahoo with divorce if she doesn't obey his commands, and then he does divorce her (through verbal repudiation). The Islamic cleric acts aggressively against Ahoo with threats and attempts to shame her. She is, according to him, "riding on the devil's mount," and since she has broken men's pride, God will punish her. She is told that her brothers will break her down, and indeed they do at the end. Why the desperation for Ahoo's return to the traditions of married life? In short, if one woman makes her escape, then others will follow.

ISLAMIC DRESS CODE: HIJAB

Viewed from a Western perspective, one of the more noticeable aspects of contemporary Iranian films is the uniformity in dress for adult female characters. Whether on a public street or in the privacy of one's home, females in Iranian film conform to hijab regulations, which, in Iran, consists of the black chador (loose-fitting robe-like outer clothing) or a head scarf with a manteau (a loose-fitting overcoat worn over long slacks). The setting or activity in the film doesn't matter: women wear hijab while chopping vegetables in their kitchens, lying on a gurney giving birth, or dying on the street after being hit by a car. In real life, however, Iranian women dress as they please in their own homes.

The word "hijab" comes from the Arabic word for curtain or cover, and it is used generically to mean modest Islamic clothing involving a veil or head covering.[22] Hijab incorporates Islamic principles of modesty, and, depending on the culture or country, hijab (or veiling) for women can range from just a head scarf that allows the face (but not hair) to be visible to a full-body covering with loose-fitting garments. The rationale for veiling is subject to debate, as Islamic scholars have questioned whether passages in the Quran that refer to the importance of modesty should be interpreted literally as an obligation for female veiling or more generally as meaning that females (and males) should maintain a sense of modesty in their clothing choices.[23] Nonetheless, in contemporary Iran, hijab is compulsory for females. The rules of hijab in Iran require that women wear clothing that presents a modest image in public. Women can choose to wear either a black chador or long pants, head scarf, and a manteau. Whatever the choice, covering of hair is critical; even the slightest strand of exposed hair can lead to punishment.

Hijab regulations begin at puberty in conjunction with rules that restrict public association of post-pubertal females and males. In public, women wear hijab (or are veiled) in the presence of unrelated men, and men must avert their eyes in the presence of unrelated women. Within their family home, females do not need to wear hijab.

According to Ashraf Zahedi, Iranian women are divided about wearing hijab. On the one hand, some women object to the compulsory requirement of hijab:

> These women find imposed Islamic attire suffocating as well as socially and politically unacceptable. They see this imposition as a violation of their rights. In fact, the imposition of hijab and the violation of women's human rights have served as the impetus for gender consciousness among Iranian women who continue to challenge the imposition of hijab. Some have chosen a life in self-imposed exile, compulsory veiling being the main reason for their emigration from Iran.[24]

Other women have found the Iranian dress code liberating, as it provides greater opportunities to engage in the public sphere. Meredith Winn states:

> Wearing chador and Islamic hijab, women have turned to education and higher education in great numbers. Likewise, they have sought employment in various jobs. They have become involved in politics and held high offices. These are women whose parents or husbands would mostly likely not have allowed them to pursue education and employment without the chador or the modern Islamic hijab. The Islamic hijab has given them the opportunity to be socially active. The protective shield, in the form of either chador or manteau and scarf, has provided women with a personal space. This attire conceals the female hair and body and diverts attention from their sexuality. Islamic attire projects an image of inaccessibility, thereby reducing the possibility of sexual harassment.[25]

The Last Supper (Shaam-e-akhar)

Year: 2002; *Director:* Fereydoun Jeyrani; *Cast:* Mehan (Katayoun Riahi)—woman aged 45; Mohsen (Atila Pesiani)—man in his late 50s; Mani (Mohammad Reza Golzar)—man aged 24; Setare (Hanie Tavassoli)—woman in her early 20s; *Length:* 96 minutes; *Setting:* large urban city (Tehran); upper class

SYNOPSIS

Mehan is a 45-year-old professor of architecture at a university in Tehran. She is married to Mohsen, who has long resented his wife for her intellectual superiority. She, too, is resentful about her loveless marriage, which was arranged some twenty years ago by her father. She has remained in the marriage for the sake of their daughter, Setare, who is now a university student.

At the beginning of the film, an ugly scene unfolds: Mehan is at her university, giving a lecture to her class. He husband barges in and hectors her about her neglect of family duties. Setare is a student in this class and is ashamed. Also in the class is Mani, a handsome 24-year-old protégé who comes to the defense of Mehan. Setare urges her mother to divorce her father following the humiliating incident. Eventually, Mehan does divorce Mohsen, and she and her daughter move to a new home.

Mani and Setare are friends, and Mani spends considerable time with both mother and daughter. A love triangle develops: Setare is romantically interested in Mani, and she believes her interest is reciprocated, as he spends so much time with the family. But Mani has fallen in love with Mehan, and Mehan is doing little to discourage his advances. She is flattered by the attention of a bright, handsome, younger man. Against her better judgment and disregarding the possibility of alienating her daughter, Mehan chooses to reciprocate Mani's attention—teacher/student boundaries be damned. Much to the displeasure of Setare, Mani proposes marriage and Mehan accepts.

At the film's conclusion, an agitated Setare, armed with a rifle, is an unexpected visitor at Mehan and Mani's home following their wedding. Mehan attempts to calm her daughter and apparently believes she has succeeded, as she and her new husband repair to their upstairs bedroom, leaving Setare below in her bedroom. But Setare does not sleep, instead creeping up the stairs with the rifle. In the final scenes, it is understood that the newlyweds are dead, with Setare in prison awaiting her sentencing.

Patriarchal Traditions and Religious Laws

This film portrays the Iranian emphasis on gender segregation in schools. At the university level, males and females are permitted to attend the same classes but must be divided. In this film, all the males are seated on the right side of the room and all the females on the left. Dress modesty codes are likewise in effect, with all females wearing the black chador and head scarfs.

Male privilege in Iranian legal codes is also evident in *The Last Supper*. The law permits men to restrict their wives from participating in outside activities; however, Mohsen, in his benevolence, has allowed his wife to pursue her academic goals. He explains this to his daughter: "Do you think your mom is a born scientist? She got her master's and her doctorate while living in my house. I allowed her to work. According to the law, I could have forbid it. But I didn't. I was patient."

Traditional Gender Stereotypes

There are numerous examples in *The Last Supper* of how the male voice carries importance and female voice is disrespected. Mohsen, the husband of Mehan, represents male prerogative and entitlement in a society that ensures male dominance. He cannot deal with the reality that his wife has a more important job than him and that she is more intelligent. He also cannot accept that she is not in love with him and wishes to divorce him. After all, it is the man who should have the important career and who should sue for divorce. In his arrogance, he destroys his wife's manuscript, claiming that her writing was trash and worth nothing. Mohsen also invokes his masculine privilege at his wife's university by barging in on her lecture and harassing her in front of her students. At another point in the film, Mohsen again confronts his wife at the university. This time, with her students as witnesses, he slaps her in the face and pushes her against the wall.

Nontraditional Gender Attributes

Setare, the daughter of Mohsen and Mehan, is headstrong and not afraid of confronting either of her equally headstrong parents. She insists that divorce for her parents would be desirable after witnessing her father's harassment of her mother in public: "What you did was not nice, Dad. I cannot forgive you for it. Don't bring excuses, you have none. I didn't think you would be that bad to drag the name of your daughter's mother through the mud. Don't speak, Dad, I do not want to hear anymore."

Mehan, the film's protagonist, is as headstrong as her daughter. She does not fear to confront her overbearing husband, who has filed a charge accusing her of misconduct with a male student. Mehan defends herself to police and university administrators: "My private life is no business of the university. As far as the university is concerned, there have been no problems in my work.... Why do you look at divorced women differently? Why do you insist on proving that we have a special relationship? I won't allow you to drag a decent relationship through the dirt."

Mehan has fallen for her student Mani but is conflicted about the challenges of an older woman being involved with a younger man. She speaks to Mani's father about the difficulty: "Do you know I have a daughter your son's age? ... I am 45 years old, your son is 24. We have an age difference of 21 years.... In five years I will be a woman of 50 and your son is a young man of 29. I don't want to be the sacrifice of a male desire again."

Censorship in Iranian Film

Iran is the major cinematic force in the Middle East, and many Iranian films have received awards from prominent film festivals, attracting international attention and thus funding for distribution in the West. But a discussion of Iranian cinema must start with a discussion of censorship. Najmeh Moradiyan Rizi[26] provides an analysis of changes that occurred in cinema following the 1979 Iranian Revolution, when "modesty" regulations, established by Islamic conservatives, forced filmmakers to conform to specific rules affecting film narratives that involved gender relationships and depictions of women. These modesty regulations mandated that women be veiled in film and that affectionate physical contact between men and women would not be shown. Since women in film are subject to the public (male) gaze, they must be veiled in all scenes, even while alone in their homes. Violations of modesty codes could result in disapproval of screenplays by Iranian authorities or denial of a state permit to release a film for exhibition. Censorship violations have resulted in forced exile or even arrest and imprisonment of filmmakers.

Censorship regulations and their enforcement are, however, in a continual state of flux as Iran undergoes changes in its religious-political climate. Following the 1997 Reformist movement, for example, the morality codes were eased somewhat, allowing a more tolerant cinema with reference to gender relationships and gender roles. Women now have careers outside the home, unrelated women and men interact in public, and both genders challenge (to some degree) Islamic codes that mandate gender segregation in public spaces.

Two Women (Do zan)

Year: 2000; *Director:* Tahmineh Milani; *Cast:* Fereshteh (Niki Karimi)—woman in her late 20s; Roya (Merila Zare'i)—woman in her late 20s; Ahmad (Atila Pesiani)—man in his 30s; *Length:* 96 minutes; *Setting:* urban cities in Iran; middle class

SYNOPSIS

The eponymous two women of this film are childhood friends, Roya and Fereshteh. In the opening scenes, Roya and Fereshteh are discussing their future careers. They are university students and plan to be architects. As the narrative develops, we learn that Roya's life has turned out well: she has successful career and has married the man she loves. Fereshteh's life, however, has become hell. A deranged man, armed with acid and a knife, is stalking her and threatens her if she does not accept his proposal of marriage. In a dramatic scene, the stalker attacks Fereshteh's cousin with acid, mistaking him for her suitor. As the family gathers by the cousin's hospital bed, it is Fereshteh who is blamed for the attack by her father, for she has brought shame to the family.

Fereshteh realizes that she cannot stay in her family home and moves to another city. But events do not fare well there, as the stalker has followed her and involves her in a car accident in which one child is hurt and another killed. Both Fereshteh and her stalker are arrested and must plead their case in court. The stalker is sentenced to prison and she is released, as her father has vouched for her and agrees to pay a steep fine. Ahmad, a man in attendance at court, offers to pay the fine if Fereshteh marries him. The pressure to marry from both Ahmad and her family is intense, and she reluctantly agrees.

Fereshteh soon learns that agreeing to this marriage was not in her best interest. She becomes virtually enslaved by Ahmad, who verbally abuses her and forbids her to leave their house. He declares that he will not allow her to resume her university education and does not let her contact her family. She tries to divorce him, but her husband does not meet the "correct" criteria that allow a woman in Iran to obtain a divorce.

At the film's conclusion, Fereshteh has taken enough abuse from her husband and runs away. Ahmad cannot permit this and follows her, only for both of them to encounter the stalker, who has just been released from prison. An argument ensues, and Fereshteh's husband is murdered by the stalker. She is now alone and finds her way to the home of her childhood friend. She wonders whether she will retain custody of her children or whether her husband's brother or father will be awarded custody. She questions what will become of her life after suffering so many injustices.

PATRIARCHAL TRADITIONS AND RELIGIOUS LAWS

Divorce

Iranian law allows a woman to obtain a judiciary divorce provided she can demonstrate that the marriage created intolerable suffering or hardship (see below). The judicial system has discretionary powers to determine if the wife's petition meets the legal criteria. In *Two Women*, Fereshteh's marriage has become intolerable and she is seeking a divorce. Her husband refuses, and Fereshteh turns to the courts for a ruling to favor the divorce over her husband's objections. The judge asks two questions: "Does your husband fail to pay the bills? Has he ever laid a hand on you?" Fereshteh is truthful and answers no to each question. Her divorce petition is denied.

Right to Employment and Education

Under Iran's constitution, women are granted rights to education and employment outside the home. However, there are conditions: a woman needs consent from her husband (or father) to attend a university or to work outside the home. According to Iran's Civil Code, "The husband can prevent his wife from an occupation or technical profession which is incompatible with the family's interests or the dignity of him or his wife."[27] There is no comparable code that allows a wife to prevent her husband from engaging in an occupation that she would deem undesirable. Note that a woman establishing her marriage contract can frequently add binding conditions stipulating that her husband cannot prohibit her from working or attending school. In *Two Women*, Ahmad is aware of Fereshteh's intention of finishing her university degree, and he threatens to withhold his permission for her to return to school.

Child Guardianship

Under Iranian law based on Sharia, in the event of a father's death, the mother cannot become her child's natural guardian. Rather, the child's paternal grandfather will be appointed as guardian and can demand that the child be raised in his household. Fereshteh is concerned that now that her husband is dead, her children will be taken away from her and awarded to her husband's family.

TRADITIONAL GENDER STEREOTYPES

Male control of women is a major theme of *Two Women*. The men in Fereshteh's life exert their control in numerous ways. Fereshteh's father repeatedly asks her to sacrifice herself to protect the reputation of his family. She is asked to accept the blame for the stalker's acid attack, to atone for the accidental injury to a child, and to marry a man she barely knows in order to pay a debt and prevent familial disgrace. Her obedience does not serve her well. A reluctant Fereshteh agrees to marry Ahmad, who turns out to be an authoritarian, possessive and punitive husband. She is not allowed to use the telephone, she can no longer read books, and she is not permitted to talk to other men. She is his prisoner. Throughout her entire life, it seems, she has been the victim of a highly patriarchal society that legally sanctions gender inequality and oppression.

NONTRADITIONAL GENDER ATTRIBUTES

Fereshteh is a strong woman who must contend with males who want to deny her self-agency in the service of patriarchy. Her father, her husband, and even the man who stalks her all seek to silence her and ensure her obedience. But she forcefully speaks up for her rights to all the men who want to oppress her. She has plans for a career and, despite the desires of her family, she does not want marriage to be her sole destiny. She challenges her authoritarian father, refusing to accept his claim that she disgraced the family by bringing public attention to the stalker's acid attack. She doesn't allow him to rationalize his authoritarian behavior by stating that he just wanted her to be happy: "No, Father, you wanted to get rid of me." She is adamant in her refusal to marry a man whom she does not love—though in the end she gives in. She rails at the judge who denies her divorce petition. She challenges her husband's possessiveness and irrationality whenever she can and is met with even more draconian restrictions on her freedom. At the end, she simply runs away. What Fereshteh has come to realize is that the threat of a shift in power from male dominance to female empowerment is dangerous in a patriarchal system. The more a woman presses for autonomy, the more the system intensifies its resistance.

Divorce in Iran

Under Iranian law, women are allowed to sue their husbands for divorce for hardship and suffering. The wife's reasons for initiating the divorce must be verified as valid by the court. The following instances are permissible reasons as defined in the Iranian Civil Code:

1. Husband's desertion of the marital home for at least six successive months or nine months in a year without reasonable excuse;

2. Husband's addiction to drugs or alcohol that is detrimental to marriage and his refusal or the impossibility to force him to quit during a period assessed by a doctor as necessary for him to quit;

3. Husband's final sentencing to imprisonment for five years or more;

4. Husband's beating or any kind of repeated maltreatment that is intolerable to the wife, given custom and her situation;

5. His affliction by an incurable or contagious disease or any other affliction disrupting marital life.[28]

Under the Skin of the City
(Zir-e poost-e shahr)

Year: 2001; *Director:* Rakhshan Bani-Etemad; *Cast:* Tuba (Golab Adineh)—woman in her 50s; Abbas (Mohammad Reza Foroutan)—man in his early 30s; Hamideh (Homeira Riazi)—woman in her 20s; Maboubeh (Baran Kosari)—teenage girl; *Length:* 92 minutes; *Setting:* large urban city (Tehran) in Iran; working class

SYNOPSIS

Under the Skin of the City, set in a poor section of Tehran, is a story about familial relationships. The film centers on Tuba, the family matriarch,

Tuba (Golab Adineh) is the family matriarch, living with her disabled husband and dependent children in an impoverished area of Iran. She must deal with the tragic choices that her beloved son Abbas (Mohammad Reza Foroutan) has made (*Under the Skin of the City* DVD cover—released in 2001).

who is first seen being interviewed for a television spot about the plight of working women in a reform-minded Iran. She comes off as ill prepared and inarticulate and leaves the interview disappointed.

Tuba works in a textile factory; she is the family breadwinner and caretaker. Tuba's husband is disabled due to a damaged foot and does not work. They are parents of two sons and two daughters. Abbas, the oldest son, is out on his own and assumes the role of protector for his mother and younger siblings. Abbas shields his sister from her abusive husband, he chastises his younger brother about missing school and neglecting his studies, and he cautions his youngest sister about covering her hair in public.

Tuba's family is slowly unraveling. Her youngest son is in trouble for skipping school to attend political activities; her married daughter, Hamideh, has left her husband's home due to his latest beating; and Tuba's husband and Abbas are secretly planning to sell the family home for what they believe will be a windfall. It is only Maboubeh, the youngest daughter, who is not troubled or in trouble. Tuba tries desperately to hold her family together, and she pays a price. She is worn out and haggard, and she suffers from periodic attacks of crippling back pain and asthma.

As the story unfolds, adversity strikes the family. The family home is sold at a loss, and Tuba's dream of the stability that an owned house can bring is ruined. Tuba's children also do not fare well. Hamideh has no other recourse than to return to her abusive husband, and Maboubeh, trying to help her best friend who has run away, is falsely arrested by the morality police. Abbas' story is most tragic, as he has destroyed his life with his decision to transport narcotics to earn money for his family.

There are no happy endings. At the film's conclusion, Tuba is at her factory and is once again being interviewed on television about her views on working women and an upcoming election. This time she is articulate, bold, and defiant. But, as the film implies, what's the point?

PATRIARCHAL TRADITIONS AND RELIGIOUS LAWS

Domestic violence against women is a frequent occurrence in patriarchal systems that consider females property of fathers, brothers, and husbands. In *Under the Skin of the City*, Hamideh has experienced another beating from her husband and returns to her parents' home with her five-year-old daughter to escape his brutality. Her family reacts to this violence in different ways. For Hamideh's brothers and sister, his actions are unacceptable, and they want her to permanently leave her husband. Hamideh's father, however, minimizes the abuse, and Hamideh's mother views it as a necessary evil in a marriage. Both parents exhort their daughter to return to her abusive husband but for different reasons. For her father, she must return because it is her duty as an obedient wife; for her mother, she must return out of economic necessity, as the family cannot afford to house two more people. It is Hamideh's mother who returns her to her husband's home, speaking with the shrewish mother-in-law who blames Hamideh for the abuse, as she was too "fresh" and had not learned to behave with her husband.

Hamideh's young daughter's reaction to the domestic violence she witnesses is telling. When asked why she and her mother have returned to the family home, the girl is indifferent and casually relates that her mother was beaten again by her father. Hamideh's daughter lacks a positive model of female agency. What she sees and experiences in her home forms her own acceptance of victimization as normal.

TRADITIONAL GENDER STEREOTYPES

While Tuba is head of her household, she embodies the role of the traditional wife and the predicament that many of wives face in patriarchal systems. Like many other women, Tuba is engaged in work activities outside the home, but her indolent husband does nothing to assist with the household duties. She must do it all. Tuba is also subordinate to men in business negotiations. Her house is sold by her husband without her knowledge or permission; when she confronts the buyer to cancel the sale, she is informed that the buyer only deals with men. Tuba, like the other female factory workers, is efficient and hard working. Yet there are no female supervisors on the factory line—only men.

NONTRADITIONAL GENDER ATTRIBUTES

Tuba and her youngest daughter, Maboubeh, are the female protagonists in *Under the Skin of the City* and they are strong, responsible, and level headed. They violate patriarchal norms that maintain that females should be passive, obedient, and subservient to males. Maboubeh is outspoken in her condemnation of her older sister's husband and his abuse. Her best friend, who lives next door, has been beaten by her brother for attending a concert. Maboubeh confronts the brother and actually hits him hard in his face after he calls her a "bitch" and a "slut." (It is interesting that affectionate physical contact is prohibited between the sexes in Iranian cinema, but aggressive physical contact is apparently permitted.) Tuba is a hard worker, both at her factory job and in her home. She rules her family and especially her husband, who is weak and ineffectual. Tuba's leadership qualities are noted by others, as she is selected to represent the working women of her factory for the television interview.

DOMESTIC VIOLENCE

Domestic violence is a global problem of epidemic proportions. International organizations collect data from most countries regarding the frequency of female-targeted intimate partner violence, both physical and sexual, and data from the Muslim-majority countries demonstrate that these nations are not exempt from high rates of domestic violence. In Iran, for example, surveys of married women in two different large cities found a prevalence rate of wife abuse averaging around 37 percent. Among the different types of abuse reported, incidents of physical assaults averaged around 30 percent.[29]

In Pakistan, it is estimated that more than 5,000 women are killed annually as victims of domestic violence.[30] Surveys of Pakistani married women indicate that domestic violence may be endemic. In a population-based epidemiological study of more than 200 women patients in an obstetric hospital, only seven women did not report any type of domestic violence in their lives. The rest of the respondents reported multiple types of violence, and about one-fourth reported that violence increased during their pregnancy. Nonconsensual sex was reported by almost half of the women.[31] In another survey of married women, around 40 percent reported spousal abuse, with about one-fourth experiencing physical assaults. In this survey, women and men were queried about their attitudes on wife beating. A sizeable number of both men (33 percent) and women (43 percent) agreed that there were justifiable reasons for a man to beat his wife, including "if she argues with him, neglects the children, refuses to have sex with him, goes out without telling him, neglects the in-laws, or burns the food."[32] Reports from Bangladesh show similar high prevalence rates of domestic violence. Recent surveys in largely rural areas reveal that more than three-fourths of women reported incidences of verbal abuse from their spouses, and 41 percent reported physical abuse.[33]

Turkey, Egypt, and Afghanistan also witness high rates of domestic violence. For Turkey, various forms of violence have been detailed that are problematic for women on a daily basis. These include honor killing, sexual harassment, rape, and physical and verbal abuse.[34] With reference to domestic violence, a survey of married women found that more than one-third of Turkish women reported experiencing violence from their husbands.[35] In Egypt, according to a 2005 report, physical violence by the husband was the most common form of domestic violence, with one-third of married women reporting at least one incidence of physical assault by their husbands. The more common forms of assault included being hit or punched with a fist or another object, being slapped or having one's arm twisted, or being pushed or shaken.[36] In Afghanistan, a 2008 survey of several provinces found that 87 percent of women reported having at some point experienced at least one form of sexual, physical, or psychological abuse from their husbands, and 62 percent reported more than one form of abuse occurring in their homes. More than half of the women reported physical violence, with over a third stating that their husbands had hit them in the past year.[37]

There is considerable debate as to whether Islam tolerates some forms of violence against women. The Quranic text *Sura* 4, verse 34, is often cited as supportive of this practice:

> Men have authority over women by [right of] what Allah has given one over the other and what they spend [for maintenance] from their wealth. So righteous women are devoutly obedient, guarding in [the husband's] absence what Allah would have them guard. But those [wives] from whom you fear arrogance—[first] advise them; [then if they persist], forsake them in bed; and [finally], strike them. But if they obey you [once more], seek no means against them. Indeed, Allah is ever Exalted and Grand.[38]

Zahia Smail Salhi discusses how this Quranic verse can lend itself to four different interpretations:

> First, the verse explicates that wife battering is permitted in Islam as a corrective measure if the wife fails to obey her husband. The interpretation that allows wife battering is based on other verses in the Qur'an that assign men the role of being in charge of women and therefore their protectors. The collective interpretation of these verses grants men a position of superiority over women, and views this power relationship as God-given.
>
> A second interpretation argues that wife battering is permissible in Islam only as a last resort, in cases when the wife is unfaithful and violence should be resorted to after admonishing or reprimanding her and abandoning her bed....
>
> The third interpretation argues that the verse about wife battering addresses exceptional cases and that it is allowed though not desirable. It supports this view with Prophet's description of husbands who beat their wife as lacking in faith.
>
> Finally, the fourth interpretation builds on linguistic rules to argue that the verse does not refer to wife battering. (Certain words have) a range of meaning of which only one refers to wife battering.[39]

Unwanted Woman (Zan-e ziadi)

Year: 2005; *Director:* Tahmineh Milani; *Cast:* Sima (Merila Zare'i)—woman in her late 20s; Ahmad (Amin Hayayee)—man in his mid–20s; Saba (Elsa Firouzazar)—woman in her mid–20s; *Length:* 103 minutes; *Setting:* large urban city in Iran; working class

SYNOPSIS

Sima, a woman in her late 20s, is a teacher whose meager salary supports her husband and their five-year-old daughter. She is married to Ahmad, who is lazy and irresponsible. He spends his time preening in mirrors, flirting with women, and hustling at odd jobs of dubious legality. He engages in self-pity: "They wedded me a wife when I was 20, and then the child came along. They said a family will tame you. I didn't get tamed." Sima is a traditional wife. She is passive and compliant, allowing Ahmad to aggress verbally and physically against her.

Ahmad is currently involved with another woman, Saba, and he plans for the two of them to take a romantic trip to visit her hometown, some distance away. Ahmad lies to his wife about Saba and claims that she is the widow of a good friend of his and needs his help in settling an estate. But there is a problem. In Iran, an unmarried (and unrelated) couple can be arrested if seen together in public, and Saba and Ahmad have already been detained by the morality police. Ahmad presses Sima to claim that the young woman is a relation. Though aware of her husband's true relationship with Saba, she begrudgingly lies for Ahmad.

Sima (with her daughter in tow) now insists on traveling with Ahmad and his girlfriend. This is the beginning of Sima's newly discovered assertiveness, and Ahmad is not pleased. On the way, a storm forces the travelers to stop for the night at a hotel. Police are there, warning guests that a man who has just killed his wife is on the loose. Later, during the night, Sima encounters the killer and takes pity on him. She drives him to an isolated cabin in the countryside, allowing him to hide from the police. As this part of the story unfolds, Sima, Saba, and the killer connect and conspire against the male chauvinism of Ahmad.

In the ending scenes, a violent confrontation between Ahmad and the killer leaves the killer dead. Sima has finally had enough and, with her daughter, walks away from Ahmad, realizing that it is better to be single than to be in a loveless and abusive marriage. Saba, in female solidarity, joins Sima, leaving Ahmad alone to deal with a dead body and broken-down car. The two women realize that the suffering they have experienced from life's injustices can be liberating, as they are empowered to exert control over their own lives. They learn that they can escape the tyranny of a male-dominated society.

PATRIARCHAL TRADITIONS AND RELIGIOUS LAW

The Iranian penal code (Article 630) under Islamic law (Sharia) allows a husband to kill his wife and her lover if they are caught in the act. If his wife was coerced, however, he may kill only her rapist. In cases of adultery, the husband is exempt from retaliation. (There is no provision in the penal code that applies to a wife killing her husband and his lover if caught *in flagrante delicto*. In such cases, the wife would be charged with murder.)

In *Unwanted Woman*, a subplot involves the murder of a woman by her husband, who suspected that she was having an affair with a family friend. A public debate is held about the husband's culpability. On the one hand, it is argued that "the husband had a right to enact God's order and kill his adulterous wife.... After all, she was a filthy woman." On the other hand, the husband himself casts doubt on the moral certitude of the murder. He is unsure of his wife's guilt, as he did not catch them in the act. He admits that he only saw the way she looked at the family friend and the way she talked to him. Did his wife really have an affair? He is ridden with guilt that she may have been innocent.

TRADITIONAL GENDER STEREOTYPES

At the beginning of the film, Sima, Ahmad's wife, is depicted working as a teacher to a classroom of teenage girls. She is the breadwinner of the family. However, despite her career and financial capability, she embodies the role of the traditional wife. She is passive, tolerant of her husband's flaws, and deferential. Her husband demands that she accept his mistress, Saba, and she does. He demands that she lie to the morality police about his relationship to Saba, and she tells them that Saba is her niece. The male characters in *Unwanted Woman* do not represent the virtues of manhood. They lie, cheat, beat up their girlfriends, and murder their wives.

NONTRADITIONAL GENDER ATTRIBUTES

Saba, the mistress of Ahmad, is bold, assertive, and at times aggressive. She chastises Ahmad for his oafish behavior and dismissive treatment of his wife. During their trip to Saba's home, Ahmad at various points becomes physically and verbally abusive toward his wife. Each time, Saba intervenes and rebukes him. During a stop at a restaurant, a fight has broken out between a man and his female friend. The man is loudly berating the woman and threatens to leave her. Saba is not one to stand by and allow a man to aggress against a woman. She reacts, screaming insults at the man and pushing him out a door.

Ahmad's wife asserts her voice as well. On this trip, Sima comes to understand that the traditional ways may not best serve her and her daughter's

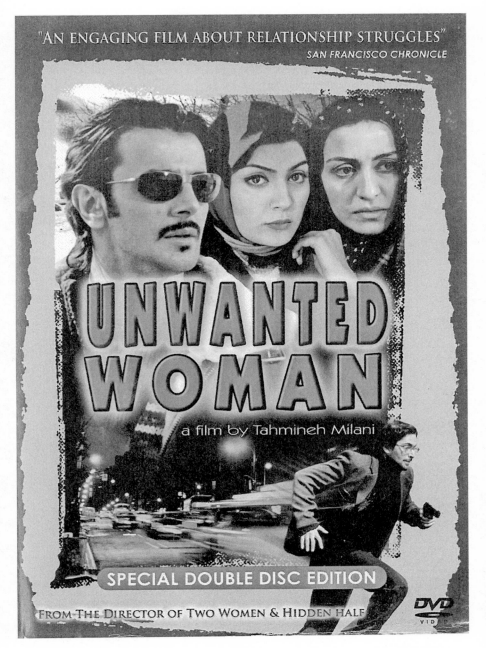

"AN ENGAGING FILM ABOUT RELATIONSHIP STRUGGLES"
SAN FRANCISCO CHRONICLE

UNWANTED WOMAN

a film by Tahmineh Milani

SPECIAL DOUBLE DISC EDITION

FROM THE DIRECTOR OF TWO WOMEN & HIDDEN HALF

DVD
VIDEO

In *Unwanted Woman*, Ahmad (Amin Hayayee) is an abusive and selfish husband who invites his mistress (Elsa Firouzazar) to join him on a vacation. As it is against Iranian law for women to fraternize with unrelated men, Ahmad's wife Sima (Merila Zare'i) is forced to accompany them as a chaperone (*Unwanted Woman* DVD cover—released in 2005).

interests. At various points, Ahmad attempts to assert his masculinity, but to no avail, as the women have the last word. In one scene, Sima tells Ahmad that she wants to accompany him on his trip with his mistress. Ahmad puffs up and yells, "When I say no, it means no!" But Sima goes anyway. At another point, Ahmad complains to Sima that she gets on his nerves, to which she retorts, "You have gotten on my nerves my whole life; now it's my turn." Ahmad is shocked by the new Sima and tells her that she has become so bold. He is sincerely befuddled by Sima's displays of agency. This isn't the way it's supposed to be.

7

Iraq

COUNTRY PROFILE

BACKGROUND[1]

The Republic of Iraq is a Middle Eastern country bordering on the Persian Gulf. Iraq is a member of the Arab League. Its population is majority Arab and minority Kurdish (15–20 percent), and the official languages are Arabic and Kurdish. Muslims constitute 99 percent of the population (Shia 60–65 percent, Sunni 32–37 percent). Around 70 percent of Iraqis live in urban areas. Iraq's form of government is a federal parliamentary republic.

IRAQ KURDISTAN

The Kurdish people of Iraq reside in mountainous areas of northeastern Iraq. They constitute Iraq's second largest ethnic group, with a population of five million. The majority of Kurds are Sunni Muslim. Currently, Iraq recognizes an autonomous Kurdish regional government. As Devrim Kilic reports on his website, KurdishMedia.com (December 26, 2005):

> Currently Iraq is the only country where the Kurds enjoy a degree of moderate national freedom.... There is now one united Kurdistan Regional Government in north of Iraq. Also, the present president of Iraq, Jalal Talabani is of Kurdish descent, and the latest Iraq Constitution recognizes autonomy for Iraqi Kurdistan. So it could be said that at least the Kurds in Iraq are now enjoying their freedom despite the intimidation of Turkey, Iran and other dominant forces in the region.

In 2011, the Kurdistan regional government passed the Family Violence Bill, which includes provisions criminalizing domestic violence, forced and child marriages, FGM/C, and honor killings.

SOCIOPOLITICAL AND RELIGIOUS ISSUES RELATED TO GENDER

Efforts have been made to ensure that the information presented here reflects current law and policies. However, it must be noted that many Muslim-majority countries are currently contending with challenges to their civil and criminal laws that stem from competing constituencies of those favoring greater freedoms for women and those espousing conservative Islamic principles. As such, governmental policies are continually evolving, and laws relevant to gender issues may be added, deleted, or amended in subsequent years.

Law

The constitution, adopted in 1979, declared Islam to be the national religion. A new constitution was approved in 2005, which identified Islamic law as the national law.[2] In 1959, the Personal Status Law was adopted, which draws on Sharia law (Ja'fari and Hanafi schools) and applies to both Sunni and Shia Iraqis. Iraq ratified the Convention to Eliminate All Forms of Discrimination Against Women (CEDAW) in 1986, with reservations that included Article 16, which calls for "the elimination of discrimination in all matters relating to marriage, divorce, and family relations." Concerns about contradicting Sharia law in family matters prompted the reservation.

Some key points of the Personal Status Law with reference to gender are as follows:

- The minimum age of marriage is 18 for both females and males
- Polygyny is allowed (up to 4 wives) with judicial permission
- Men have the right to divorce without any justification and can divorce unilaterally (*talaq*, or verbal repudiation); women can obtain a divorce only under certain conditions (e.g., conflict; husband marries another wife without judicial permission)
- Women can obtain a divorce unilaterally but forfeit dowry if they do so (*khul'* divorce)
- The father is the guardian of the children
- Women are granted custody of children up to the age of 10 (this can be extended up to the age of 15 if it is in the child's best interests); a mother does not automatically lose physical custody of children if she remarries
- Females typically inherit less than males; daughters inherit one half of their brother's or other male relative's share

- Women must have their guardian's approval to obtain a passport
- Abortion is prohibited, but exceptions are made to preserve the life and health of the woman, for reasons of fetal defect, and for reasons of incest and rape

Laws Regulating Homosexuality

The 2016 report on sexual orientation laws compiled by the International Lesbian, Gay, Bisexual, Trans and Intersex Association identified the following items in Iranian penal law:

> After the American invasion in 2003 the Penal Code of 1969 was reinstated in Iraq. This code does not prohibit same-sex relations…. [However,] non-state actors in Iraq including Sharia judges, are known to order executions of men and women for same-sex sexual behaviour, despite the fact that Iraq's civil code makes no reference to same-sex sexual behaviour, does not criminalize it, and neither does the country's (civil law) legal system defer to the Sharia court.[3]

Additional Issues

Women in Iraq are disadvantaged by social norms that restrict their freedom of movement, thus denying them access to education and to jobs. This is especially problematic in war-torn Iraq, as there are significant numbers of widows with children who are without financial assistance. Reasons for movement restrictions involve the political instability within Iraq and pressures from fundamentalist Islamists concerned about the moral conduct of females. As reported by the OECD Development Centre, "The physical integrity of women in Iraq has been systematically compromised as a result of the on-going conflict, and women in many parts of Iraq are at risk of physical and sexual violence on a day-to-day basis. Women have faced physical attack on the streets from ordinary men, as well as from members of armed Islamist militias, who accuse them of not adhering to strict Islamic moral codes."[4]

Exacerbating the plight of Iraqi women is the failure of national law to criminalize violence. As examples, under the 1969 Penal Code,[5] the law gives a husband the right to physically punish his wife and provides a lenient sentence to a man who kills his wife (or a close female relative) caught in the act of "unlawful sexual relations."

While rape is a criminal offense, a rapist can escape prosecution by marrying the victim. The penal code does not recognize the concept of marital rape: a husband has the right to have sex with his wife unless she is ill or has a "compelling reason" to refuse.

FILMS

Ahlaam

Year: 2006; *Director:* Mohamed Al Daradji; *Cast:* Ahlaam (Aseel Adel)—woman
in her 20s; Ali (Bashir Al Majid)—man in his 20s; *Length:* 110 minutes; *Setting:*
large urban city (Baghdad) in Iraq; middle class

SYNOPSIS

Ahlaam takes place in Baghdad, Iraq, and depicts the terror of living
among the anarchy during and following the downfall of Saddam Hussein.
The film, based on a true story, recounts in parallel narratives the story of two
friends who have been conscripted into Saddam's military and the story of a
young woman, Ahlaam, who is preparing to marry the man she loves. The
two young soldiers are encamped in the desert and bitterly complain about
fighting for the Baathists. The camp is bombed, and Ali, one of the friends,
survives, only to be arrested by the military for desertion. As punishment,
his ear is severed (in a gruesome scene) and he is imprisoned in a Baghdad
mental hospital.

A parallel story features Ahlaam, who is preparing to join her fiancé for
their wedding vows. A joyous party has gathered, but they are suddenly interrupted by a car full of armed men who brutally attack the fiancé and drag
him away to an unknown location for an unknown reason. Ahlaam's anguish
is unrelenting, and she is confined to the same mental hospital where Ali lies
cowering in his small cell, calling out for his dead friend. Ahlaam, still in her
wedding dress, sees her fiancé everywhere—inside her cell at the psychiatric
hospital, in the face of the man who later rapes her, on the deserted streets
of Baghdad. Is she mad? Maybe, but maybe not. How else could she manage
in an insane world where all is chaos and nothing is understood and where
loved ones disappear in an instant?

The hospital is shelled and many patients escape, including Ahlaam and
Ali. The city is dangerous, filled with armed marauders, looters and snipers.
Ahlaam wanders through the ravaged and deserted city streets, searching for
her fiancé. She is lost, disoriented, and terrified, and eventually she is lured
by looters to an abandoned building, where she is raped. Ali roams the city
streets as well, as he is on a mission to find the patients and return them
safely to the hospital. But the film concludes on a hopeless note. Just as Ali
has gathered and calmed the frightened patients, he is murdered by a sniper.
Ahlaam is last seen on the rooftop of an abandoned building, looking off
into the distance at the wreckage of the city.

"America's 'Shock and Awe' campaign has been
BEAUTIFULLY CAPTURED..."
INDIEWIRE

AHLAAM

(Utopia) a film by Mohamed Al-Daradji

IRAQ'S
OFFICIAL
ENTRY
IN THE
79TH
ANNUAL
ACADEMY
AWARDS

"Filmed under truly
hellish conditions,
including repeated
kidnappings
of cast and crew...
**A MATURE,
VISUALLY
STUNNING
TRIUMPH"**
SEATTLE
INTERNATIONAL
FILM FESTIVAL

"That any film should
be made under such
circumstances is extraordinary...
that the film should also be so
COMPELLING
is nothing short of
A MIRACLE"
ANTON BITEL,
CHANNEL 4 FILMS

PATHFINDER
Home Entertainment

The terror of living in the anarchy that occurred during and following the downfall
of Saddam Hussein in Iraq is experienced by Ahlaam (Aseel Adel), a young woman
soon to marry her childhood sweetheart, and Ali (Bashir Al Majid), a young man
serving in Saddam's army (*Ahlaam* DVD cover—released in 2006).

TRADITIONAL GENDER STEREOTYPES

Ahlaam represents the epitome of female vulnerability and powerlessness. She is a victim of male aggression at her wedding, in the mental hospital, and on the streets of Baghdad. Following the loss of her fiancé, Ahlaam exhibits an existential vulnerability, a sense of incompleteness made all the more intense by her strong desire for belongingness. Her hallucinations of her (presumed) dead lover are ever present throughout the film and in context understandable.

On display in *Ahlaam* are males who are arrogant and callous. Men are depicted as predators of the vulnerable. Physicians, soldiers, and civilians are all complicit. A doctor in the mental hospital orders electric shock therapy for his patients and watches impassively as they are dragged, struggling and screaming, to the equipment. Another doctor in surgical garb carries out a court-ordered punishment and indifferently cuts off the ear of a non-anesthetized man. An observer to the procedure asks the doctor how he could possibly justify his actions; the doctor replies that the prisoner deserved it, as it was his punishment. The witness is not convinced: "Sir, how can you say that as a doctor? He is a human being. How do you expect him to live after you've cut off his ear?" At other points in the film, Iraqi soldiers attack a wedding party and shoot civilians, engaging in the ultimate male privilege of deciding who lives and who dies. Iraqi male civilians are also aggressive, as they trap a frightened young woman in a deserted building, rape her, and dispose of her on the street. A rooftop sniper at the end of the film randomly fires at and kills passersby below.

Half Moon (Niwemang)

Year: 2007; *Director:* Bahman Ghobadi; *Cast:* Mamo (Ismail Ghaffari)—man in his 70s; Hesho (Hediyeh Tehrani)—woman in her 40s; *Length:* 107 minutes; *Setting:* small villages in rural Kurdistan region of Iraq and Iran

SYNOPSIS

In *Half Moon*, Mamo, an elderly man, is famous throughout the Kurdish region of Iran for his folk music. Mamo is planning to give a concert in the Kurdish region of Iraq, which is now allowed following the demise of Saddam Hussein. Mamo enlists the services of his twelve musician sons, a bright orange bus, and a not-too-bright bus driver who comes equipped with a video camera and a pet rooster.

On the way to the Iran/Iraq border, Mamo insists on stopping at a remote mountain village that is the home of women singers who have been exiled for singing in public. Mamo is searching for Hesho, whose "celestial" singing voice is needed to accompany his voice at the concert in Iraq. Hesho is located, and the bus resumes its journey to the border. Mamo and his sons know full well that women are forbidden to sing in public and that it is illegal to transport females for that purpose. At the Iran/Iraq border, they hide Hesho under floorboards in the bus, but she is detected by specially trained female-detecting dogs and is arrested and taken away. Mamo is dejected and orders his troupe to find another route to Iraq.

When all hope seems lost, Mamo meets (or hallucinates) a muse who supplies him with an instrument, promises to take him to the concert in Iraq, and agrees to sing with him. The film ends in the spirit of magic realism: Mamo dies peacefully in the countryside in the company of his muse, and his troupe performs their concert—perhaps in Iraq, perhaps in the next world.

PATRIARCHAL TRADITIONS AND RELIGIOUS LAWS

After the 1979 revolution, Iranian leaders instituted a thorough Islamization of the state as a counterpoint to the former regime of the shah, which was deemed morally corrupted by Western values. Clerics in Iran have ruled that it is forbidden for a woman to sing in the presence of a man to whom she is not related, as this could incite male lust. In *Half Moon*, the mountain village retreat housing a thousand or so exiled women singers does not in reality exist.

TRADITIONAL GENDER STEREOTYPES

Within patriarchal societies, females are confined to private spheres of the home and restricted to activities of homemaking and childcare. It is reasoned that these restrictions will protect the honor of women, who thus will not be subjected to the sexual attentions of unrelated men. It is forbidden in Iran for females to travel in the company of men without a male relative or a husband being present. In *Half Moon*, both the men and Hesho have violated this rule; yet it is Hesho who is arrested, not the men who smuggled her on the bus. And it was female-detecting dogs that snared her, not male-detecting dogs.

NONTRADITIONAL GENDER ATTRIBUTES

Although Iraq/Kurdistan is clearly patriarchal and males are dominant, in *Half Moon*, females are valued for their important contributions to the social structure. Mamo tells Hesho that he is not leaving without her and will protect her from the Iranian border guards, even if they are arrested. He states that their performance would not be complete without her.

Female Solo Singing in Iran

With the advent of the 1979 Iranian revolution, many restrictions were placed on artistic endeavors in Iran, with censorship criteria rigidly applied and regulated by the state-appointed Ministry of Culture and Islamic Guidance Board. Public resentment and political regime changes in the following years led to a decrease in restrictions and censorship standards for many of the arts, including cinema and music.[6] However, the ban placed on females singing solo in public is still in place. Parmis Mozafari[7] provides an analysis of how professional female singers in Iran resist/work around the ban, detailing scenarios that serve as "sites of resistance." The first scenario involves females singing in a chorus, which may be permitted if the female voice is unrecognizable. The second scenario involves co-singing—that is, a female singing alongside a second or third voice, with the rationale being that each individual voice would then be unrecognizable. Female singers may also be allowed to sing publicly if they sing with a changed voice, which can occur if they alter their voice to sound like children (used in commercials and children programming) or if they sing soprano (as used in film music). Other means that female singers have used to sidestep the prohibitions on solo singing are performing in private homes and performing at female-only music festivals. A final "site of resistance" for females desiring to sing publicly is holding public performances outside Iran. With the musical black market in Iran and the ubiquity of social media, this method of resisting censorship is a popular one.

Marooned in Iraq

Year: 2006; *Director:* Bahman Ghobadi; *Cast:* Mirza (Shahab Ebrahimi)—man in his 70s; Barat (Faegh Mohamadi)—man in his 40s; Audeh (Allah-Morad Rashtian)—man in his 40s; *Length:* 108 minutes; *Setting:* rural villages in Iran and Iraq Kurdistan

SYNOPSIS

Mirza and his two adult sons, Barat and Audeh, are on a quest to find Hanareh, Mirza's ex-wife, who is said to be in a refugee camp in Iraqi Kurdistan following the 1988 Iran-Iraq war. Mirza is a wizened septuagenarian who is famed for his singing in his home region of Iranian Kurdistan. His two sons, who are also musicians, don't appear to have much to do. Audeh bemoans his fate of having no sons: his marriage to seven wives has yielded 11 daughters and no sons. Barat is not married and spends much of his time traveling from village to village on his motorbike. Though somewhat buffoonish, the two brothers are immensely likeable.

The three men set off on their trek to the Iraq border; along the way, they encounter a number of comedic events: a wedding party interrupted by a gun-toting spurned suitor; the theft of their motorbike by marauders; and the attempted sale of said motorbike at a market. The film, however, turns dark when the three finally reach the border and encounter, first, an overcrowded orphanage and, next, a recently excavated mass grave with numerous refugees searching for their dead.

Mirza continues on alone to find the refugee camp where his wife is said to reside. At the camp, dozens of displaced women are living in horrific conditions. These women have survived Saddam Hussein's chemical bomb attacks and many are disfigured, including Mirza's wife, Hanareh, who not only is horrendously disfigured but also has lost her voice. Hanareh recognizes Mirza but chooses not to reveal her true identity to him. Instead, Mirza is told by the others that Hanareh is dead and has left a young daughter who is now an orphan. At the film's conclusion, Mirza has made a decision. He is last seen crossing the border to return home, trudging through knee-high snow and carrying Hanareh's young daughter on his back.

Traditional Gender Stereotypes

Males are valued and females are devalued in *Marooned in Iraq*. The importance of males in this Kurdistan culture (in contrast to females) is illustrated through Audeh's desperate desire to have a son. His desire was so great that he married seven times, only to beget 11 daughters. He tells his father about a dream he had: "Last night I was happy, I couldn't sleep. I only managed to sleep five minutes, but thanks to God I dreamed that God was giving me two sons. I hope I won't make anyone jealous! Thank God, two sons! Two at the same time, and no wife." Later, he explains to an employee at the orphanage where he is seeking another wife, "Yes, I have seven wives and eleven daughters.... It was just to have a son! The first one couldn't give me one. Neither could the second one, same for the third one and same again until my seventh wife. I promised myself never to leave women alone until I had a son.... He will become a singer like me. And a great artist!" Audeh learns that he can adopt two boys at the orphanage camp, and he is overjoyed. Not one son but two! And no wife!

The females in Audeh's village (ostensibly his wives and daughters) are mostly invisible, serving as background for the film's main action, which centers on the three male protagonists. The girls and women are employed in all sorts of menial labor. They work in the fields, construct a house, and prepare food. Audeh's daughters help him shower and wash the motorbike. Barat at one point receives a request from a woman with whom he is infatuated to teach her how to sing. "Sing?" he asks. "Singing is forbidden for women."

Though there are comedic elements present throughout *Marooned in Iraq*, males frequently display aggressive behavior that is directed toward other men.

In their journey to Iraq, Mirza and his sons encounter a man struggling with his motorbike. When they offer their assistance, he responds angrily, "This is none of your business. Get lost! Go away!" Mirza takes it upon himself to inspect the bike anyway. The man lunges at them: "I told you to get lost!" And the fistfight begins. Later marauders dressed as soldiers discover the three men on an isolated road and accuse them of stealing a motorbike and smuggling clothes. They are kicked, slapped, pushed, tied up, and then robbed. The thieves are eventually apprehended, and yet another fistfight ensues.

NONTRADITIONAL GENDER ATTRIBUTES

Despite mass graves, chemical attacks, and overrun orphanages, there is a glimmer of optimism as the patriarchal-dictated mentality of the male protagonists is exposed to reveal traits of caring and generosity. Barat is in love with a woman with a beautiful singing voice. He asks for her hand in marriage, and she agrees on one condition: that he teach her how to sing. At first he refuses because of the tradition that women should not sing in public, but he quickly admits his error in holding to that tradition. Audeh realizes that he does not need another wife to conceive a son, as he can adopt, and Mirza takes Hanareh's daughter under his protection.

Chemical Attacks

The following account of the 1988 destruction of the city of Halabja in Iraq, which left thousands disfigured, maimed, or dead, is provided by BBC:

Thousands of people are reported to have been killed and many others injured in a poison gas attack on a Kurdish city in northern Iraq.... According to experts, the chemicals dropped by the planes may have included mustard gas, the nerve agents sarin, tabun and VX and possibly cyanide.... Iraq was said to be keen to avenge the fall of Halabja, which is seen as an important centre for Kurdish resistance in their struggle for autonomy.... Most of the wounded, who were taken to hospital in the Iranian capital Tehran, were suffering from mustard gas exposure. Those who escaped death have developed respiratory or visual problems from the cocktail of chemicals dropped on the city. According to some reports, up to 75% of the victims were women and children. The injured survivors seen by reporters showed the classic symptoms of mustard gas poisoning—ugly skin lesions and breathing difficulties.... Although there is some evidence Saddam Hussein's forces had used chemical agents before this date, the attack on Halabja is thought to be the first documented assault using chemicals.[8]

One Candle Two Candles
(Êk Momik, Du Momik)

Year: 2014; *Director:* Jano Rosebiani; *Cast:* Viyan (Katrin Ender)—a teenage girl; Haji Hemmo (Enwer Shexani)—a man in his 60s; *Length:* 105 minutes; *Setting:* small urban city in Kurdistan region of Iraq; middle class

SYNOPSIS

One Candle Two Candles is a seriocomedic film that presents the story of Viyan, a young girl who is trapped between the dictates of traditional Kurdish beliefs and the modern values that favor gender equality. Viyan is a Westernized teenager who dresses in jeans, listens to popular music, gossips about boys, and shops with her friends. On one of their outings, she meets a young aspiring artist, and it is obvious that the two have fallen for each other. Unfortunately, Viyan's father has arranged her marriage to a wealthy businessman, Haji Hemmo, a man some 50 years her senior. Haji wants a young, pretty wife (she would be his fourth) and is well aware that Viyan's greedy father is only too willing to trade his daughter for the considerable dowry that he will receive. Viyan is distraught at this prospect and, along with her mother and grandmother, begs her father not to force her to marry Haji. Irritated by Viyan's presumption that she has any say in the matter, Haji orders Viyan's father to control his daughter, and the marriage proceeds.

On the wedding night, a leering Haji attempts to bed Viyan, but she'll have nothing to do with him and, in her puffy white wedding dress, runs away and climbs a tree. The neighbors, Haji's wives and daughters, and even the local imam witness Haji's humiliation, and he becomes the village laughingstock. Haji's honor and his manhood have been tarnished; in retribution, he locks Viyan in a small room for weeks. Alone and in despair, she fantasizes about escaping with her young artist, but to no avail, as Haji resorts to beatings and other brutalities to force Viyan into obedience. Still, she will not yield to him, and finally he's had enough. In a rage, he divorces her (by repeating "I divorce you" three times), locks her in a shed, and sets it on fire. But Viyan escapes unharmed, and Haji wants her back. He is reminded, however, that he divorced her and that there were witnesses. If he wishes to remarry her, he must abide by the Islamic doctrine that requires an intermediate marriage. As the imam explains, for a remarriage to occur, Viyan must marry another man for one day and one night, and then be divorced by that man. Haji is not happy with this solution and asks if the law can be softened a bit. "No," he is informed, "the Sharia is non-negotiable."

At the end, there is optimism for Viyan, who has eloped with the man she loves, and there is revenge for Haji, with a visit from the "Ball Buster," a woman vigilante who escaped her own bad marriage by killing her husband in a gruesome way.

PATRIARCHAL TRADITIONS AND RELIGIOUS LAWS

Laws concerning polygyny and divorce are depicted in *One Candle Two Candles*. In several Muslim-majority countries, a husband is allowed to marry as many as four wives. This practice is allowed in Sharia and based on Quranic text. Polygyny is permitted in Iraq civil law but has been prohibited in Iraq Kurdistan since 2008 (with an exception made if the first wife is unable to bear children). In some countries under Sharia law, husbands are also allowed to divorce their wives unilaterally through repudiation. Haji exercises his right to marry other wives, though whether he obtained the obligatory permission from his other wives was not depicted. Haji also engages in a private divorce of Viyan whereby he repeats "I divorce you" three times in the presence of witnesses.

TRADITIONAL GENDER STEREOTYPES

Haji, the imam, the council of village elders, and Viyan's father are dominant characters in this film. All collude to force Viyan to marry Haji. Although the women are in solidarity with Viyan (an amusing scene has them hurling insults at Haji and Viyan's father), they know that, once the men have decided, they are powerless to prevent the marriage. In one scene, during a premarital meeting at which Haji and Viyan's father agree to the marriage, Viyan is dragged into the room, only to run away in disgust. Haji complains about

Viyan's insult to him, to which her father replies, "Give me a few days, and I'll put her in her place." Later, he lectures his daughter about her objections to the marriage and speaks of his humiliation and shame: "Did I bring you up so you'll spread mud on my face?"

NONTRADITIONAL GENDER ATTRIBUTES

Viyan experiences considerable social pressure from traditional Kurdistan custom to marry the man her father chooses for her. Viyan's mother, grandmother, friends, and love interest all voice their objections to the marriage, but to no avail, as the men of this village dictate the fate of women. But Viyan will have none of it. She fights the wedding and the marital bed despite the brutality of her husband and pressures from his family. Viyan's persistence ultimately pays off. In the end, she escapes Haji before he can remarry her and elopes with her love interest.

DIVORCE BY REPUDIATION AND INTERMEDIATE MARRIAGE

Some Muslim-majority countries governed by Sharia law provide the husband with the unilateral right to divorce his wife with or without her consent (or even her presence). This type of divorce is termed divorce by verbal repudiation (*talaq*) and is noted as a pre–Islamic Arab tradition that was later modified by the Quran and modern law. Wives are not allowed this type of divorce, which, according to Kecia Ali, privileges males by giving them greater say in the status of their marriages.[9] Emily L. Thompson and F. Soniya Yunus explain that, in a *talaq* divorce, the husband states the word *talaq* ("I divorce you" or "I cast you off") and the marriage contract is dissolved. There is also the triple *talaq* situation, in which the husband divorces his wife by pronouncing three repudiations.

A *talaq* divorce can be revocable or irrevocable. In a revocable divorce, the husband can return to his wife after her obligatory waiting period (*iddah*), which is three menstrual periods. In an irrevocable divorce, divorce can be either major or minor. In a minor irrevocable divorce, the husband may remarry his former wife with a new marital contract. In a major irrevocable divorce, the husband cannot remarry his former wife if he has repudiated her on three separate occasions. Hence, a couple can divorce and remarry only twice; their third divorce then becomes irrevocable. But there is a loophole: if an intermediate marriage has occurred in which the former wife has married another man but then was divorced by that person, she may remarry the first husband.[10]

In *One Candle Two Candles*, Haji divorced Viyan by repeating "I divorce you" three times, but he subsequently decides to remarry her. He and his advisors (who include the imam) plot to arrange an intermediate marriage of Viyan to another man who will promise to immediately divorce her. This film appears to violate the Islamic law that in a *talaq* divorce a woman must wait three months to remarry. Obviously, Haji did not intend for Viyan to observe the required waiting period.

Qarantina

Year: 2010; *Director:* Oday Rasheed; *Cast:* Silah (Hattam Auda)—man in his mid–40s; Kerima (Alaa Najem)—woman in her early 30s; unnamed assassin (Asaad Abdul Majeed)—man in his mid–30s; Meriam (Rawan Abdullah)—teenage girl; *Length:* 90 minutes; *Setting:* large urban city (Baghdad) in Iraq; working class

Synopsis

Silah, a middle-aged man; his younger wife, Kerima, and his two children (the oldest being from a previous marriage) are living in a dilapidated building in postwar Iraq. They have rented the upstairs to an unnamed and enigmatic professional killer. The family lives in poverty, and what little money they earn comes from Silah's job as trash collector, his 8-year-old son's shoe-shine job, and his wife's cleaning and cooking for the lodger.

The men in this film are aggressive. Silah is angry with life and abusive to his wife and his teenage daughter, Meriam, whom he has raped and who is now pregnant. Both women strive in their own way to escape Silah's brutality—Kerima through an affair with the killer and the daughter by refusing to eat and speak. The assassin remains largely silent throughout the film making limited contact with the family as he carries out various contracted murders. The film is about the choices each character makes, which will determine their fate.

Traditional Gender Stereotypes

Qarantina portrays how males and females are trapped by conformity to gender stereotypes and gender role restrictions. The wife, Kerima, is trapped by the tradition of subordination to her husband. She is ordered by her husband to clean and cook for the family and for the lodger, and she does. She is literally confined to the house by his order. The daughter, Meriam, is

In postwar Iraq, an impoverished family struggles to deal with the everyday violence both on the streets and within their home. Pictured here is Muhanad (Sajad Ali), the youngest member of the family (*Qarantina* DVD cover—released in 2010).

trapped in tradition stating that her body is not her own but is the property of a man—in this case, the property of her father, who rapes her. Both the assassin and Silah are trapped through conformity to masculine role expectations. The assassin witnesses the abuse of his lover by her husband and does nothing, as wife abuse is a husband's right in a patriarchal society. The husband assumes the prerogative of controlling his family through brutality and abuse.

The men in *Qarantina* are brutish, violent, and soul-less. Silah rapes his daughter and verbally abuses her when she becomes mute. He hits his wife with a belt when she threatens to leave him. The assassin accepts assignments to kill, and he murders with no show of remorse. He is also aggressive to his landlord, who visits him one day in his room: "Do you want something? Speak. What is it? Listen carefully. Don't bring your problems here. I will break your legs if I ever find you up here again. Understand? Get out."

NONTRADITIONAL GENDER ATTRIBUTES

Kerima transforms from an obedient, subservient wife at the onset of the film to a woman with an independent voice. She asserts herself to her lover, the assassin: "Why must there always be a man? What do I want from Silah? What do I want from you? He is an old man and you are young. But there is no difference. I hate him and I hate you. I go down to him and up to you until I hate myself. I hate it. In the end ... I want to say what I want, not what you all want." Kerima, at the end, chooses to deny her husband's prerogative to abuse both Meriam and herself. After discovering that her stepdaughter is pregnant and that Silah had raped her, Kerima and Meriam pack to leave. "Look, Silah, you won't touch Meriam. Put that out of your mind. Only over my dead body. I know you and your no-good brother plan to kill the poor child. Why? She is just a poor kid."

Violence has consequences. The assassin is fully aware that he will be killed by the men who have employed him. Silah soon realizes his isolation when Kerima and his daughter abandon him. In the end, though, there is a glimmer of hope. The young boy, a spectator to the violence around him, has the chance to escape the dictates of a brutalized masculinity. He is given the choice of staying with his father or leaving with his mother and sister, and he chooses to go with the women.

8

Pakistan

COUNTRY PROFILE

BACKGROUND[1]

The Islamic Republic of Pakistan, located in Southern Asia, gained independence in 1947 after separating from British India. Pakistan has adopted the title of Islamic Republic (one of five countries in the world to do so). The national language is Urdu, and the form of government is parliamentary. Pakistan is home to several ethnic groups, the largest being the Punjabi. Pakistan's national religion is Islam; 96 percent of the population is Muslim. About one-third of Pakistanis live in urban areas.

SOCIOPOLITICAL AND RELIGIOUS ISSUES RELATED TO GENDER

Efforts have been made to ensure that the information presented here reflects current law and policies. However, it must be noted that many Muslim-majority countries are currently contending with challenges to their civil and criminal laws that stem from competing constituencies of those favoring greater freedoms for women and those espousing conservative Islamic principles. As such, governmental policies are continually evolving, and laws relevant to gender issues may be added, deleted, or amended in subsequent years.

Law

Pakistan's constitution[2] was established in 1973; since then, it has been subject to suspension and restoration several times. Pakistan governs by civil law and Islamic Sharia (predominantly the Hanafi school of thought). A

Council of Islamic Ideology ensures that secular laws are compatible with the laws of Islam. Pakistan's constitution recognizes gender equality; yet several laws guided by the Muslim Family Laws Ordinance (1961) disadvantage women. Pakistan ratified the Convention to Eliminate All Forms of Discrimination Against Women (CEDAW) in 1996, stating that the ratification is subject to provisions in its constitution.

Some key points of the Muslim Family Laws Ordinance with reference to gender are as follows:

- The minimum age of marriage is 16 for females and 18 for males
- Polygyny is allowed (up to 4 wives) with the consent of all wives and validation by a local court
- Men can repudiate (i.e., divorce their wives unilaterally), although there is a requirement to go through a three-month arbitration process with the local council
- Women have limited rights to divorce, which can only be granted under certain circumstances (e.g., if the woman has been deserted, if the husband is abusive, or if the marriage was never consummated); a wife can also divorce by *khul'* with forfeit of her dowry
- In the event of divorce, mothers retain custody of sons until the age of seven and of daughters until the age of sixteen, at which time custody reverts to the father or his family
- Women are entitled to inherit one half of a brother's or another male relative's share
- Abortion is permitted to save the life of the woman, to preserve physical health, or to preserve mental health; it is prohibited in cases of rape or incest or for reasons of fetal impairment

Laws Regulating Homosexuality

The 2016 report on sexual orientation laws compiled by the International Lesbian, Gay, Bisexual, Trans and Intersex Association identified the following items in Pakistani penal law: "Whoever voluntarily has carnal intercourse against the order of nature with any man, woman or animal, shall be punished with imprisonment for life, or with imprisonment of either description for a term which shall not be less than two years nor more than ten years, and shall also be liable to a fine. Explanation: Penetration is sufficient to constitute the carnal intercourse necessary to the offence described in this section."[3]

Additional Issues

Pakistan has been listed as one of worst countries for women to live in according to gender experts surveyed by TrustLaw, a news service of Thomson

Reuters Foundation (June 2011). Pakistan earns this distinction due in part to the 1979 implementation of Hudood ordinances, which were applied disproportionately against women.[4] Hudood ordinances, based on Sharia law, added zina offenses (adultery and fornication) to the criminal code and included punishments of whipping and death by stoning for these offenses. In 2006, Pakistan amended the Hudood ordinances and eliminated the punishment of whipping for zina offenses, but death by stoning as punishment for adultery was retained. In a 2010 Pew Research study on Muslim political beliefs, a majority of people in Pakistan endorsed the practice of stoning of those who commit adultery.[5] In 2006, however, regulations concerning victims of rape were changed so that victims were no longer jailed if unable to prove rape, and victims could also establish rape through DNA evidence and not just through reliance on witnesses to the rape.

Though the government of Pakistan has moved to reform some laws unfavorable to females, many harmful cultural and religious practices still exist. Pakistan reports a high number of acid attacks against females and high numbers of child and forced marriages and honor killings. According to the UNICEF (2016), child bride rates in Pakistan range around 24 percent.[6] Many of these child marriages occur in rural areas. Though Pakistan has criminalized the practice of *swara* and *vani* (forced marriage of young girls to settle tribal feuds), increased the penalty for acid throwing to life imprisonment, and categorized honor killings as murder, these practices continue to occur at high rates due to a combination of factors, including police inaction and the preeminence of tribal law over national law.[7] (Notably, at the time of this writing, the legal forgiveness loophole, in which a family member of the victim of an honor killing can pardon the perpetrator, is no longer permitted.)

FILMS

Bol

Year: 2011; *Director:* Shoaib Mansoor; *Cast:* Zainab (Humaima Malik)—woman in her 20s; Hakim Shafatullah (Manzar Sehbai)—man in his 50s; *Length:* 165 minutes; *Setting:* large urban city (Lahore) in Pakistan; working-class family

SYNOPSIS

Zainab, a woman in her 20s, is on death row in a Pakistani prison for the murder of her father. She is to be executed but has been granted an opportunity to tell her story. In defiance, she sheds her head scarf and walks out to the

Bol relates the interconnecting stories of three Pakistani women who suffer under the dictates of a religiously conservative and patriarchal system that restricts women's freedom. Ayesha (Mahira Khan), Zainab (Humaima Malik), and Meena (Iman Ali) each act in their own way to defy the system (*Bol* DVD cover—released in 2011).

gathered media to begin with a portrait of Hakim, her father, and the birth of her brother.

Hakim, she relates, was a brutal patriarch who confined his daughters and wife to purdah (seclusion in their home). He believed himself to be a devout and conservative Muslim and would expound on his fundamentalist views to his family and anyone else whom he happened to encounter. In his worldview, females were by nature weak, submissive, incompetent, and morally corruptible and served only one purpose: to reproduce and to obey and revere men. For Hakim, the more anodyne terms "masculinity" and "manliness" translated to misogyny and chauvinism.

To his great disappointment, Hakim had sired seven daughters with his wife, a meek, haggard-looking woman who was expected to be sexually available to him at his command. Hakim was overjoyed when finally a boy was born. However, the boy, named Saifee, was not exactly what his father had expected, as he was born with female-appearing genitals.

As Saifee grew older, his effeminate traits delighted his sisters but shamed Hakim, who mostly ignored him. Saifee endured taunts from other males in his neighborhood about his femininity. At one point, he was raped by a group of men; upon discovering the rape, Hakim killed Saifee out of shame.

Hakim was subsequently arrested and learned from the local police chief that he could be absolved of the murder if he paid a substantial amount of money. He was too poor to afford the bribe, but he did have one asset—siring females—and the local brothel owner needed females to replenish his business. The two made a deal: Hakim would impregnate a brothel prostitute, and if she gave birth to a girl, Hakim would get his money.

The prostitute did in fact give birth to a girl; however, Hakim had a crisis of conscience and was ashamed of his actions—after all, he was a pious Muslim and confining his daughter to a life of prostitution was morally unacceptable. The mother was convinced to give the baby girl to Hakim, and he tried to kill the proof of his sin by killing the baby. Zainab, however, interceded to prevent another death at the hands of her father and struck him on his head, killing him. Convicted of his murder, she was sentenced to die.

Zainab denounces the hypocrisy of a patriarchal system which condemns infanticide yet obligates women to breed children, often at the expense of their lives. Before her execution Zainab asks, "Why give birth to children when you can't feed them? My father killed eight children.... Why is it a crime to kill but not to give birth?"

In the final scenes, the execution has been carried out, and the president is watching a news report about Zainab and her last words. He phones his assistant and requests him to convene a meeting that will include his full cabinet and religious leaders. His agenda: "Why is only taking a life a crime? Why not giving life as well?"

PATRIARCHAL TRADITIONS AND RELIGIOUS LAWS

Obedience of Wives and Daughters

Religious scholars are divided as to interpretations of certain Quranic verses about marital relations with reference to wifely obedience and polygyny. In verses relevant to the roles of wives and husbands in marriage, Hakim's conservative interpretation gives him license to demand sexual obedience from his wife at all times in exchange for her maintenance. The Quran allows a husband more than one wife, and Hakim takes advantage of this by marrying a prostitute in order to legitimize their sexual relations and any offspring that might result. Pakistani Sharia law also gives the father custodial rights over his children. Hakim exercises this privilege in restricting his daughters' access to education, movement outside the home, and even listening to radio broadcasts of a cricket game.

TRADITIONAL GENDER STEREOTYPES

In rigidly patriarchal systems, such as the one Hakim espouses, women have little value, other than tending to domestic tasks and (in the case of his wife) tending to his sexual needs. The women affirm patriarchal expectations in their compliance with his demands. Hakim insists on female modesty even within the privacy of their home. The women comply by hastily covering their heads with scarves whenever he enters a room. Even during the evening supper, the women are veiled while the father eats his meal at a special place off to the side. Hakim forbids his daughters to attend school after the fifth grade, and they comply. His wife and daughters are also confined to their home. After all, as Hakim explains, females are too incompetent to work outside the home. In matters of marriage, Hakim insists his daughters marry men in whom they have no interest. In a patriarchal system, boys are valued over girls. When Hakim has killed his only son, the police officer commiserates with him that he cannot use an honor defense. After all, "daughters can be killed in the name of honor."

Females are portrayed as sex objects in *Bol* and males are their predators. The women in *Bol* are either chaste and irreproachable or whores and morally corrupt. Hakim's family of women is, of course, chaste, as they are confined to their home. Although one daughter "escaped" and married a man she loved, she is now estranged from the family and disposable. The brothel owner also offers his favorite prostitute in marriage to Hakim, stating that his business runs on girls. The prostitute is essentially "othered" as nothing more than a breeder.

Nontraditional Gender Attributes

Zainab is not afraid of her father, though she is well aware of the consequences if he is challenged. At one point, she questions his need for numerous children and cites the toll that multiple pregnancies are taking on her mother. At another point, she threatens to kill him if he physically assaults her mother or sisters. And Zainab certainly has a voice when she does indeed kill her father to prevent him from killing her baby sister.

Zainab's voice is not silenced in prison. She exhorts other female prisoners to take off their veils, which are symbols of gender oppression. Zainab's telling of her story at the execution stage is meant to challenge and perhaps change society.

Dukhtar

Year: 2015; *Director:* Afia Nathaniel; *Cast:* Allah Rakhi (Samiya Mumtaz)— woman in her late 20s; Sohail (Mohib Mirza)—man in his early 40s; *Length:* 93 minutes; *Setting:* rural villages in Pakistan and large urban city (Lahore) in Pakistan

Synopsis

Allah Rakhi, a young mother in her 20s, defies patriarchal tradition by refusing her husband's order to marry their 10-year-old daughter to the powerful and elderly tribal leader of a neighboring village. The father has offered his child to the elder in order to settle a blood feud. Allah Rakhi is well aware of the life in store for her beloved daughter, as she herself was forced into marriage at age 15 (this, she says, "was when my story ended").

On the day of her daughter's marriage, Allah Rakhi escapes her husband's house with her daughter in hand. Her goal is to reach the city of Lahore, where her mother lives. The two make it to the main highway, but, with no money and no resources, they are at the mercy of passers-by. They are lucky to find Sohail, a young truck driver, who hides them in his truck. Allah Rakhi convinces a reluctant Sohail to drive them to Lahore, though both are aware of their probable fate if caught.

The tribal leader has suffered a grave insult with the desertion of his child bride on his wedding day. Honor is everything, and he orders his men to find the pair and kill the mother and capture the child. Throughout the film, the gunmen are in close pursuit and finally trap the three in Lahore.

The film's ending is ambiguous. Sohail defends Allah Rakhi and her daughter, but Allah Rakhi is shot and dies while being rushed to the hospital. The concluding scene shows a grieved Sohail looking at the murdered woman's daughter, who is holding her dead mother's hand.

PATRIARCHAL TRADITIONS AND RELIGIOUS LAWS

Child Marriages: Swara and Vani

Child marriages are not legally permitted in most of the world, including Muslim-majority countries. However, child marriages do occur in many regions, especially where patriarchal systems are strong (see commentary below). Child marriages are often considered forced marriages, as the right of consent is violated. In the practice of *swara* or *vani*, seen in some tribes in Pakistan and Afghanistan, a young girl from one tribal family is forced to marry a man from a rival tribe to end a feud. Often the groom is a tribal elder who holds a position of power. Essentially, the girl becomes the property of that man and his tribe. In *Dukhtar*, a war between tribes has caused many deaths, and the elder of one tribe proposes an alliance between the tribes to be built upon the bond of marriage between himself and Khan's prepubertal daughter. At first, Khan initially protests that his daughter is just a child and not yet of age. The elder states, "Daurat Khan, this is a decision between us men; you decide now, and this Friday, we will have the marriage." Khan agrees.

TRADITIONAL GENDER STEREOTYPES

There are several points in this film when males' dominance is asserted over females, who are subjugated and powerless. Khan, the husband of Allah Rakhi, has complete control over his wife and daughter. He forces the marriage of his prepubertal daughter without the knowledge or consent of his wife. He also refuses to let his wife visit her mother, whom she has not seen in more than 10 years. The maintenance of male and tribal honor is of utmost importance. As Khan's wife and daughter have escaped, he has insulted the honor of the rival tribe and the elder. The elder tells Khan that he will find the pair: "I will find her. And you know how we deal with an insult of honor. She was yours. Now she is ours." Orders are given to kill Khan's wife, as she is dispensable. Only the daughter has value, as she was purchased and is now the property of a tribal elder.

A theme of *Dukhtar* is that females, being powerless and vulnerable, are in constant need of male protection. Allah Rakhi has defied the authority of both her husband and the rival village elder by running away with her daughter. She is now in peril. As masculine authority must be restored in order to maintain the "natural" order of patriarchy, a male is required to save her. Sohail, the truck driver, serves as the film's gallant male rescuer. He hides the two females in his truck and protects them from discovery by the armed men sent by the elder to capture the girl. Though aware of the great peril to himself, he agrees to transport them to Lahore. In Lahore, Sohail again rescues Allah Rakhi and her daughter, who have been captured by a gunman. He kills the gunman and frees the two. However, Allah Rakhi has accidently been shot. En route to a hospital, Allah Rakhi dies, held by her daughter. Will Sohail come to the rescue one more time and adopt the daughter? The fate of the daughter is unknown at the film's conclusion.

Nontraditional Gender Attributes

Allah Rakhi departs from traditional gender stereotypes in her disobedience to her husband and her refusal to permit the marriage of her young daughter. She is determined to escape, even knowing that she is without resources, a plan, or assistance. Consequences to gender violations of patriarchal systems are dire: she dies in the end from a gunshot wound, and the fate of her daughter is unknown.

Child Marriage

The Convention on the Elimination of All Forms of Discrimination Against Women (CEDAW) prohibits child marriage and has set the age of 18 as the minimum age of marriage for females and males.[8] CEDAW grants both men and women the right to freely choose a spouse and to enter into marriage only with free and full consent. The Convention on the Rights of the Child does not explicitly prohibit child marriage, but it does specify guaranteed rights of children that would be contravened by early marriage, including the right to education; the right to be protected from all forms of physical or mental violence, injury or abuse (including sexual abuse) and from all forms of sexual exploitation; the right to the enjoyment of the highest attainable standard of health; the right to educational and vocational information and guidance; the right to seek, receive and impart information and ideas; the right to not be separated from their parents against their will; and the right to protection against all forms of exploitation affecting any aspect of the child's welfare.[9]

Despite the establishment of 18 as the minimum age recognized by many countries, child marriages are widespread. United Nations Population Fund estimates that about one in three girls in the developing world is married before age 18.[10] The problem of child marriage is exacerbated by the civil codes of some countries, which allow child marriage (age 15 or younger) with the consent of the child's guardian, and by tribal law and custom that supersede national civil law. Girls often marry at younger ages than boys, and girls are especially at risk when married early. Girls in early marriages are denied an education and a future career, as they are essentially indentured to their husband's family as additional household help.[11] As reported by Nawal M. Nour, girls married before 18 have an increased risk of contracting the human immunodeficiency virus (HIV) and experiencing pregnancy and childbirth complications, including maternal mortality. Infants born to girls under age 18 have a 60 percent higher mortality rate. Psychologically, girls married at early ages can be traumatized by sexual experiences for which they are not prepared.[12]

The question of whether child marriage is permissible according to Islamic tenets is controversial. According to Andrea Büchler and Christina Schlatter:

> Some Muslims who follow a conservative interpretation of Sharia argue that Islam permits child marriage as the Quran specifies that girls can be married upon reaching maturity, which conservative scholars define as puberty. However, there is debate within Islam about at what age a girl reaches maturity. Many Muslim communities and Islamic scholars agree with the internationally recognized age of maturity, eighteen. Moreover, many Muslims argue against child marriage because Islam mandates that men and women should choose their partners freely, and children are unable to do so.[13]

In the Name of God (Khuda Kay Liye)

Year: 2007; *Director:* Shoaib Mansoor; *Cast:* Hussain Khan (Humayun Kazmi)—man in his late 30s; Maryam (Iman Ali)—woman in her 20s; Sarmad Khan (Fawad Khan)—man in his 20s; *Length:* 167 minutes; *Setting:* large urban cities (London and Lahore) and rural Afghanistan

SYNOPSIS

Maryam, a university student, and her father, a well-to-do Pakistani shop owner, reside in London. Maryam has acculturated to Western norms and enjoys an indulgent and carefree life. She wants to marry a fellow student who is Christian, but her father is reaffirming his Islamic faith after being

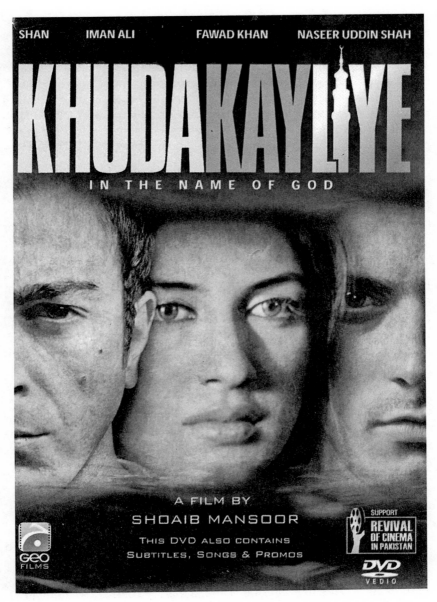

Two brothers, Mansoor (Shaan Shahid) and Sarmad (Fawad Khan), are Pakistani musicians who follow very different paths in dealing with the political realities of contemporary Pakistan. Maryam (Iman Ali) is a young British Pakistani woman who, in her father's eyes, may be too Westernized; she is enjoined to travel to Pakistan to meet Mansoor and Sarmad, her cousins (*In the Name of God* DVD cover—released in 2007).

shamed by the local Muslim community for being too Western. He is vehement in his objections to the marriage, citing Islamic law that prohibits a Muslim woman from marrying a non–Muslim man.

Maryam's story intercuts with that of two brothers who live in Lahore, Pakistan. One of the brothers, Sarmad, is a popular musician who is questioning his "decadent" way of life. (The other brother's story is not included in this film summary.) Sarmad meets a charismatic cleric who expounds on the "virtues" of an extremist Islamic ideology (one such virtue is the prohibition on music). This appeals to Sarmad, who is drafted to fight for the ideology as a militant jihadi.

In the meantime, in London, Maryam's father has devised a scheme to marry his daughter to a devout Muslim. He convinces Maryam to attend a family reunion in Pakistan; while there, she meets Sarmad, her cousin. Unbeknownst to Maryam, her father has persuaded Sarmad to marry her ("for her own good"). The three travel to a remote area of Afghanistan for a day outing, ostensibly to visit the countryside. But once there Maryam learns that she has been duped. She is forced to marry Sarmad (who is now aligned with Islamic terrorists), her passport is confiscated, and she is enslaved in a primitive Afghan terrorist camp with no means of contacting the outside world.

As the film evolves, Maryam is eventually rescued from the camp, and both she and Sarmad come to terms with their enslavement. A shamed Sarmad renounces the extremist movement to which he had once devoted his life, divorces Maryam, and returns to his former life. Maryam now understands that life provides a purpose beyond oneself and returns to the village of her imprisonment to teach Afghan girls. At the film's conclusion, the tensions between two countervailing ideologies, moderate Islam and fundamentalist Islam, are addressed by a Muslim cleric who tells his audience that the true voice of Islam is moderation and acceptance and not violence and intolerance, as taught by extremists.

PATRIARCHAL TRADITIONS AND RELIGIOUS LAWS

Islamic law allows Muslim men to marry outside their faith provided that they marry women from monotheistic religions, such as Christianity or Judaism ("People of the Book"). Muslim women, however, are forbidden to marry men who are non–Muslim. Though there is controversy among religious scholars as to whether this proscription is supported by the Quran,[14] many Muslim-majority countries have codified the regulations concerning mixed marriages into their family laws. In *In the Name of God*, Hussain, Maryam's father, is chastised by a man from the local Muslim community for allowing Maryam to date, and possibly marry, a non–Muslim:

Have some shame, Hussain Khan. You are named after a prophet. And your deeds are so bad. Because of people like you today Muslims are like this. We are ruined. You have spent your life with white people. Now your daughter is too following your footsteps. Were you not content with white people? Now you are getting a white son in law! Why are you tarnishing your religion, Hussain Khan? Become a Catholic. Leave us and our religion alone. Imam Hussain won't spare you! Go to hell!

Traditional Gender Stereotypes

The gendered dominance-subjugation binary that exists in rigidly entrenched patriarchies reveals that men are *expected* to control and dominate women. Women are regarded as nothing more than objects that exist to serve men. In *In the Name of God*, Maryam is enslaved in an Afghan camp and treated no differently from the other women who live there. The women are forbidden to leave the camp, while the men go off for military training. Women are forbidden to show their faces in the presence of unrelated men or to be educated. Maryam rebels, attempting to teach the alphabet to young girls of the village, but she and the girls are severely rebuked by the village elder for the impropriety of educating females. The females of the village enforce the patriarchal rules through shaming Maryam. She is seen unveiled one day in a public space, and the women admonish her: "You are shameless! You do not even have a veil on your head. What will the villagers say to us? You are defaming us."

Maryam rebels in her marriage as well, refusing to have any sexual contact with her husband Sarmad. The village elder informs Sarmad that the best way to deal with Maryam is to impregnate her, as "once a girl is a mother, then she will settle down and be obedient." Though Maryam does become pregnant and gives birth, she does not "settle down."

Nontraditional Gender Attributes

During her enslavement in the Afghan camp, Maryam rails against the traditions of femininity that are forced upon her. She challenges the patriarchy and engages in acts of civil disobedience that include protesting her forced marriage, refusing to have sexual relations with her husband, unveiling outdoors, teaching girls the alphabet, and the ultimate disobedience—attempting to escape. Even though the punishments for these indiscretions are harsh, she shows little acknowledgment of a basic reality that if an oppressed or marginalized person or group challenges patriarchy in any form, then the patriarchal response is to leverage even more control over the oppressed.

Silent Waters (Khamosh Pani)

Year: 2003; *Director:* Sabiha Sumar; *Cast:* Saleem (Aamir Ali Malik)—man in his early 20s; Zubeida (Shilpa Shukla)—woman in her early 20s; Ayesha Khan (Kiron Kher)—woman in her 40s; *Length:* 99 minutes; *Setting:* small rural village in Pakistan; working class

SYNOPSIS

Silent Waters spans a time period from the 1940s to contemporary times. The film begins in the 1970s and tells the story of Ayesha, a middle-aged widow, and her adolescent son, the somewhat indulged Saleem. Ayesha and Saleem live in a small home located in a peaceful Pakistani village. Ayesha spends her days tending to their home and teaching young girls about the Quran. She is devoted to Saleem. She has plans for his future and arranges job prospects for him with local business owners. Ayesha is also concerned about a future wife for Saleem and hopes for a daughter-in-law who will assist her with household duties. Saleem, for his part, is not interested in his mother's vision of his future career, which he perceives as tedious and unexciting. He is also not interested in her matchmaking, as he is secretly courting Zubeida, a young woman with ambitions of attending college and securing a career. Saleem is adrift and confused, unsure of his identity and uncertain about his future.

As the story unfolds, Saleem meets two young Islamic extremists who are on assignment in his village to recruit men to their movement. At first skeptical about their messages of militancy, Saleem soon finds the men's arguments persuasive. As he becomes more involved and more indoctrinated to the fundamentalist philosophy of the extremists, he discovers an identity and adopts a new purpose in his life: that of making Pakistan an Islamic state. As a result of his conversion and acceptance of the pernicious judgments of his new "brothers," Saleem finds himself alienated from his mother and his girlfriend. Since his girlfriend once accepted his kisses, she is no longer a chaste and pious Muslim woman, and she has disgraced him. Since his mother refused to publicly express her allegiance to Islamic precepts, she is suspect and he can no longer be her protector.

At this point in the narrative, a group of Sikh men visit the village, intending to celebrate a religious event at a local temple. The village was once their home before their forced exile to India during the time of the 1947 partition. For Ayesha, their return triggers memories of events that she has long suppressed. At the time of the partition, fathers had ordered the young girls of their families to protect their chastity from Muslim invaders by drowning themselves in the village well. Ayesha was one of these girls. She refused her

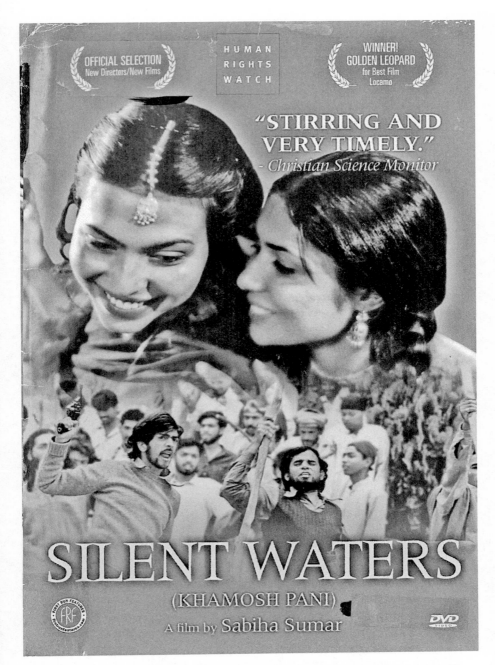

"STIRRING AND
VERY TIMELY."
- *Christian Science Monitor*

SILENT WATERS

(KHAMOSH PANI)

A film by Sabiha Sumar

DVD
VIDEO

Silent Waters spans a time period from the 1940s to contemporary times in a small village in Pakistan. The narrative contrasts the peaceful and harmonious environs of the village prior to the 1970s with the turbulence and chaos that ensued with the arrival of fundamentalist extremists (*Silent Waters* DVD cover—released in 2003).

father's order and ran away, only to be later raped by the invaders. One of the men took pity on her and married her; since then, in her village, she became one of the many ordinary Muslim women living a peaceful life. Ayesha is now faced with a decision: Should she reveal her secret to her son and risk his censure and ostracism from the village, or should she bury the secret and return to the well? She chooses death.

The film finally shifts forward to the 2000s. Saleem is now a leader of the extremist movement, and Zubeida is working in an office in a large modern city. She has turned on a television and witnesses Saleem exhorting his followers to commit terrorist acts against the state.

TRADITIONAL GENDER STEREOTYPES

Fundamentalist extremists of any religion prey on young men who are disaffected and disenfranchised from a mainstream society that has marginalized them. Saleem is one of those young men. His is aimless and unsure about his identity, making him an easy target for those who offer a mindless and structured life with the promise of a simplistic solution to existential alienation. Saleem is seduced by an Islamic fundamentalist ideology that preaches violent jihad against those holding contrary beliefs.

Saleem's aggression is depicted at several points during the film. He aggressively denounces both his love interest, Zubeida, and his mother for their lack of fidelity to Islamic ideals. He also participates in the rhetoric of mob violence at the time of the Sikh visitation to the village and threatens those who do not conform to his fundamentalist beliefs. Later, Saleem has assumed leadership of the extremists and his rhetoric of aggression has become even more vitriolic.

NONTRADITIONAL GENDER ATTRIBUTES

Ayesha has a strong voice from the beginning of her narrative. As a young girl, she watches her sisters as they one by one kill themselves by jumping into the well. She refuses her father's order to do so as well and runs away. Later Ayesha opposes her son's affiliation with Islamic extremists, and she is quite vocal about her disdain for the movement. Although she risks losing her son, Ayesha refuses to stand in the public square and declare that she is Muslim. Ayesha has a voice in determining her own fate, choosing at the end to kill herself to protect the secret of her true identity.

9

Turkey

COUNTRY PROFILE

BACKGROUND[1]

The Republic of Turkey is a Middle Eastern country that stretches across Southeastern Europe and Southwestern Asia. Modern Turkey was founded in 1923 under the leadership of Mustafa Kemal (later titled Ataturk). Almost three-fourths of Turkey's population lives in urban areas. There are a number of ethnic minorities in Turkey, the largest being the Kurds. The form of government is a parliamentary republic, and the official language is Turkish. Although the vast majority (99 percent) of population is Sunni Muslim, Turkey is one of the few Muslim-majority countries with a secular legal system.

TURKISH KURDISTAN

Turkey is home to the largest concentration of Kurdish people, with a population estimated to range from 10 to 20 million. The Turkish Kurds reside in the mountainous areas of eastern Turkey and are predominantly Sunni Muslim. The Kurds have experienced a long history of persecution. As Devrim Kilic reports on his website, KurdishMedia.com (December 26, 2005):

> There is no official or accurate information about the Kurdish population in Turkey on account of the Turkish state's historical denial of the existence of Kurds as a distinct culture and people. The official Turkish ideology claims that there is no such ethnicity as Kurds and there is no language as Kurdish ... the life for Kurds has not been easy in Turkey. As a result of Turkey's recent demand to join the European Union the oppression on the Kurdish language and culture has been eased, but by no means can it be said

that the Kurds are free in Turkey. However, the Kurds have at least become a reality that can no longer be denied by Turkish state.

SOCIOPOLITICAL AND RELIGIOUS ISSUES RELATED TO GENDER

Efforts have been made to ensure that the information presented here reflects current law and policies. However, it must be noted that many Muslim-majority countries are currently contending with challenges to their civil and criminal laws that stem from competing constituencies of those favoring greater freedoms for women and those espousing conservative Islamic principles. As such, governmental policies are continually evolving, and laws relevant to gender issues may be added, deleted, or amended in subsequent years.

Law

Turkey, though a Muslim-majority country, is known for its secular government. Sharia law was abolished in 1924. In 2004, the constitution was amended to ensure that men and women have equal rights.[2] The civil code, amended in 2001 and 2009, deleted language that declared the husband to be head of the household and wives their husbands' designated helpers. The penal code was amended in 2005 to eliminate the reduction of prison sentences to relatives who commit honor killings. Currently, there is considerable Islamist-secularist polarization in Turkey, and whether these amendments will be revised is unknown.[3] In 1985, Turkey signed and ratified the Convention on the Elimination of All Forms of Discrimination Against Women (CEDAW). Turkey initially had reservations against CEDAW's Articles 15 and 16 but approved all articles in 1999.

Some key points of the revised family code with reference to gender are as follows:

- The minimum age of marriage is 18 for both sexes
- Polygyny is not allowed and is a criminal offense
- Women and men have equal divorce rights
- The judiciary decides who receives custody of children in a divorce; joint custody is not allowed
- Males and females inherit equally
- Women have the right to travel freely
- Adultery is not a criminal offense
- Abortion is legal until the tenth week of the pregnancy

Additional Issues

Patriarchal and religious traditions that contravene law are still prevalent in Turkey, especially in eastern and southeastern regions and in rural communities. Research conducted by WWHR in these regions found that the practices of polygyny, forced marriages, and child marriage still occur with some regularity.[4] As reported in the OECD Development Centre's Social Institutions and Gender Index, an estimated 40–50 percent of girls may be married before the age of 18. Early marriage is particularly common in rural areas of Turkey and is seen as an acceptable way to "relieve families of the economic burden of caring for their daughters, while ensuring that girls do not engage in premarital sexual activities."[5]

Criminal Behavior and Punishment

Turkey amended its penal code in 2004 to criminalize several acts of violence against women. Sexual assault and rape carry penalties of imprisonment, ranging from two to seven years for assault and from seven to twelve years if the assault included penetration. The penal code also criminalizes sexual harassment with a penalty of a fine or imprisonment. Turkey recognizes marital rape as a crime and does not criminalize homosexual acts. Many Turks, in contrast to other Muslim-majority countries, take a moderate position on criminal law. According to 2010 Pew Research poll, the majority of Turks did not feel that laws should strictly follow the Quran. As an example, most Turks opposed stoning as punishment for adultery.[6]

FILMS

A Step into the Darkness (Büyük oyun)

Year: 2010; *Director:* Atil Inac; *Cast:* Cennet (Suzan Genç)—woman in her 20s; *Length:* 120 minutes; *Setting:* large urban city (Kirkuk) in Iraq; large urban city (Istanbul) in Turkey

SYNOPSIS

A Step into the Darkness is about the violence of war and its aftermath. Cennet, a young unmarried woman living in rural Iraq, witnesses the slaughter of her family and other villagers in a raid led by American soldiers who have mistaken the village for a terrorist holdout. Her brother, who works in

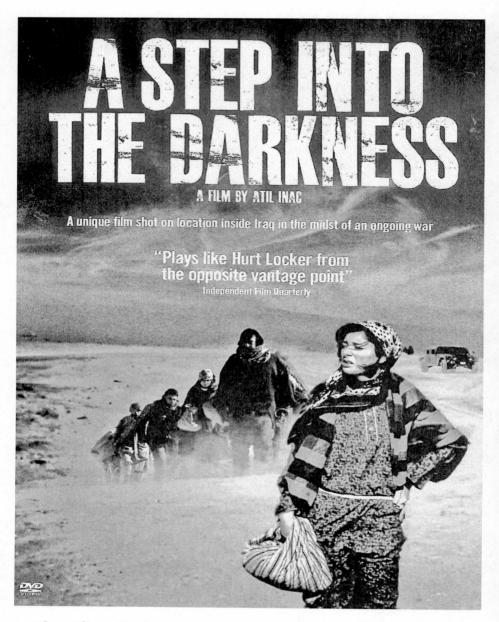

Cennet (Suzan Genç), a young woman living in rural Iraq, has witnessed the slaughter of her family and entire village in a raid led by American soldiers who mistook the village for a terrorist holdout. She sets out on foot searching for her brother, who works in a distant city on the Turkish border (*A Step into the Darkness* DVD cover—released in 2010).

a distant city on the Turkish border, is her only surviving relative, and she sets out on foot to find him. Finding his employer, she learns that her brother has been wounded in a bomb explosion and taken to hospital in neighboring Turkey. Cennet is determined to find him, as he is all she has.

Lacking a passport, she arranges passage to Turkey with Kurdish smugglers, one of whom rapes her during their trek. In despair, she attempts to kill herself but is rescued by another group of men who are crossing into Turkey illegally. Cennet and another woman who is unnamed are delivered to an enclave in Istanbul that houses an extremist fundamentalist Islamic sect. The women are sequestered in one room of the enclave and the men in another, where they receive a lecture from the sect's leader about the "virtues" of jihad through suicide bombing of innocent civilians. Plans are made for the women to carry out suicide attacks at public sites in Istanbul, and the jihadist leader must convince Cennet to commit these attacks. He has promised to find her brother, but he lies, stating that her brother has been found and that he is dead. The jihadist wants Cennet to experience emptiness so profound that she will have no willpower and no desire to live. He wants her to be a lamb, and indeed she is. The two women, as well as others residing in the women's sector, are utterly joyless and trapped in despair. Their eyes are dead and their faces are flat. They are barely animated figures who creep about listlessly or sit silently in a room.

The film's ending is as bleak as its beginning. While one woman completes her assignment and blows up her target and herself, Cennet cannot bring herself to detonate her explosives. In a final shot, Cennet has discarded her vest and wanders isolated and alone through the streets of Istanbul.

Patriarchal Traditions and Religious Laws

Gender Segregation

Restrictions placed on the mixing of sexes in public are common in many highly patriarchal Muslim-majority countries. Depending on the country or region, rules governing gender segregation are enforced in such spheres as public transportation, educational institutions, work environments, places of worship, and even public parks (as in Iran). In many mosques gender segregation is likewise observed. Women are separated from men by a barrier of some sort, or else women are assigned to a separate room or balcony.

In *A Step into the Darkness*, gender segregation is strictly enforced at fundamentalist Islamic enclave in Istanbul. Meeting rooms and much of the courtyard are reserved for men, who discuss political and religious matters. The women are assigned to separate quarters and full hijab is enforced. When

Cennet must be fitted with a suicide jacket, only females are allowed to attend to her. At a funeral, gender segregation is also observed. Men carry the coffin to the burial ground, while women and children follow. As the men near the cemetery, the women and children turn back to the house, where they lament the deceased.

TRADITIONAL GENDER STEREOTYPES

Males exercise complete control over the fates of the two women who have been selected to carry out the suicide bombings. The women themselves are of no importance to the men who deliver them to the jihadist leader. Cennet's desperate attempts to find her wounded brother are unacknowledged. The jihadist wants Cennet to have little to live for, so he falsely informs her that her only surviving relative, her brother, is dead. She is referred to as a "lamb" who will obediently and without question follow the leader's command to detonate explosives in a suicide attack on Istanbul's populace. Although the leader has attracted a considerable following, with male apprentices who intently listen to his diatribe, it is women who are volunteered for the suicide missions, not men. Women are dispensable.

FUNDAMENTALIST ISLAM

Similar to adherents of all religious faiths, Muslims vary considerably as to their ideological beliefs, and efforts to classify people by religious philosophy results in a variety of groupings. One such grouping divides Muslim ideologies into traditionalism, fundamentalism, extremism, and modernism. Traditionalists are conservatives who advocate for strict teachings of traditional Islam. Fundamentalists go beyond tradition, calling for "radical political change," and extremists represent a subset of fundamentalists who advocate for political change through violence. Modernists are those Muslims who support reform of Islam in efforts to modernize their countries. Traditional and fundamentalist approaches ascribe to a more literal interpretation of the Quran, whereas modernists maintain that contextual understandings can lead to different interpretations of Quranic messages. With reference to Islamic fundamentalism, Lina Khatib[7] elucidates that this ideology is not represented by one monolithic entity but rather by a combination of several groups that vary by country of origin, historical context, and tradition. What all fundamentalist groups share, Khatib asserts, is a belief in Islamic authenticity and an opposition to secular modernity, which is said to be indifferent to core religious values. Within fundamentalist groups, jihad (holy war) is necessary to instill Islamic authenticity through either nonviolent or militant means.

Many Muslims across the world have expressed concern about the rise of Islamic extremism. Surveys of Muslims in several different countries found little support for violence used against civilians. According to a 2010 Pew survey:

> Eight-in-ten Muslims in Pakistan say suicide bombing and other acts of violence against civilian targets in order to defend Islam from its enemies are never justified; majorities in Turkey (77%), Indonesia (69%) and Jordan (54%) share this view. Support for suicide bombing has declined considerably over the years. For example, while 74% of Muslims in Lebanon said these violent acts were at least sometimes justified in 2002, just 39% say that is the case now; double-digit declines have also occurred in Jordan, Pakistan, Nigeria and Indonesia.[8]

Bliss (Mutluluk)

Year: 2007; *Director:* Abdullah Oguz; *Cast:* Meryem (Özgü Namal)—teenage girl; Cemal (Murat Han)—man in his late 20s; Ali Riza Amca (Mustafa Avki-ran)—man in his 50s; *Length:* 105 minutes; *Setting:* rural village and large urban city (Istanbul) in Turkey

SYNOPSIS

Meryem, a 17-year-old girl, has been found raped and barely conscious on a beach outside her small village in eastern Turkey. As tradition dictates, she must die for the shame she has brought upon herself, her family and the village. The village elder, Ali Riza, a distant cousin of Meryem, orders her honor killing and imprisons her in a small hut to await her execution. She is alone and alienated from others, receiving no kindnesses from anyone, including the women of the village, who encourage her to kill herself to atone for her shame. Ali Riza commands his son Cemal to take Meryem to Istanbul and kill her en route. Cemal is a brooding, taciturn young man who has just returned from military duties. Without question, he accepts the assignment. After all, who is he to challenge the "natural" order of the patriarchy that places the importance of honor above all else?

On their journey, Cemal attempts to kill Meryem but, at the last moment, finds that he cannot. Cemal is developing some empathy for Meryem and the two escape, followed by hitmen hired by Ali Riza to find and kill the girl. They encounter an ex–university professor who is embarking on a sailing trip, and he hires them for his crew. As the three begin a tour along the coast of Turkey, the relationship between Cemal and Meryem subtly and slowly evolves to reveal a mutual appreciation of each other. Cemal begins to realize how much he truly cares for Meryem at a moment of peril for her.

When the gunmen find Meryem and attempt to drown her, Cemal comes to her rescue. He witnesses her reliving the rape and realizes that the perpetrator was his father, Ali Riza. He needs to confront his father, whom he now finds despicable, and they return to the village. Cemal, with gun in hand, threatens his father. But he cannot shoot. However, Meryem's father is present and he can. Honor is restored.

PATRIARCHAL TRADITIONS AND RELIGIOUS LAWS

Rape and Honor Killing

A central theme of *Bliss* concerns the patriarchal tradition dictating that a man is duty bound to protect honor of his family. Much of that honor is dependent on the moral propriety of the family's female members, and moral propriety is dependent on their chastity. A sexual transgression—real or imagined—demands that a woman's male protectors (whether father, son, brother, or husband) restore the family's honor through punishing her, which could include her murder.

In *Bliss*, Meryem has been raped and is now impure. Ali Riza blames her for the rape and orders her execution: "What was she doing all the way out there? Seeing she was being a whore, she could at least have died.... It's her sin." Her loving father also acknowledges the rape as her sin but asks for mercy, as she is just a "simple girl." Cemal, the man ordered to kill her, tells her, "It's going to be your graveyard. You're stained with sin, Meryem. You've brought shame to us." The village women are complicit in upholding the honor killing of Meryem. They are as gender oppressive as the men. Meryem's stepmother encourages her to take her own life and brings her a noose, stating, "You're soiled, Meryem. You've sinned badly. You know that too. They've given the verdict. God forgive you. You know the custom.... If you do the job yourself, maybe you'll go to heaven.... You know how to do it, don't you?"

TRADITIONAL GENDER STEREOTYPES

Cemal represents the embodiment of masculinity. He is stoic, in control, and quick to react with aggression when his absolute male privilege is challenged. Cemal is taking Meryem to Istanbul, where he plans to kill her. On the train, he falls asleep and wakes from a dream about Meryem that is tinged with sexual overtones. He is angry with Meryem about his dream: "Are you my devil? You no-good pile of trouble! Come on, who did you flirt with, bitch? You have to tell me, damn you! You're soiled." Cemal's quick anger is also evident when he observes his employer, Ifran, giving Meryem a gift of a necklace and placing on her neck. He is enraged:

> What is that around your neck? How could you let a stranger touch you?"
> "I couldn't put it on. He helped. I was all confused."
> "Confused, huh? Yes, you are confused! I'll smash your head now. It's all my fault not to punish you before. You whore! If you aren't ashamed of yourself, at least be ashamed of me."

Meryem is the personification of passivity and subservience. She takes orders without question, cringes at the slightest criticism, and presents a sense of unworthiness. Meryem's subservience is shown in her interactions with Cemal. When walking, she follows; in interactions with the world, he is in charge and she is silent. She proclaimed her innocence about her rape, but her meekness did not persuade the villagers, Cemal, nor even her father of her innocence.

Nontraditional Gender Attributes

Cemal is a transformational character in *Bliss*. In his interactions with Meryem and Ifran, he comes to realize that masculine bravado does not always serve him well. Toward the conclusion of the film, he is softer with Meryem and empathizes with her. He cries when he learns that his own father raped her. He seeks to avenge Meryem's rape and threatens to kill his father yet ultimately chooses not to, acting out of his newly discovered inner strength.

Meryem is also a transformational character in *Bliss*. She is learning at the film's conclusion to assert an identity of her own, unshaped by the restrictions of a cruel past. At one point, Meryem asks where she and Cemal are going. He tells her to just "shut up." But this time Meryem retorts, "You're always telling me to shut up, Cemal Abi, but I'm not going to!" She tells Cemal in the film's last frame, "Life is amazing. Don't ask what I'm going to do or what will happen. I don't know. But this life is mine."

Honor and Its Importance in Patriarchy

In patriarchal societies, the honor of one's family is of central importance, and if honor is compromised through a woman's sexual misconduct (or suspicions thereof), the family faces social restrictions and may be expelled from the community. There are, however, mechanisms for restoring a family's social privileges. The man who engaged the woman in sexual misconduct could marry her (even if against her wishes), or she could be killed by a male family member. A forced suicide could also substitute for an honor killing in some communities. In this scenario, family members do not directly kill the victim but force her to commit suicide, in order to avoid punishment. Such suicides are reportedly common across the Middle East.[9]

Honor killings are not sanctioned by Islamic law or principle. The practice is thought to stem from pre–Islamic patriarchal traditions that served to protect patrilineal communities. Suzanne Ruggi cites Sharif Kanaana, a professor of anthropology, who claims that the practice of honor killing has more to do with reproduction than sexual impropriety: "What the men of the family, clan, or tribe seek control of in a patrilineal society is reproductive power. Women for the tribe were considered a factory for making men. The honour killing is not a means to control sexual power or behavior. What's behind it is the issue of fertility, or reproductive power."[10]

The practice of honor killings is rigidly entrenched in rural areas of many Muslim-majority and non–Muslim countries. According to the World Health Organization, honor killings have occurred recently in all parts of the world, including Bangladesh, Brazil, Ecuador, Egypt, Great Britain, India, Israel, Italy, Jordan, Pakistan, Morocco, Sweden, Turkey, and Uganda.[11] In examining the frequency of these practices, Ihsan Cetin emphasizes the importance of distinguishing "crimes of passion" from honor killings. Murder as a crime of passion results from a woman's own agency in the conduct of her life (e.g., divorcing her spouse, spurning a lover's advances), whereas a woman's murder in an honor killing results from the premeditated decision of the family or community.[12]

In some Muslim-majority countries, laws have been enacted to criminalize the practice of honor killing. In Turkey, persons found guilty of this crime are sentenced to life in prison. In 2002, the Kurdistan region of Iraq (though not Iraq proper) removed the provision for lighter sentencing for killers who claimed to act with honorable motives. In Pakistan, honor killings are punishable by a prison term or death, and a loophole allowing the perpetrators of honor killings to escape prosecution if the family of the victim forgave them has been voided.

Majority (Cogunluk)

Year: 2010; Director: Seren Yüce; Cast: Mertkan (Bartu Küçükçağlayan)—man in his 20s; Gul (Esme Madra)—woman in her 20s; Kemal (Settar Tanrıöğen)—man in his late 40s; Length: 111 minutes; Setting: large urban city (Istanbul) in Turkey; middle-class and working-class communities

Synopsis

The narrative revolves around Mertkan, a young man who lives with his parents in a middle-class suburb of Istanbul. Mertkan is a slacker. He is not in school, nor is he employed full time; other than doing the occasional odd job at a construction company his father owns, he spends time with his male friends, drinking, smoking marijuana, and aimlessly cruising bars, malls, and cafés. Mertkan's purposeless existence is periodically challenged by Kemal, his father, a harsh and humorless disciplinarian who threatens to enroll Mertkan in compulsory military service.

Kemal at various points imparts lessons to his son about what it takes to be a man. He introduces Mertkan to his cronies at a Turkish bath, where the men engage in self-promoting banter and tease Mertkan about male virility. Mertkan learns from his father that those with lower standing in life are to be treated with contempt and violence. And careless mistakes—like wrecking one's father's car while driving under the influence—can easily be remedied with the right amount of money paid to the right person.

When Mertkan meets Gul, a young Kurdish woman working as a waitress to support her university studies, he is provided with the opportunity to assert himself and become his own man. Redemption, however, is elusive, and by the end of the film, Mertkan has become his father.

Traditional Gender Stereotypes

The dominance, aggression, and non-nurturance of males is expressed throughout the film in the characters of Kemal, the father, and his son Mertkan. Kemal is a tyrant who rules his wife through silence and his son through shame and belittlement. Both Mertkan and his mother are subject to Kemal's authority in all matters. Mertkan's mother stays at home, and she is on call to prepare meals, wash clothes, and perform other household activities. She is a household fixture and acknowledged only when her husband or her son needs something.

Kurds are the largest minority group in Turkey and are subject to prejudice and discrimination. As such, Kemal orders his son to break up with his girlfriend, who, being Kurdish, is seen as socially unfit: "Just break up with her, I don't like her. I don't want to see her again ... you should hang around with people who are like yourself. We are all Muslims, Turks, you should be with people who are worthy of our family ... people like these they seek to divide our nation. Being with these people will hurt us all."

Throughout the film, messages are communicated that male aggression is an acceptable social response when one's desires are frustrated. In the film's opening scenes, a preteen Mertkan bullies the family's housekeeper. He yanks the cord from the wall as she vacuums and slams a door in her face. As she continues her chores, he kicks her, knocking her against the wall. No one admonishes the young Mertkan for his behavior. The posturing and misogyny of male adolescents is likewise illustrated in scenes where Mertkan and his friends are commenting on the purpose of females: "They are only good to fuck and then be disposed of … those miserable bitches, you just fuck them and dump them." Mertkan is admired by his friends ("You did good, man") when he brags about his girlfriend: "I fucked her—long and hard—then I left her."

Those who challenge male privilege are subject to violence. A car blocking the driveway is vandalized by Kemal. A taxi driver who politely asks for fair treatment following the destruction of his taxi by a drunken Mertkan is beaten by Kemal and his older son. Kemal physically accosts another taxi driver for the perceived insult to his masculinity in suggesting that his son could not pay the taxi fare.

Males are also non-emotional and non-nurturing. Kemal, the family patriarch, is unkind and impassive. His coldness is illustrated at the dinner table when he tells his wife to shut up after she asks him to acknowledge that she exists, telling him that she all she wants is "just a welcoming hello … a question about how my day was." When Mertkan and Gul have sex in her bedroom, it is unemotional, mechanical, and quickly over with Mertkan's orgasm. Afterward, Gul attempts to cuddle with Mertkan as he dispassionately watches television and drinks tea.

ADDITIONAL POINT

Majority is set in an environment not unlike any urban environment in the United States. Mertkan and his slacker friends could easily be American teens, struggling with identity issues, holding misogynistic attitudes about females, and reveling in a pervasive sense of entitlement. Add drugs, deep-seated conflicts with parents, and prejudice toward marginalized minority groups (just substitute any American minority group for Kurds), and you have the American *Majority*.

Mustang

Year: 2015; *Director:* Deniz Gamze Ergüven; *Cast:* Lale (Güneş Şensoy)—girl around age 12; *Length:* 97 minutes; *Setting:* small village on Black Sea in Turkey; upper class

SYNOPSIS

School is out, and five attractive sisters, ranging in ages from about 12 to 17, celebrate their freedom. On the way home, dressed in school uniforms, they run into the sea to join their fellow classmates, a group of boys, in a game of "shoulder war." The village gossips are scandalized by this shameful behavior of girls and boys intermixing and alert the girls' grandmother, who, though ordinarily loving, beats them one by one for their "obscene" behavior with boys. The girls' uncle (their guardian, as they are orphans) calls them whores and forces the older three to take virginity tests at a medical clinic to prove their chastity. This is a patriarchal system, and the uncle rules. He places the girls under house arrest. Perhaps this would not be so bad under ordinary circumstances, as the house is spacious and comfortable, and food is plentiful. But doors are locked or nailed shut, and computers, phones, cosmetics, revealing clothing and other potentially corrupting materials are locked in cabinets.

The only way to protect the girls is to arrange quick marriages for them. The sisters are clothed in formless, drab smocks and forced to attend lessons in cooking, cleaning, and other female duties in a house that has turned into a "wife factory." The girls' spirits, however, are undaunted. They are restless and rebellious and soon find ways to escape, with the oldest sister escaping the house at night to join her boyfriend, all the sisters attending a forbidden football game, and one sister even learning to drive a car. But the plan is to marry off the oldest four girls. The oldest two are duly married (one to the man of her choice, the other to a virtual stranger), while the third sister ultimately kills herself and the younger two escape to Istanbul.

PATRIARCHAL TRADITIONS AND RELIGIOUS LAWS

Imposed Virginity Test

Female virginity prior to marriage is of paramount importance in many countries and reflects patriarchal valuation of familial honor through the preservation of female chastity and purity. In many patriarchal systems, proof of virginity is required before a marriage can proceed. This proof is obtained either by gynecological exam or by a posteriori evidence observed following the consummation of the marriage. In the gynecological exam, a health practitioner looks for an unbroken hymen at the vaginal opening. If the hymen is torn or absent, this is taken as evidence that the female was not a virgin. With reference to marital consummation, the presence of vaginal bleeding after a woman's first intercourse indicates that the hymen was intact and that she was a virgin.

In *Mustang*, the sanctity of virginity is a main theme, and the girls' uncle forces the oldest sisters to undergo virginity tests following their public flirtation with boys. The girls are certified as virgins, and certificates of virginity are issued to the family. Later in the story, one of the sisters marries; following the wedding night, her husband's family members knock on the couple's bedroom door, demanding proof of her virginity: "Show us the sheet!" The newly wed husband is frantic as he strips the bedding, looking for the tell-tale evidence, and beseechs his new wife, "Where is the blood? Where is the blood?" The two are rushed to a medical clinic, where the in-laws explain to the clerk, "We just married our son and the girl didn't bleed."

Arranged Marriage

Arranged marriages are common in Muslim-majority countries (as they are throughout the world). There is considerable variation in how marriages are arranged, but, in many situations, a family elder (male or female) arranges for families of the prospective bride and groom to meet in a private gathering; if both families are in agreement, decisions are made about conditions that are to be included in the marriage contract. These initial meetings may occur in the presence or absence of prospective spouses. In Muslim marriages, Islamic principles make it clear that marriages must be consensual. Several arranged marriages occur in *Mustang* that are organized by the grandmother. The oldest daughter actually arranges to marry her boyfriend, the second oldest daughter reluctantly agrees to marry a man she barely knows, and another daughter refuses to marry and runs away on the day of her marriage ceremony. Only the youngest daughter escapes marriage arrangements—but only for a while.

TRADITIONAL GENDER STEREOTYPES

The female sexual binary of chastity versus impurity (virgin-whore) is portrayed in *Mustang*. The sisters are normal girls, experimenting with their feminine identities and with their sexuality. They flirt with boys, talk about sexual body parts, and pad their bras. They explore sexuality with innocence, fun and curiosity, and they are indeed chaste. Ironically, the adults in the film, in their obsession with the sanctity of virginity, make the girls impure through their doubts and attempts to shame. Upon discovering that the girls were sitting on the shoulders of boys while playing an innocent game in the sea, their uncle calls them whores and their grandmother calls them obscene: "My granddaughters, pleasuring themselves on boys' necks ... you're depraved, you're disgusting ... rubbing your parts on boys' necks." The older girls are forced to take a virginity test, and after the girls return with hospital documents documenting their virginity, the grandmother insists that the test was for their own good. "If ever there was the slightest doubt," she tells them, "you'd never be able to get married."

The sisters in *Mustang* are sexually objectified. The sisters receive clear messages that their value is a function of a sexual body part—an intact hymen—and that males, by their innate nature, desire nothing more than to sexually prey on females. Males, they are told, act without conscience and without morality when it comes to sex. The sisters are imprisoned in their home to protect them from these predators. But, ironically, the real predator is inside. The uncle has sexually abused one of the sisters, who eventually commits suicide. That does not deter him, as he continues his sexual abuse with another sister. It is ironic that the grandmother, who is so shamed by the innocent flirtations of the girls with neighborhood boys, is not troubled by her son's sexual molestations (of which she is aware).

NONTRADITIONAL GENDER ATTRIBUTES

Lale is the hero of this film. She is the youngest sister and has considerable agency. She is inquisitive, rebellious, and stubborn, circumventing the rules that require the sisters to remain indoors. She wants to attend a football game, and she does. She wants to learn how to drive, and she does. She does not want her last remaining sister to marry, and she arranges their escape. At the end, Lale rescues her sister and herself.

VIRGINITY TESTS AND THE HYMEN

In many countries, both Muslim-majority and non–Muslim, women and girls have been subjected to virginity tests to verify their sexual purity. In many instances, the woman's family asks a health practitioner to perform a vaginal examination on the woman to confirm that her hymen is intact. As part of a prenuptial agreement, the family of a prospective husband can request proof of virginity. Upon examination, if the hymen is torn or absent, it is assumed that the female has had sexual intercourse, as the hymen is typically torn in vaginal-penile intercourse, with consequent bleeding.

But this is not always the case, as the hymen can be torn through strenuous physical activity or may never have developed. In older times, the absence of the torn hymen (as detected by lack of vaginal blood after intercourse) was proof that the female was not a virgin on her wedding day; as such, her penalty was severe and could range from ostracism to divorce, and even death.

There are modern procedures to reconstruct a hymen. If a woman's goal is to bleed from engagement in penile intercourse (providing proof that she is virgin), hymen reconstruction surgery is a simple procedure that involves stitching together remnants of a torn hymen. The stitches are not detectable and will dissolve. Or an artificial hymen can be purchased on the Internet. The artificial hymen (also known as a "Chinese hymen" or "fake hymen") is a small plastic device that is inserted in the vagina. On contact with a penis, it releases a liquid that looks like blood.

Watchtower (Gözetleme Kulesi)

Year: 2012; *Director:* Pelin Esmer; *Cast:* Seher (Nilay Erdönmez)—woman in her 20s; Nihat (Olgun Simsek)—man in his 30s; *Length:* 100 minutes; *Setting:* rural Turkey; working class

Synopsis

Watchtower relates the parallel stories of two people isolated in sorrow from trauma they have experienced. Nihat, a 30-something-year-old man, has taken a job as fire guard in a watchtower situated in the forests of Turkey. He lives alone in the remote tower with infrequent radio contact from his supervisor—his only contact with the outside world. The job provides the solitude that Nihat needs to cope with the deaths of his wife and son in an auto accident for which he feels responsible. He has cut himself off from humanity. The grief and guilt are too intense, and the possibility of connecting to another human is unthinkable.

Seher, a young woman in her 20s, has left her university studies and her uncle's home to take a job as a hostess for a bus company that is located in the same area as Nihat's watchtower. Like Nihat, she lives alone in a small room adjacent to the bus depot and adjoining café, and she, too, is in need of solitude. She is unmarried and pregnant, a victim of rape by her uncle. She is cut off from humanity in her rage against the circumstances that brought her to this remote bus stop seeking solitude. Seher hides her pregnancy with oversized clothing and tells no one of her condition or the rape. She spends each day working on the bus or serving customers at the café and returns each night to the seclusion of her room, awaiting the birth of the child.

Nihat, on occasion, dines at the café, where he encounters Seher, about whom he is curious. On a day that he is at the café, he observes her rushing out of the diner. Later, he observes her crossing the café's lot with a bundle in her arms. She has given birth (unassisted) in a storeroom and abandons the infant in a deserted field. Soon after, Nihat finds her on a highway, stumbling in pain with blood on her clothes. He provides her with shelter in the watchtower and returns for the baby. They are at cross-purposes: she wants to rid herself of her uncle's sin, and he wants to redeem himself by keeping this infant alive. The two come to a sort of tacit understanding. Seher will reluctantly and perfunctorily perform the duties needed to keep the infant alive, and Nihat will provide shelter and sustenance for both of them.

At the beginning of their tenuous relationship, she is defiant and remote, while he is judgmental. However, slowly and subtly, the dynamics of their relationship begin to change. Nihat starts to see Seher as a wounded individual in need of solace, and she is becoming more aware of the solidness and kindness of this quiet man. However, the ending promises no assured resolution to the relationship between them. Whether Nihat can resolve his grief and allow himself to fully connect with another is unknown. Whether Seher can accept the tragedy in her life and realize the humanity of Nihat is equally unknown.

TRADITIONAL GENDER STEREOTYPES

The roles prescribed to mothers and fathers in patriarchal societies are precise. Mothers are assigned to the private sphere, responsible for the household and the care of children. In some societies, purdah is observed, and women are confined to their homes, rarely being allowed to go out in public. Fathers, as heads of the household, are responsible for the financial maintenance of their families and for important family decisions. Although mothers are caretakers, father are the legal guardians of their children in some Muslim-majority countries. Parents who shirk their responsibilities to their children are censured, though there is greater tolerance for fathers than for mothers who deviate from parental responsibilities. After all, the father has competing demands on his time due to the necessity of his agency in the world.

NONTRADITIONAL GENDER ATTRIBUTES

The gendered stereotypes of feminine helplessness and masculine callousness are not found in *Watchtower*. Seher is not a helpless woman. In response to her rape and subsequent pregnancy, she makes choices. Knowing that her family would be shamed, she realizes that there is no one she can turn to for help and that she can only rely on herself. She leaves the university and her uncle's home and finds a job and a place to live while waiting out the pregnancy. She delivers the infant alone and chooses to abandon it. Nihat is the nurturing character in this film. He rescues the infant and Seher and provides both with shelter. He is instrumental in the infant's care, bathing and diapering him and persuading Seher to feed him. He is protective of both of them.

Fate (Yazgi)

Year: 2001; *Director:* Zeki Demirkubuz; *Cast:* Musa (Serdar Orçin)—man in his mid–20s; Necati (Engin Günaydın)—man in his 30s; *Length:* 119 minutes; *Setting:* large urban city in Turkey; middle class

SYNOPSIS

In the opening scenes, Musa, who shares an apartment with his elderly mother, is preparing to leave for work. The mother is usually up and fixing his breakfast, but not this day. Musa appears unconcerned and continues on to his job as a customs clerk. He returns home at the end of a long day and discovers the next morning that his mother is dead. Her death doesn't affect him—he loves her, he says, and he's glad she's dead. His only concern is that he lacks the know-how required to organize a funeral. Musa's two co-workers, his boss, and his neighbor Necati (a thuggish man in his 30s) sympathize with him, but he is indifferent. The female co-worker, whom Musa barely knows, asks him to marry her, so he does. Necati wants Musa to carry his gun, so he does. Musa's boss and others accuse him of murdering the boss' wife and children, and he makes no attempt to defend himself after his arrest. Even in prison, upon learning that the judiciary has sentenced him to death, he is undisturbed. Musa, modeled on Camus' protagonist in *The Stranger*, has no interiority, no curiosity, no emotionality. He is an apatheist. Fate is fate, and events will happen regardless of one's agency. Existence is meaninglessness.

TRADITIONAL GENDER STEREOTYPES

Physical aggression, force, and contempt are linked to conceptualizations of masculinity in patriarchal societies. One theme in *Fate* is the contempt that men have for women, which is exemplified by the aggression that Musa, his neighbor Necati, and Musa's boss (the customs agent) display. Necati is overly aggressive in his response about a woman whom he believes has betrayed him. He is vulgar and threatening when he talks to Musa about her betrayal: "I smashed her face in and told her she was a whore, and then I left. Beating her up hasn't stopped me from being angry.... I'll bring her home and fuck the bitch and just as she's about to come I'll pull out and spit in her mouth and throw her out." The customs agent is engaged in a clandestine affair and callously treats his wife with disdain when she questions his late nights and furtive phone calls. His wife threatens to leave him, and, in a fit of rage, he murders her and his children. Musa's aggression toward his own wife is more passive and perhaps the most destructive of all. In his non-acknowledgment of her (and later their child), he negates her existence. She is simply an object in his apartment and in his bed—it really could be anyone or no one.

COMPULSIVE MASCULINITY

In patriarchal societies, males are socialized for compulsive masculinity, a term used to encapsulate the hostility that males direct toward females.[13] Males, at young ages, learn that attributes deemed by society to be feminine are inferior and shameful; as a defense against their own feminine attributes, boys compulsively adopt masculine traits in opposition to the traits they perceive as female ones. Some believe that compulsive masculinity stems from a fear of women and that this fear results in misogyny and oppression of women. Men can also be victims of their own dominance schema. As Pierre Bourdieu summarizes:

> Manliness must be validated by other men, in its reality as actual or potential violence, and certified by recognition of membership of the group of "real men" ... Manliness, it can be seen, is an eminently relational notion, constructed in front of and for other men and against femininity, in a kind of fear of the female, firstly in oneself.... If women, subjected to a labour of socialization which tends to diminish and deny them, learn the negative virtues of self-denial, resignation and silence, men are also prisoners, and insidiously victims, of the dominant representation.[14]

10

Summary

Muslim-majority countries have their own distinctive cultural identities, and each differs historically, linguistically, and politically. Yet Muslim nations have an important point of commonality in their shared Islamic faith and their embrace of patriarchal custom as established in tradition and in law. Are there commonalities shared by/in Muslim-majority countries regarding gender constructions that transcend a national cultural distinctiveness? An examination of the cinematic output from the countries reviewed in this filmography reveals commonalities with reference to traditional gender stereotypes, prescribed gender roles, and gendered violence.

GENDER AND PATRIARCHY IN FILM

With reference to traditional gender stereotypes, a prevalent binary discovered in these films depicted males as dominant and females as subordinate. Regardless of the country of origin, or socioeconomic status, age, and occupational status of characters, females complied (or were forced to comply) with patriarchal standards that empowered male domination. Female subjugation to male dominance and control was especially pronounced in rural areas. The women residing in rural communities of Afghanistan, Iran, Turkey, Kurdistan, and Bangladesh were much alike. They were silent, obedient, hard working, self-sacrificial, chaste, and in many ways slaves of men who enforced their adherence to traditional feminine roles that disadvantaged them and advantaged men.

Within the gendered binary of male dominance–female subjugation, many female film characters rebelled against their oppression. But only a few of those characters who attempted to break the bonds of patriarchy succeeded at the end. The female protagonists of *Secret Ballot, Border Café, Enough!, Donya, Unwanted Woman, Cairo 678,* and *Mustang* sought empowerment and gained it, often at the expense of males. These females were in the minority, however, as many others suffered adverse consequences in response to their rebellion, some of them quite severe. In films from Afghanistan, female characters experienced threats of honor killing, incarceration, and forced abortion as a result of their transgressions against hegemonic masculine traditions. Pakistani female characters who transgressed were kidnapped, murdered by hired gunmen, executed by the state, or driven to commit suicide. Turkish females experienced forced marriage, murder, threats of honor killing, and suicide. In Egyptian films, women who challenged male control faced female genital mutilation/cutting, physical and sexual assault, and murder.

Many contemporary Iranian films appeared ambivalent about women's attempt to discard patriarchal norms. For most of the films, female characters who stepped outside the normative boundaries were punished or had their fates left unresolved. Of the 18 Iranian films analyzed in this filmography, nine female characters violated a patriarchal tradition or religious law and suffered for it at the end of the narrative. These transgressive characters experienced death by murder or suicide, paralysis, loss of children, and incarceration. The fates of other Iranian women who rebelled were ambiguous. In *Daughters of the Sun*, for example, the female protagonist walks slowly away following her act of arson at the film's conclusion. Though she has liberated herself from enslavement, it is unclear what will happen to her. As another example, the woman in *My Tehran for Sale* has experienced personal loss and rejection. At the conclusion, she wanders the streets of Tehran, lost and alienated. In contemporary Iranian films, it seems, the happy ending is absent.

It has been said that women are often their own worst enemies, and this trope is apparent in many of the films. In films from Afghanistan, Turkey, Pakistan, and Iran, female characters actively participated in their own subordination and devaluation. These women appeared to have internalized the culture of patriarchy and accepted paternalistic sentiments regarding their supposedly inferior capabilities and their duty to obey and to serve men. This concept is exemplified in the Turkish film *Bliss*, in which the young village girl, Meryem, is blamed for her rape and sentenced to die to protect the honor of the village and her family. The women villagers are complicit with this patriarchal tradition and encourage the girl, now considered impure, to kill herself. The motive for their complicity is unclear. Have these women internalized patriarchal beliefs that a female's sexual impurity, regardless of the cause, threatens the natural order of the community and must be "corrected"? Do these women identify with the power of masculine hegemony as a defense against their own powerlessness? Are they simply jealous of Meryem's youth and beauty? Whatever the motive, destroying the solidarity among women that should naturally exist is perhaps one of the greatest sins of patriarchy.

FEMALE SEXUALITY IN FILM

Female sexuality was a prominent theme of several films, and many conveyed the message that female sexuality is strong and dangerous and therefore must be restrained. Methods of restraint illustrated in these films range from veiling to purdah (house seclusion) to female genital mutilation/cutting. Only a handful of films portrayed females as sexual entities with their own agency. *Patience Stone*, *Viva Laldjérie*, and *Dunia* were notable in this regard. The Egyptian and Algerian films were the most explicit in their frank depictions of sexual topics, while Iranian women (for the most part) were desexualized—undoubtedly a function of state censorship. It is interesting to note how many contemporary films featured topics related to the hymen.

MALES AND AGGRESSION AND GENDERED VIOLENCE IN FILM

This filmography examined the concept of "masculine compulsivity," which refers to the need of males in patriarchal societies to distinguish themselves from females, who are considered weak, powerless, and vulnerable. Males are thus compelled (whether innately or through learning) to adopt traits and engage in behaviors that are opposite to feminine traits and behaviors. Aggression is a masculine behavior that is oppositional to feminine empathy and nurturance, and aggression against women is a signifier of masculinity.

Scholars have commented on the gender-based violence that occurs in Muslim-majority countries. Zahia Smail Salhi, in an analysis of MENA (Middle East and North African) countries, remarks on the experience of Muslim women who reside in these countries:

> Women experience numerous if not all forms of gender-based violence at various levels and with varied intensity from one country to another. The spectrum of violence fluctuates from female foeticide and infanticide to segregation against female girls in terms of food and access to health and education, to female genital mutilation which in some countries amount to infibulations, forced marriages ... child abuse and incest, sexual harassment at school, at work and in the street, intimidation in the streets and at work, acid attacks in the street, domestic violence, rape (including gang rape and marital rape) and femicide in the form of honor killing and terrorist/Islamist femicide."[1]

Salhi connects gendered violence with entrenched patriarchal traditions and with the proliferation of extremist Islamist ideology in many Muslim-majority countries. Women, she claims, live in fear from early childhood to the end of their lives and experience constant gender inequality and oppression, which she attributes in part to the discriminatory legal codes and legislative processes that have been fostered by Islamist ideology.

Is Salhi's summation of gendered violence in MENA countries reflected in the films analyzed in this filmography? An analysis of the gender themes found in contemporary films supports her conclusions. With the exception of Bangladesh (with only three films), all the countries examined here had films that featured gendered violence, with males primarily serving as the aggressors. Physical aggression, sexual aggression, or institutionalized aggression were depicted. Females in these films experienced genital mutilation/cutting, forced marriage, child abuse and incest, street sexual harassment, domestic violence, incarceration for adultery, honor killing, gang rape and marital rape. Females also experienced physical aggression in the form of murder, beatings, punching, and slapping. In only four films, women were depicted as aggressors against men (*The Last Supper, Cairo 678, Bol,* and *Scheherazade, Tell Me a Story*).

Given findings that Muslim females experience gender oppression and gender-based inequality both cinematically and in real life, two important questions are raised. The first concerns the relative contributions of patriarchy and religion to the gender oppression and gendered violence that affect females in many Muslim-majority countries. As Farhad Kazemi elaborates:

> Broadly speaking, two related gender issues exacerbate the problem: one is attitudinal and based on beliefs and values, the other relates to legal doctrines. The attitudinal component concerns the prevalence in much of the Middle East of certain patriarchal values, learned through the socialization experience, on women and gender roles. The legal dimension pertains to the essentially discriminatory nature of Islamic personal status laws and the criminal code when applied to women. The combination of these two factors—patriarchal attitudes and legal strictures—places women in a highly disadvantaged position in the social order. Clearly, many Islamic countries do not apply either the full Islamic criminal code or the complete version of personal state laws to their citizens. The intensity of patriarchal values also varies both within one country and from one Islamic society to another. Nonetheless, the two themes of patriarchy and legal discrimination continue to remain central to the debate on Islam and gender.[2]

A second question concerns filmmakers' motivation in portraying gendered dominance and violence. Is the purpose to tell a story of women's victimization and suffering that mirrors the experienced reality of the country of origin? Or is it to tell a story that will appeal to an audience, including viewers in the West who might expect such fare? While discussions of these issues are beyond the scope of this book, it is hoped that these findings will spur further analysis, investigation, and discussion of the influence of patriarchy and religion on gender and gender relationships.

FILM COMPARISONS

Films from Iran

Some of the issues illustrated in Iranian films concerned temporary marriage, the imposition of religiously dictated dress code for females, gender segregation in public, and obsession with female hair. Hair represents a female's sexual identity, and in Iran, the modest female must hide her femininity. In the Iranian films, themes of obligatory veiling (*The Day I Became a Woman*), forced cutting of hair as punishment (*Under the Skin of the City*) or for economic gain (*Daughters of the Sun*), and concern for female propriety (*Born Under Libra*) are observed.

Iranian films often conclude with an ambiguous ending. Those viewers raised on the movies of Hollywood might find these endings frustrating. Although in Hollywood a big-budget film's narrative will usually wrap up with a satisfying ending, in Iran there is frequently no neat resolution. This style may reflect the influence of the famed Iranian director Abbas Kiarostami, who favored an open-ended, unresolved plot line to encourage the viewer to complete the story.

Films from Bangladesh, Iraq and Pakistan

Relative to other countries included in this filmography, many Bangladeshi, Iraqi, and Pakistani films were not included, as they were not available in the U.S. market. It may be that films from these countries have not yet garnered the international attention required to secure the necessary distribution funds for placement in Western markets. In the case of Iraq, as political upheaval and instability continue, film production will remain difficult and challenging. In Pakistan, the movie industry was shut down for some 40 years due in part to Islamization and censorship laws. Film production has been revived in contemporary Pakistan, but output is sparse in comparison to other Muslim-majority countries such as Iran. None of the three Bangladeshi films reviewed in this study were available for purchase or rental. They were instead accessed online (with English subtitles) through YouTube.

Films from Afghanistan

The Afghanistan films included in this filmography painted a picture of two distinct Afghanistans, post–Taliban rule. One Afghanistan featured modern, urban settings and showed people on busy commercial streets with current technology and Western clothing. The other Afghanistan was exceedingly primitive and impoverished, with settings in desolate, rural locales.

Films from Turkey

Gönül Dönmez-Colin, in her analysis of Turkish films, notes that gender relationships are stark and brutal and that male characters are self-absorbed and alienated from themselves.[3] The films from Turkey analyzed in this filmography conformed to her analysis. Female characters were portrayed as victims of male frustration and aggression. One character was raped and later threatened with honor killing, one was murdered for protesting her husband's affair, another was beaten for insulting male pride, and others were victims of incest.

Chapter Notes

Introduction

1. Lina Khatib, *Filming the Modern Middle East* (London: I. B. Tauris, 2006).

2. Viola Shafik, *Arab Cinema*, revised edition (Cairo: American University in Cairo Press, 2007).

3. One criteria for selection of films was a release date of around 2000 or later. This date is approximate as the production date, distribution date, and release date of a film to an international market can vary by a few years. As an example, although *Children of Heaven* was released in 1999 to the U.S. market, it was released in 2000 to certain European markets and was included in the filmography. In the event of these release date variations, an effort was made to select films with only minor date discrepancies.

4. Valentine M. Moghadam, "Patriarchy in Transition: Women and the Changing Family in the Middle East," *Journal of Comparative Family Studies* 35, no. 2 (2004): 137–62.

5. John C. Caldwell, *Theory of Fertility Decline* (London: Academic Press, 1982); Deniz Kandiyoti, "Bargaining with Patriarchy," *Gender and Society* 2, no. 3 (1988): 274–90.

6. Moghadam, "Patriarchy in Transition."

7. *Ibid.*

8. Andrea Büchler, and Christina Schlatter, "Marriage Age in Islamic and Contemporary Muslim Family Laws: A Comparative Survey," *Electronic Journal of Islamic and Middle Eastern Law* 1 (2013): 37–74.

9. Wael B. Hallaq, *An Introduction to Islamic Law* (Cambridge: Cambridge University Press, 2009).

10. Jan Michiel Otto, ed., *Sharia Incorporated* (Amsterdam: Leiden University Press, 2010).

11. Najma Chowdhury, and Barbara Nelson, "1994 Redefining Politics: Patterns of Women's Political Engagement from a Global Perspective," in *Women and Politics Worldwide*, edited by Barbara Nelson and Najma Chowdhury (New Haven, CT: Yale University Press, 1994).

12. Irshaad Hussain, "The Hermeneutics of Takfir," *Islam from Inside* (February 2002), http://www.islamfrominside.com/Pages/Articles/Hermeneutics%20of%20takfir.html.

13. Moghadam, "Patriarchy in Transition."

14. Mariam Al-Attar, "Women and Violence in Light of an Islamic Normative Ethical Theory," in *Gender and Violence in Islamic Countries*, edited by Zahia Salhi (London: I. B. Tauris, 2013), 65–74.

15. Mazna Hussain, "'Take My Riches, Give Me Justice': A Contextual Analysis of Pakistan's Honor Crimes Legislation," *Harvard Journal of Law & Gender* 29, no. 1 (2006): 223–46.

16. United Nations General Assembly, "Convention on the Elimination of All Forms of Discrimination Against Women," *United Nations, Treaty Series 1249* (December 18, 1979), http://www.refworld.org/docid/3ae6b3970.html.

Chapter 1

1. UN General Assembly, *Convention on the Elimination of All Forms of Discrimination against Women*, 18 December 1979, A/RES/34/180, http://www.refworld.org/docid/3b00f2244.html.

2. The following paragraphs are taken from the website of the Office of the United Nations High Commissioner for Human Rights (http://www.ohchr.org/EN/ProfessionalInterest/Pages/CEDAW.aspx).

Chapter 2

1. *The World Factbook 2013–14* (Washington, D.C.: Central Intelligence Agency, 2014), https://www.cia.gov/library/publications/the-world-factbook/index.html.

2. *Constitution of Afghanistan* [Afghanistan] (January 3, 2004), http://www.refworld.org/docid/404d8a594.html.

3. International Lesbian, Gay, Bisexual, Trans and Intersex Association, *State Sponsored Homophobia 2016: A World Survey of Sexual Orientation Laws: Criminalization, Protection and Recognition* (Geneva: ILGA, May 2016), http://ilga.org/downloads/02_ILGA_State_Sponsored_Homophobia_2016_ENG_WEB_150516.pdf.

4. Afghanistan Legal Education Project (ALEP), Stanford Law School (2011), https://law.stanford.edu/alep/#slsnav-publications.

5. *Max Planck Manual on Family Law in Afghanistan*, Max Planck Institute for Comparative Public Law (2012), http://www.mpipriv.de/files/pdf3/max_planck_manual_on_afghan_family_law_english.pdf.

6. Islamic Republic of Afghanistan Ministries of Women's Affairs, *First Report on the Implementation of the Elimination of Violence Against Women (EVAW) Law in Afghanistan* (January 2014), http://mowa.gov.af/Content/files/EVAW%20Law%20Report_Final_English_17%20%20March%202014.PDF, 8–9.

7. Mark Graham, *Afghanistan in the Cinema* (Urbana: University of Illinois Press, 2010).

8. "List of Types of Sartorial Hijab—Women," http://www.liquisearch.com/list_of_types_of_sartorial_hijab/women.

9. Ann Black, Hossein Esmaeili, and Nadirsyah Hosen, *Modern Perspectives on Islamic Law* (Cheltenham, UK: Edward Elgar, 2013).

10. *Ibid.*

11. Federico García Lorca, "Lament for Ignacio Sanchez Mejias," *Great Famous Poets*, http://greatfamouspoets.blogspot.com/2009/01/lorca.html#lamentfor.

12. Abdullahi A. An-Na'im, ed., *Islamic Family Law in a Changing World: A Global Resource Book* (London: Zed Books, 2002).

13. *Ibid.*

14. Black, et al., *Modern Perspectives on Islamic Law*.

15. United Nations Office on Drugs and Crime, *Afghanistan: Female Prisoners and Their Social Reintegration* (New York: UNODC, 2007), http://www.unodc.org/pdf/criminal_justice/Afghan_women_prison_web.pdf.

16. Human Rights Watch, "Afghanistan: End 'Moral Crimes' Charges, 'Virginity' Tests," May 25, 2016, https://www.hrw.org/news/2016/05/25/afghanistan-end-moral-crimes-charges-virginity-tests.

Chapter 3

1. Draft Amendment to the Algerian Constitution adopted February 3, 2016 (in French), http://www.constitutionnet.org/vl/item/draft-amendment-algerian-constitution-adopted-3-feb-2016-french.

2. Constitution of the People's Democratic Republic of Algeria, 1989 (amended by the constitutional revision of 1996), http://confinder.richmond.edu/admin/docs/local_algeria. pdf.

3. International Lesbian, Gay, Bisexual, Trans and Intersex Association, *State Sponsored Homophobia 2016: A World Survey of Sexual Orientation Laws: Criminalization, Protection and Recognition* (Geneva: ILGA, May 2016), http://ilga.org/downloads/02_ILGA_State_ Sponsored_Homophobia_2016_ENG_WEB_150516.pdf.

4. Meredeth Turshen, "Militarism and Islamism in Algeria," *Journal of Asian and African Studies* 39, no. 1 (2004): 119–32.

5. Freedom House, "Women's Rights in the Middle East and North Africa—Algeria," October 14, 2005, http://www.refworld.org/docid/47387b6a0.html.

6. Nafeez Mosaddeq Ahmed, "Algeria and the Paradox of Democracy: The 1992 Coup, Its Consequences and the Contemporary Crisis," *Media Monitors Network*, May 11, 2001, http://www.mediamonitors.net/mosaddeq4.html.

Chapter 4

1. *The World Factbook 2013–14* (Washington, D.C.: Central Intelligence Agency, 2014), https://www.cia.gov/library/publications/the-world-factbook/index.html.

2. *Constitution of the People's Republic of Bangladesh* [Bangladesh] (November 4, 1972), http://www.refworld.org/docid/3ae6b5684.html.

3. United Nations Population Division, Department of Economic and Social Affairs, *Abortion Policies: A Global View* (2002), http://www.un.org/esa/population/publications/ abortion/index.htm.

4. International Lesbian, Gay, Bisexual, Trans and Intersex Association, *State Sponsored Homophobia 2016: A World Survey of Sexual Orientation Laws: Criminalization, Protection and Recognition* (Geneva: ILGA, May 2016), http://ilga.org/downloads/02_ILGA_State_ Sponsored_Homophobia_2016_ENG_WEB_150516.pdf.

5. United Nations Children's Fund, Ending Child Marriage: Progress and prospects, UNICEF, New York, 2014, https://www.unicef.org/media/files/Child_Marriage_Report_7_ 17_LR..pdf.

6. Nathaniel Adams, "Religion and Women's Empowerment in Bangladesh," Occasional Paper, Berkley Center for Religion, Peace and World Affairs (December 2015), https://s3.amazon aws.com/berkley-center/151215WFDDReligionandWomensEmpowermentinBangladesh.pdf.

7. Avon Global Center for Women and Justice at Cornell Law School and the New York City Bar Association, "Combating Acid Violence in Bangladesh, India, and Cambodia" (2011), http://www.ohchr.org/Documents/HRBodies/CEDAW/HarmfulPractices/AvonGlobalCenter forWomenandJustice.pdf.

8. Immigration and Refugee Board of Canada, "Bangladesh: Domestic Violence, including Legislation, State Protection, and Services Available to Victims" (2007–July 2011) [BGD-103807.E], http://www.ecoi.net/local_link/203055/308008_en.html.

9. Adams, "Religion and Women's Empowerment in Bangladesh."

Chapter 5

1. *The World Factbook 2013–14* (Washington, D.C.: Central Intelligence Agency, 2014), https://www.cia.gov/library/publications/the-world-factbook/index.html.

2. *Constitution of the Arab Republic of Egypt* [Egypt] (January 18, 2014), http://www. refworld.org/docid/3ae6b5368.html.

3. International Lesbian, Gay, Bisexual, Trans and Intersex Association, *State Sponsored Homophobia 2016: A World Survey of Sexual Orientation Laws: Criminalization, Protection*

and Recognition (Geneva: ILGA, May 2016), http://ilga.org/downloads/02_ILGA_State_Sponsored_Homophobia_2016_ENG_WEB_150516.pdf.

4. "Muslim Publics Divided on Hamas and Hezbollah," Pew Research Center, Washington, D.C., December 2, 2010, http://www.pewglobal.org/2010/12/02/muslims-around-the-world-divided-on-hamas-and-hezbollah/.

5. Rasha Hassan, Komsan Nehad and Aliyaa Shoukry, "Clouds in Egypt's Sky: Sexual Harassment: From Verbal Harassment to Rape," Egyptian Center for Women's Rights (2008), http://harassmap.org/en/wp-content/uploads/2013/03/ECWR-report.pdf.

6. Seif El Mashad, "The Moral Epidemic of Egypt: 99% of Women Are Sexually Harassed," Egyptian Streets, March 5, 2015, http://egyptianstreets.com/2015/03/05/the-moral-epidemic-of-egypt-99-of-women-are-sexually-harassed/.

7. Tahmina Islam, "Causes and Consequences of Eve-teasing in Urban Bangladesh: An Empirical Study," *SUST Studies* 15, no. 1 (2012): 10–20.

8. Fatima Mareah Peoples, "Street Harassment in Cairo: A Symptom of Disintegrating Social Structures," *African Anthropologist* 15, nos. 1 and 2 (2008): 1–20.

9. Fatima Mernissi, *The Veil and the Male Elite: A Feminist Interpretation of Women's Rights in Islam* (New York: Addison-Wesley, 1991).

10. UNICEF, "Fresh Progress toward the Elimination of Female Genital Mutilation and Cutting in Egypt," July 2, 2007, https://www.unicef.org/media/media_40168.html.

11. Fatma El-Zanaty, and Ann Way, *Egypt Demographic and Health Survey 2005* (Cairo, Egypt: Ministry of Health and Population, National Population Council, El-Zanaty and Associates, and ORC Macro, 2006).

12. Thomas von der Osten-Sacken and Thomas Uwer, "Is Female Genital Mutilation an Islamic Problem?" *Middle East Quarterly* 14, no. 1 (2007): 29–36.

13. World Health Organization, "Female Genital Mutilation," February 2016, http://www.who.int/mediacentre/factsheets/fs241/en/.

14. United Nations Population Fund, "Female Genital Mutilation (FGM) Frequently Asked Questions," December 2015, http://www.unfpa.org/resources/female-genital-mutilation-fgm-frequently-asked-questions.

15. Kecia Ali, *Sexual Ethics and Islam* (London: Oneworld, 2016).

16. Sami Aldeeb, "To Mutilate in the Name of Jehovah or Allah: Legitimization of Male and Female Circumcision," *Medicine and Law* 13 (1994): 575–622.

17. El-Zanaty and Way, *Egypt Demographic and Health Survey.*

18. International Lesbian, Gay, Bisexual, Trans and Intersex Association, *State Sponsored Homophobia 2016: A World Survey of Sexual Orientation Laws: Criminalization, Protection and Recognition* (Geneva: ILGA, May 2016), http://ilga.org/downloads/02_ILGA_State_Sponsored_Homophobia_2016_ENG_WEB_150516.pdf.

Chapter 6

1. *The World Factbook 2013–14* (Washington, D.C.: Central Intelligence Agency, 2014), https://www.cia.gov/library/publications/the-world-factbook/index.html.

2. *Constitution of the Islamic Republic of Iran* (October 24, 1979), http://www.refworld.org/docid/3ae6b56710.html.

3. Mohammad Hossein Nayyeri, "Gender Inequality and Discrimination: The Case of Iranian Women," Iran Human Rights Documentation Center (2013), http://iranhrdc.org/english/publications/legal-commentary/1000000261-gender-inequality-and-discrimination-the-case-of-iranian-women.html.

4. International Lesbian, Gay, Bisexual, Trans and Intersex Association, *State Sponsored Homophobia 2016: A World Survey of Sexual Orientation Laws: Criminalization, Protection and Recognition* (Geneva: ILGA, May 2016), http://ilga.org/downloads/02_ILGA_State_Sponsored_Homophobia_2016_ENG_WEB_150516.pdf.

5. Nayyeri, "Gender Inequality and Discrimination."

6. Islamic Penal Code of Iran, Corpus of Laws, http://corpus.learningpartnership.org/?s=islamic+penal+code&Submit.x=0&Submit.y=0.

7. Mohammad Hossein Nayyeri, "New Islamic Penal Code of the Islamic Republic of Iran: An Overview," Human Rights in Iran Unit, March 13, 2012, https://www.essex.ac.uk/hri/documents/HRIU_Research_Paper-IRI_Criminal_Code-Overview.pdf.

8. Rollo Romig, "Blood Money: Crime and Punishment in 'A Separation,'" *New Yorker*, February 24, 2012, http://www.newyorker.com/culture/culture-desk/blood-money-crime-and-punishment-in-a-separation.

9. *Ibid.*

10. United Nations Population Division, Department of Economic and Social Affairs, *Abortion Policies: A Global View* (2002), http://www.un.org/esa/population/publications/abortion/index.htm.

11. Mohammad Hossein Nayyeri, "Gender Inequality and Discrimination: The Case of Iranian Women," Iran Human Rights Documentation Center (2013), http://iranhrdc.org/english/publications/legal-commentary/1000000261-gender-inequality-and-discrimination-the-case-of-iranian-women.html.

12. *Ibid.*

13. *Ibid.*

14. Ann Black, Hossein Esmaeili, and Nadirsyah Hosen, *Modern Perspectives on Islamic Law* (Cheltenham, UK: Edward Elgar, 2013).

15. *Ibid.*, 123.

16. Kecia Ali, "Marriage, Family, and Sexual Ethics," in *The Islamic World*, edited by Andrew Rippin (London: Routledge, 2008).

17. Saeid Golkar, "Manipulated Society: Paralyzing the Masses in Post-Revolutionary Iran," *International Journal of Politics, Culture, and Society* 29 (2016): 135–55.

18. Nayyeri, "Gender Inequality and Discrimination."

19. Golkar, "Manipulated Society."

20. Kamran Rastegar, "Film Studies," in *Women and Islamic Cultures*, edited by Suad Joseph (Boston: Brill, 2013).

21. Gönül Dönmez-Colin, "Cinema," in *The Islamic World*, edited by Andrew Rippin (London: Routledge, 2008), 527–48.

22. Black, et al., *Modern Perspectives on Islamic Law*.

23. Ashraf Zahedi, "Contested Meaning of the Veil and Political Ideologies of Iranian Regimes," *Journal of Middle East Women's Studies* 3, no. 3 (2007): 92.

24. *Ibid.*

25. Meredith Katherine Winn, "Women in Higher Education in Iran: How the Islamic Revolution Contributed to an Increase in Female Enrollment," *Global Tides* 10 (2016).

26. Najmeh Moradiyan Rizi, "Iranian Women, Iranian Cinema: Negotiating with Ideology and Tradition," *Journal of Religion & Film* 19, no. 1 (2015).

27. Nayyeri, "Gender Inequality and Discrimination."

28. Ziba Mir-Hosseini, *Interpreting Divorce Laws in Islam* (Copenhagen: DJOF Publishing, 2012).

29. S.M. Mousavi, and A. Eshagian, "Wife Abuse in Esfahan, Islamic Republic of Iran East," *Mediterranean Health Journal* 11, no. 5–6 (2005).

30. Robert D. Hansar, "Cross-Cultural Examination of Domestic Violence in China and Pakistan," in *Encyclopedia of Domestic Violence*, edited by Nicky Ali Jackson (London: Routledge, 2007), 211.

31. Ali Shaikh, "Is Domestic Violence Endemic in Pakistan? Perspective from Pakistani Wives," *Pakistan Journal of Medical Sciences* 19, no. 1 (2003): 23–28.

32. National Institute of Population Studies (Pakistan) and ICF International, *Pakistan Demographic and Health Survey 2012–13* (Calverton, MD: National Institute of Population Studies and ICF International, 2013), https://dhsprogram.com/pubs/pdf/FR290/FR290.pdf.

33. Koustuv Dalal, Fazlur Rahman, and Bjarne Jansson, "Wife Abuse in Rural Bangladesh," *Journal of Biosocial Science* 41 (2009): 561–73.

34. Canan Aslan-Akman, and Fatma Tutuncu, "The Struggle Against Male Violence," in *Gender and Violence in Islamic Countries*, edited by Zahia Smail Salhi (London: I. B. Tauris, 2013), 88.

35. Ayşe Gül Altınay, and Yeşim Arat, *Violence Against Women in Turkey: A Nationwide Survey* (Istanbul: Punto, 2009), http://research.sabanciuniv.edu/11418/1/Violence_Against_ Women_in_Turkey.pdf.

36. Fatma El-Zanaty and Ann Way, *Egypt Demographic and Health Survey 2005* (Cairo, Egypt: Ministry of Health and Population, National Population Council, El-Zanaty and Associates, and ORC Macro, 2006).

37. Human Rights Watch, "'I Had to Run Away': The Imprisonment of Women and Girls for 'Moral Crimes' in Afghanistan" (2012), https://www.hrw.org/sites/default/files/reports/ afghanistan0312webwcover_0.pdf.

38. "An-Nisa, 34" (translated by Abdullah Yusuf Ali), Wikipedia, https://en.wikipedia. org/wiki/An-Nisa,_34.

39 Zahia Smail Salhi, ed., *Gender and Violence in Islamic Countries* (London: I. B. Tauris, 2013), 35–36.

Chapter 7

1. *The World Factbook 2013–14* (Washington, D.C.: Central Intelligence Agency, 2014), https://www.cia.gov/library/publications/the-world-factbook/index.html.

2. *Constitution of the Republic of Iraq* [Iraq] (October 15, 2005), http://www.refworld. org/docid/454f50804.html.

3. International Lesbian, Gay, Bisexual, Trans and Intersex Association, *State Sponsored Homophobia 2016: A World Survey of Sexual Orientation Laws: Criminalization, Protection and Recognition* (Geneva: ILGA, May 2016), http://ilga.org/downloads/02_ILGA_State_ Sponsored_Homophobia_2016_ENG_WEB_150516.pdf.

4. OECD Development Centre, "Social Institutions and Gender Index: Iraq," http:// www.genderindex.org/country/iraq.

5. *Iraq: Penal Code* [Iraq], No. 111 of 1969 (July 1969), http://www.refworld.org/docid/ 452524304.html.

6. Najmeh Moradiyan Rizi, "Iranian Women, Iranian Cinema: Negotiating with Ideology and Tradition," *Journal of Religion & Film* 19, no. 1 (2015).

7 Parmis Mozafari, "Still Singing: Female Singers in Contemporary Iran," *The Middle East in London* 12, no. 2 (2016): 7–8.

8. "1988: Thousands Die in Halabja Gas Attack," BBC, March 16, 1988, http://news. bbc.co.uk/onthisday/hi/dates/stories/march/16/newsid_4304000/4304853.stm.

9. Kecia Ali, "Marriage, Family, and Sexual Ethics," in *The Islamic World*, edited by Andrew Rippin (London: Routledge, 2008), 613.

10. Emily L. Thompson, and F. Soniya Yunus, "Choice of Laws or Choice of Culture: How Western Nations Treat the Islamic Marriage Contract in Domestic Courts," *Wisconsin International Law Journal* 25, no. 2 (2007): 367–68.

Chapter 8

1. *The World Factbook 2013–14* (Washington, D.C.: Central Intelligence Agency, 2014), https://www.cia.gov/library/publications/the-world-factbook/index.html.

2. *Constitution of the Islamic Republic of Pakistan* [Pakistan] (April 10, 1973), http:// www.refworld.org/docid/47558c422.html.

3. International Lesbian, Gay, Bisexual, Trans and Intersex Association, *State Sponsored Homophobia 2016: A World Survey of Sexual Orientation Laws: Criminalization, Protection and Recognition* (Geneva: ILGA, May 2016), http://ilga.org/downloads/02_ILGA_State_ Sponsored_Homophobia_2016_ENG_WEB_150516.pdf.

4. Rahat Imran, "Legal Injustices: The Zina Hudood Ordinance of Pakistan and Its Implications for Women," *Journal of International Women's Studies* 7, no. 2 (2005): 78–100.

5. "Muslim Publics Divided on Hamas and Hezbollah," Pew Research Center, Washington, D.C., December 2, 2010, http://www.pewglobal.org/2010/12/02/muslims-around-the-world-divided-on-hamas-and-hezbollah/.

6. United Nations Children's Fund (UNICEF) June 2016 https://www.unicef.org/publications/files/UNICEF_SOWC_2016.pdf.

7. Mazna Hussain, "'Take My Riches, Give Me Justice': A Contextual Analysis of Pakistan's Honor Crimes Legislation," *Harvard Journal of Law & Gender* 29, no. 1 (2006): 223–46.

8. United Nations General Assembly, "Convention on the Elimination of All Forms of Discrimination Against Women," *United Nations, Treaty Series 1249* (December 18, 1979), http://www.refworld.org/docid/3ae6b3970.

9. United Nations General Assembly, "Convention on the Rights of the Child," *United Nations, Treaty Series 1577* (November 20, 1989), http://www.refworld.org/docid/3ae6b38f0.html.

10. United Nations Population Fund Child Marriage February 2017, http://www.unfpa.org/child-marriage.

11. Andrea Büchler, and Christina Schlatter, "Marriage Age in Islamic and Contemporary Muslim Family Laws: A Comparative Survey," *Electronic Journal of Islamic and Middle Eastern Law* 1 (2013): 37–74.

12. Nawal M. Nour, "Child Marriage: A Silent Health and Human Rights Issue," *Review of Obstetrics and Gynecology* 2, no. 1 (2009): 51–56.

13. Büchler and Schlatter, "Marriage Age in Islamic and Contemporary Muslim Family Laws."

14. Wael B. Hallaq, *An Introduction to Islamic Law* (Cambridge: Cambridge University Press, 2009).

Chapter 9

1. *The World Factbook 2013–14* (Washington, D.C.: Central Intelligence Agency, 2014), https://www.cia.gov/library/publications/the-world-factbook/index.html.

2. *Constitution of the Republic of Turkey* (November 7, 1982), http://www.refworld.org/docid/3ae6b5be0.html.

3. "Turks Divided on Erdogan and the Country's Direction," Pew Research Center, Washington, D.C., July 30, 2014, http://www.pewglobal.org/2014/07/30/turks-divided-on-erdogan-and-the-countrys-direction/.

4. Women for Women's Human Rights (WWHR)—NEW WAYS, "Gender Discrimination in the Turkish Penal Code Draft Law," translated and compiled by Liz E. Amado (2003), https://www.zwangsheirat.de/images/downloads/english/Gender_Discrimination_in_the_turkish_Penal_Code_Draft_Law.pdf.

5. OECD Development Centre, "Social Institutions and Gender Index," http://www.genderindex.org/sites/default/files/datasheets/TR.pdf.

6. "Muslim Publics Divided on Hamas and Hezbollah," Pew Research Center, Washington, D.C., December 2, 2010, http://www.pewglobal.org/2010/12/02/muslims-around-the-world-divided-on-hamas-and-hezbollah/.

7. Lina Khatib, *Filming the Modern Middle East* (London: I. B. Tauris, 2006).

8. "Muslim Publics Divided on Hamas and Hezbollah," Pew Research Center, Washington, D.C., December 2, 2010, http://www.pewglobal.org/2010/12/02/muslims-around-the-world-divided-on-hamas-and-hezbollah/.

9. Phyllis Chesler, "Worldwide Trends in Honor Killings," *Middle East Quarterly* 12, no. 2 (2010): 3–11.

10. Suzanne Ruggi, "Commodifying Honor in Female Sexuality: Honor Killings in Palestine," *Middle East Report* 28, no. 206 (1998).

11. World Health Organization, *Global and Regional Estimates of Violence Against Women: Prevalence and Health Effects of Intimate Partner Violence and Non-Partner Sexual Violence* (2013), http://www.endvawnow.org/uploads/browser/files/who_prevalence_2013.pdf.

12. Ihsan Cetin, "Defining Recent Femicide in Modern Turkey: Revolt Killing," *Journal of International Women's Studies* 16, no. 2 (2015): 346–60.

13. Gwendolyn L. Gerber, "Gender Stereotypes and the Problem of Marital Violence," in *Violence and the Prevention of Violence*, edited by Leonore Loeb Adler and Florence L. Denmark (Westport, CT: Praeger, 1995).

14 Pierre Bourdieu, *Masculine Domination*, translated by Richard Nice (Palo Alto, CA: Stanford University Press, 2002), 52–53.

Chapter 10

1. Zahia Smail Salhi, ed., *Gender and Violence in Islamic Countries* (London: I. B. Tauris, 2013).

2. Farhad Kazemi, "Gender, Islam, and Politics—Iran," Iran Chamber Society (2016), http://www.iranchamber.com/society/articles/gender_islam_politics_iran2.php.

3. Gönül Dönmez-Colin, *Women, Islam, and Cinema* (London: Reaktion Books, 2004), 13.

Bibliography

Abu-Lughod, Lila. "Do Muslim Women Really Need Saving? Anthropological Reflections on Cultural Relativism and Its Others." *American Anthropologist* 104, no. 3 (2002).

Adams, Nathaniel. "Religion and Women's Empowerment in Bangladesh." Occasional Paper, Berkley Center for Religion, Peace and World Affairs. December 2015. https://s3.amazon aws.com/berkley-center/151215WFDDReligionandWomensEmpowermentinBangladesh. pdf.

Ahmad, Ali Nobil, ed. *Cinema in Muslim Societies*. New York: Routledge, 2016.

Ahmed, Nafeez Mosaddeq. "Algeria and the Paradox of Democracy: The 1992 Coup, Its Consequences and the Contemporary Crisis." *Media Monitors Network*, May 11, 2001. http:// www.mediamonitors.net/mosaddeq4.html.

Al-Attar, Mariam. "Women and Violence in Light of an Islamic Normative Ethical Theory." In *Gender and Violence in Islamic Countries*, edited by Zahia Smail Salhi, 65–74. London: I. B. Tauris, 2013.

Aldeeb, Sami. "To Mutilate in the Name of Jehovah or Allah: Legitimization of Male and Female Circumcision." *Medicine and Law* 13 (1994): 575–622.

Ali, Kecia. "Marriage, Family, and Sexual Ethics." In *The Islamic World*, edited by Andrew Rippin. London: Routledge, 2008.

———. *Sexual Ethics and Islam*. London: Oneworld, 2016.

Altınay, Ayşe Gül, and Yeşim Arat. *Violence Against Women in Turkey: A Nationwide Survey*. Istanbul: Punto, 2009. http://research.sabanciuniv.edu/11418/1/Violence_Against_Women_ in_Turkey.pdf.

An-Na'im, Abdullahi A., ed. *Islamic Family Law in a Changing World: A Global Resource Book*. London: Zed Books, 2002.

Arat, Yesim. "Women's Rights and Islam in Turkish Politics: The Civil Code Amendment." *Middle East Journal* 64, no. 2 (2010): 235–51.

Armes, Roy. *New Voices in Arab Cinema*. Bloomington: Indiana University Press, 2015.

Aslan-Akman, Canan, and Fatma Tutuncu. "The Struggle Against Male Violence." In *Gender and Violence in Islamic Countries*, edited by Zahia Smail Salhi. London: I. B. Tauris, 2013.

Avon Global Center for Women and Justice at Cornell Law School and the New York City Bar Association. "Combating Acid Violence in Bangladesh, India, and Cambodia." 2011. http://www.ohchr.org/Documents/HRBodies/CEDAW/HarmfulPractices/AvonGlobal CenterforWomenandJustice.pdf.

Badran, Margot. *Feminism in Islam: Secular and Religious Convergences*. Oxford: Oneworld, 2009.

Black, Ann, Hossein Esmaeili, and Nadirsyah Hosen. *Modern Perspectives on Islamic Law*. Cheltenham, UK: Edward Elgar, 2013.

Bourdieu, Pierre. *Masculine Domination*. Translated by Richard Nice. Palo Alto, CA: Stanford University Press, 2002.

Büchler, Andrea, and Christina Schlatter. "Marriage Age in Islamic and Contemporary Muslim Family Laws: A Comparative Survey." *Electronic Journal of Islamic and Middle Eastern Law* 1 (2013): 37–74.

Caldwell, John. *Theory of Fertility Decline*. London: Academic Press, 1982.

Cetin, Ihsan. "Defining Recent Femicide in Modern Turkey: Revolt Killing." *Journal of International Women's Studies* 16, no. 2 (2015): 346–60.

Chesler, Phyllis. "Worldwide Trends in Honor Killings." *Middle East Quarterly* 12, no. 2 (2010): 3–11.

Chowdhury, Najma, and Barbara Nelson. "1994 Redefining Politics: Patterns of Women's Political Engagement from a Global Perspective." In *Women and Politics Worldwide*, edited by Barbara Nelson and Najma Chowdhury. New Haven, CT: Yale University Press, 1994.

Dalal, Koustuv, Fazlur Rahman, and Bjarne Jansson. "Wife Abuse in Rural Bangladesh." *Journal of Biosocial Science* 41 (2009): 561–73.

Dönmez-Colin, Gönül. "Cinema." In *The Islamic World*, edited by Andrew Rippin, 527–48. London: Routledge, 2008.

_____. *Women, Islam, and Cinema*. London: Reaktion Books, 2004.

El-Zanaty, Fatma, and Ann Way. *Egypt Demographic and Health Survey 2005*. Cairo, Egypt: Ministry of Health and Population, National Population Council, El-Zanaty and Associates, and ORC Macro, 2006.

Ennaji, Moha, and Fatima Sadiqi. *Gender and Violence in the Middle East*. London: Routledge, 2011.

Faegheh, Shirazi. "Educating Iranian Women." *International Journal of Education and Social Science* 1, no. 2 (2014).

Fahmy, Ashraf, M.T. El-Mouelhy, and A.R. Ragab. "Female Genital Mutilation/Cutting and Issue of Sexuality in Egypt." *Reproductive Health Matters* 18, no. 36 (2010): 181–90.

Freedom House. "Women's Rights in the Middle East and North Africa—Algeria." October 14, 2005. http://www.refworld.org/docid/47387b6a0.html.

Gerber, Gwendolyn L. "Gender Stereotypes and the Problem of Marital Violence." In *Violence and the Prevention of Violence*, edited by Leonore Loeb Adler and Florence L. Denmark. Westport, CT: Praeger, 1995.

Ghanim, David. *Gender and Violence in the Middle East*. Westport, CT: Praeger, 2009.

Ginsberg, Terri, and Chris Lippard. *Historical Dictionary of Middle Eastern Cinema*. Lanham, MD: Scarecrow Press, 2010.

Golkar, Saeid. "Manipulated Society: Paralyzing the Masses in Post-Revolutionary Iran." *International Journal of Politics, Culture, and Society* 29 (2016): 135–55.

Graham, Mark. *Afghanistan in the Cinema*. Urbana: University of Illinois Press, 2010.

Hallaq, Wael B. *An Introduction to Islamic Law*. Cambridge: Cambridge University Press, 2009.

Hansar, Robert D. "Cross-Cultural Examination of Domestic Violence in China and Pakistan." In *Encyclopedia of Domestic Violence*, edited by Nicky Ali Jackson. London: Routledge, 2007.

Hassan, Rasha, Komsan Nehad, and Aliyaa Shoukry. "Clouds in Egypt's Sky: Sexual Harassment: From Verbal Harassment to Rape." Egyptian Center for Women's Rights, 2008. http://harassmap.org/en/wp-content/uploads/2013/03/ECWR-report.pdf.

Human Rights Watch. "Afghanistan: End 'Moral Crimes' Charges, 'Virginity' Tests." May 25, 2016. https://www.hrw.org/news/2016/05/25/afghanistan-end-moral-crimes-charges-virginity-tests.

_____. "'I Had to Run Away': The Imprisonment of Women and Girls for 'Moral Crimes' in Afghanistan." 2012. https://www.hrw.org/sites/default/files/reports/afghanistan0312 webwcover_0.pdf.

Hussain, Irshaad. "The Hermeneutics of Takfir." *Islam from Inside* (February 2002). http://www.islamfrominside.com/Pages/Articles/Hermeneutics%20of%20takfir.html.

Hussain, Mazna. "'Take My Riches, Give Me Justice': A Contextual Analysis of Pakistan's Honor Crimes Legislation." *Harvard Journal of Law & Gender* 29, no. 1 (2006): 223–46.

Immigration and Refugee Board of Canada. "Bangladesh: Domestic Violence, including Legislation, State Protection, and Services Available to Victims." 2007–July 2011 [BGD-103807.E]. http://www.ecoi.net/local_link/203055/308008_en.html.

Imran, Rahat. "Legal Injustices: The Zina Hudood Ordinance of Pakistan and Its Implications for Women." *Journal of International Women's Studies* 7, no. 2 (2005): 78–100.

International Lesbian, Gay, Bisexual, Trans and Intersex Association. *State Sponsored Homophobia 2016: A World Survey of Sexual Orientation Laws: Criminalization, Protection and Recognition.* Geneva: ILGA, May 2016. http://ilga.org/downloads/02_ILGA_State_Sponsored_Homophobia_2016_ENG_WEB_150516.pdf.

Islam, Tahmina. "Causes and Consequences of Eve-teasing in Urban Bangladesh: An Empirical Study." *SUST Studies* 15, no. 1 (2012): 10–20.

Islamic Republic of Afghanistan Ministries of Women's Affairs. *First Report on the Implementation of the Elimination of Violence Against Women (EVAW) Law in Afghanistan.* January 2014. http://mowa.gov.af/Content/files/EVAW%20Law%20Report_Final_English_17%20%20March%202014.PDF.

Kandiyoti, Deniz. "Bargaining with Patriarchy." *Gender and Society* 2, no. 3 (1988): 274–90.

Kazemi, Farhad. "Gender, Islam, and Politics—Iran." Iran Chamber Society, 2016. http://www.iranchamber.com/society/articles/gender_islam_politics_iran2.php.

Khatib, Lina. *Filming the Modern Middle East.* London: I. B. Tauris, 2006.

Macey, Marie. "Religion, Male Violence, and the Control of Women: Pakistani Muslim Men in Bradford, UK." *Gender and Development* 7, no. 1 (1999): 48–55.

Mashad, Seif El. "The Moral Epidemic of Egypt: 99% of Women Are Sexually Harassed." Egyptian Streets, March 5, 2015. http://egyptianstreets.com/2015/03/05/the-moral-epidemic-of-egypt-99-of-women-are-sexually-harassed/.

Max Planck Manual on Family Law in Afghanistan. Max Planck Institute for Comparative Public Law, 2012. http://www.mpipriv.de/files/pdf3/max_planck_manual_on_afghan_family_law_english.pdf.

Mernissi, Fatema. *The Veil and the Male Elite: A Feminist Interpretation of Women's Rights in Islam.* New York: Addison-Wesley, 1991.

Mir-Hosseini, Ziba. *Interpreting Divorce Laws in Islam.* Copenhagen: DJOF Publishing, 2012.

Moghadam, Valentine M. *Modernizing Women: Gender and Social Change in the Middle East.* Boulder, CO: Lynne Rienner, 2003.

———. "Patriarchy in Transition: Women and the Changing Family in the Middle East." *Journal of Comparative Family Studies* 35, no. 2 (2004): 137–62.

Mousavi, S.M., and A. Eshagian. "Wife Abuse in Esfahan, Islamic Republic of Iran East." *Mediterranean Health Journal* 11, no. 5–6 (2005).

Mozafari, Parmis. "Still Singing: Female Singers in Contemporary Iran." *The Middle East in London* 12, no. 2 (2016).

"Muslim Publics Divided on Hamas and Hezbollah." Pew Research Center, Washington, DC, December 2, 2010. http://www.pewglobal.org/2010/12/02/muslims-around-the-world-divided-on-hamas-and-hezbollah/.

National Institute of Population Studies (Pakistan) and ICF International. *Pakistan Demographic and Health Survey 2012–13.* Calverton, MD: National Institute of Population Studies and ICF International, 2013. https://dhsprogram.com/pubs/pdf/FR290/FR290.pdf.

Nayyeri, Mohammad Hossein. "Gender Inequality and Discrimination: The Case of Iranian Women." Iran Human Rights Documentation Center (2013). http://iranhrdc.org/english/publications/legal-commentary/1000000261-gender-inequality-and-discrimination-the-case-of-iranian-women.html.

———. "New Islamic Penal Code of the Islamic Republic of Iran: An Overview." Human Rights in Iran Unit, March 13, 2012. https://www.essex.ac.uk/hri/documents/HRIU_Research_Paper-IRI_Criminal_Code-Overview.pdf.

"1988: Thousands Die in Halabja Gas Attack." BBC, March 16, 1988. http://news.bbc.co.uk/onthisday/hi/dates/stories/march/16/newsid_4304000/4304853.stm.

Nour, Nawal M. "Child Marriage: A Silent Health and Human Rights Issue." *Review of Obstetrics and Gynecology* 2, no. 1 (2009): 51–56.

OECD Development Centre. "Social Institutions and Gender Index." http://www.genderindex.org/sites/default/files/datasheets/TR.pdf.

Osten-Sacken, Thomas von der, and Thomas Uwer. "Is Female Genital Mutilation an Islamic Problem?" *Middle East Quarterly* 14, no. 1 (2007): 29–36.

Otto, Jan Michiel. *Sharia and National Law in Muslim Countries.* Copenhagen: Amsterdam University Press, 2008.

_____, ed. *Sharia Incorporated.* Amsterdam: Leiden University Press, 2010.

Peoples, Fatima Mareah. "Street Harassment in Cairo: A Symptom of Disintegrating Social Structures." *African Anthropologist* 15, nos. 1 and 2 (2008): 1–20.

Rastegar, Kamran. "Film Studies." In *Women and Islamic Cultures,* edited by Suad Joseph. Boston: Brill, 2013.

Rizi, Najmeh Moradiyan. "Iranian Women, Iranian Cinema: Negotiating with Ideology and Tradition." *Journal of Religion & Film* 19, no. 1 (2015).

Romig, Rollo. "Blood Money: Crime and Punishment in 'A Separation.'" *New Yorker*, February 24, 2012. http://www.newyorker.com/culture/culture-desk/blood-money-crime-and-punishment-in-a-separation.

Ruggi, Suzanne. "Commodifying Honor in Female Sexuality: Honor Killings in Palestine." *Middle East Report* 28, no. 206 (1998).

Sadiqi, Fatima, and M. Ennaji. *Women in the Middle East and North Africa: Agents of Change.* London: Routledge, 2010.

Salhi, Zahia Smail. "The Algerian Feminist Movement between Nationalism, Patriarchy and Islamism." *Women's Studies International Forum* 33, no. 2 (2010): 113–24.

_____, ed. *Gender and Diversity in the Middle East and North Africa.* New York: Routledge, 2010.

_____, ed. *Gender and Violence in Islamic Countries.* London: I. B. Tauris, 2013.

Shafik, Viola. *Arab Cinema.* Revised edition. Cairo: American University in Cairo Press, 2007.

Shaikh, Ali. "Is Domestic Violence Endemic in Pakistan? Perspective from Pakistani Wives." *Pakistan Journal of Medical Sciences* 19, no. 1 (2003): 23–28.

Shirazi, Faegheh. "Educating Iranian Women." *International Journal of Education and Social Science* 1, no. 2 (2014): 28–42.

Thompson, Emily L., and F. Soniya Yunus. "Choice of Laws or Choice of Culture: How Western Nations Treat the Islamic Marriage Contract in Domestic Courts." *Wisconsin International Law Journal* 25, no. 2 (2007): 361–95.

"Turks Divided on Erdogan and the Country's Direction." Pew Research Center, Washington, D.C., July 30, 2014. http://www.pewglobal.org/2014/07/30/turks-divided-on-erdogan-and-the-countrys-direction/.

Turshen, Meredeth. "Militarism and Islamism in Algeria." *Journal of Asian and African Studies* 39, no. 1 (2004): 119–32.

UNICEF. "Fresh Progress toward the Elimination of Female Genital Mutilation and Cutting in Egypt." July 2, 2007. https://www.unicef.org/media/media_40168.html.

_____. "Women and Girls in Bangladesh." 2010. http://www.unicef.org/bangladesh/Women_and_girls_in_Bangladesh.pdf.

United Nations General Assembly. "Convention on the Elimination of All Forms of Discrimination Against Women." *United Nations, Treaty Series 1249,* December 18, 1979. http://www.refworld.org/docid/3ae6b3970.html.

United Nations Office on Drugs and Crime. *Afghanistan: Female Prisoners and Their Social Reintegration.* New York: UNODC, 2007. http://www.unodc.org/pdf/criminal_justice/Afghan_women_prison_web.pdf.

United Nations Population Division, Department of Economic and Social Affairs. *Abortion Policies: A Global View.* 2002. http://www.un.org/esa/population/publications/abortion/index.htm.

United Nations Population Fund. "Female Genital Mutilation (FGM) Frequently Asked Questions." December 2015. http://www.unfpa.org/resources/female-genital-mutilation-fgm-frequently-asked-questions.

Vick, Tom. *Asian Cinema Guide*. New York: HarperCollins, 2007.

Winn, Meredith Katherine. "Women in Higher Education in Iran: How the Islamic Revolution Contributed to an Increase in Female Enrollment." *Global Tides* 10 (2016).

Women for Women's Human Rights (WWHR)—NEW WAYS. "Gender Discrimination in the Turkish Penal Code Draft Law." Translated and compiled by Liz E. Amado. 2003. https://www.zwangsheirat.de/images/downloads/english/Gender_Discrimination_in_the_turkish_Penal_Code_Draft_Law.pdf.

The World Factbook 2013-14. Washington, D.C.: Central Intelligence Agency, 2014.

World Health Organization. "Female Genital Mutilation." February 2016. http://www.who.int/mediacentre/factsheets/fs241/en/.

_____. *Global and Regional Estimates of Violence Against Women: Prevalence and Health Effects of Intimate Partner Violence and Non-Partner Sexual Violence*. 2013. http://www.endvawnow.org/uploads/browser/files/who_prevalence_2013.pdf.

Zahedi, Ashraf. "Contested Meaning of the Veil and Political Ideologies of Iranian Regimes." *Journal of Middle East Women's Studies* 3, no. 3 (2007): 75–98.

Index